RECONSIDERING POLICY
Complexity, Governance and the State

Kate Crowley, Jenny Stewart, Adrian Kay and Brian W. Head

P

First published in Great Britain in 2021 by

Policy Press, an imprint of
Bristol University Press
University of Bristol
1-9 Old Park Hill
Bristol
BS2 8BB
UK
t: +44 (0)117 954 5940
e: bup-info@bristol.ac.uk

Details of international sales and distribution partners are available at
policy.bristoluniversitypress.co.uk

© Bristol University Press 2021

British Library Cataloguing in Publication Data
A catalogue record for this book is available from the British Library

ISBN 978-1-4473-3311-1 hardcover
ISBN 978-1-4473-3316-6 paperback
ISBN 978-1-4473-3313-5 ePub
ISBN 978-1-4473-3312-8 ePdf

The right of Kate Crowley, Jenny Stewart, Adrian Kay and Brian W. Head to be identified as authors of this work has been asserted by them in accordance with the Copyright, Designs and Patents Act 1988.

All rights reserved: no part of this publication may be reproduced, stored in a retrieval system, or transmitted in any form or by any means, electronic, mechanical, photocopying, recording, or otherwise without the prior permission of Bristol University Press.

Every reasonable effort has been made to obtain permission to reproduce copyrighted material. If, however, anyone knows of an oversight, please contact the publisher.

The statements and opinions contained within this publication are solely those of the authors and not of the University of Bristol or Bristol University Press. The University of Bristol and Bristol University Press disclaim responsibility for any injury to persons or property resulting from any material published in this publication.

Bristol University Press and Policy Press work to counter discrimination on grounds of gender, race, disability, age and sexuality.

Cover design: Hayes Design
Front cover image: Jillian Mitchell, Alamy Stock Photo

Contents

Detailed contents list		v
List of tables		viii
List of abbreviations		ix
Notes on authors		x
Preface		xi
1	Reconsidering policy – *our agenda*	1
2	Reconsidering *policy systems*	11
3	Reconsidering *institutions*	33
4	Reconsidering *the state*	55
5	Reconsidering *borders*	75
6	Reconsidering *advice and advisory systems*	97
7	Reconsidering *information*	119
8	Reconsidering *implementation*	141
9	Reconsidering *policy change*	163
10	Reconsidering policy – *our agenda revisited*	185
Index		233

Detailed contents list

1	Reconsidering policy – *our agenda*	1
	Introduction	1
	Why bother with public policy studies?	4
	Bringing the state back in	6
	Organisation of the book	9
2	Reconsidering *policy systems*	11
	Introduction	11
	The evolution of systems thinking in the policy sciences	12
	Systems thinking in policy studies	15
	Making sense of complexity	17
	Complexity in policy studies	20
	Application of systems thinking – an overview	24
	Conclusions	30
3	Reconsidering *institutions*	33
	Introduction	33
	Why institutions matter	35
	Institutions and institutional analysis	38
	Governance, networks, systems dynamics	43
	Policy shaping, problem-solving and institutions	48
	Conclusions	52
4	Reconsidering *the state*	55
	Why the state matters	55
	Crisis, resilience and the state	58
	The state in the concept of governance	61
	The changing state and its implications for policy studies	63
	Future directions for policy studies after reconsidering the state	67
	Conclusions	72
5	Reconsidering *borders*	75
	Why borders matter	75
	Borders, global governance and policy studies	78
	Borders and policymaking	81
	Global public policy	82
	A political economy of cross-border policymaking	85
	Global policy processes	88
	Conclusions	95

6	Reconsidering *advice and advisory systems*	97
	Introduction	97
	Policy advising matters	99
	Policy advisory systems	102
	Governance, systems and policy advice	107
	Expert advice and systems-based problem-solving	112
	Conclusions	116
7	Reconsidering *information*	119
	Introduction	119
	What is 'information'?	120
	Policymaking as an informational process	122
	Information and governance	127
	Information, accountability and the state	131
	Applying the informational perspective	134
	Conclusions	138
8	Reconsidering *implementation*	141
	Introduction	141
	Implementation matters	143
	The evolving history of implementation studies	146
	Changing contexts and challenges for implementation	149
	Factors influencing implementation	152
	Improving capacities for successful implementation	155
	Performing, evaluating and learning	157
	Conclusions	161
9	Reconsidering *policy change*	163
	Introduction	163
	Explaining policy change in recent scholarship	165
	Crises and responses to policy challenges	167
	The role of policy ideas	171
	Conflicts in framing policy problems	174
	Success and failure in policy design and change	177
	Policy learning and policy change	180
	Conclusions	183
10	Reconsidering policy – *our agenda revisited*	185
	Introduction	185
	Complexity, governance and the state	186
	Towards better outcomes	188
	Future research options	190

Detailed contents list

The challenges of change	192
Conclusions	194

List of tables

3.1	Hard/formal and soft/informal institutions	39
3.2	Old, behavioural and new institutionalism	41
6.1	Policy advisory system actors classified by policy types	105
6.2	Exploring advisory subsystems – scope for future research	111
6.3	The 'externalisation' of idealised advisory bodies	114

List of abbreviations

CCTV	closed-circuit television
COP	UNFCCC Conference of Parties
GDP	Gross Domestic Product
GFC	Global Financial Crisis
ICPP	Intergovernmental Panel on Climate Change
ILO	International Labor Organisation
IO	International Organisation
IPE	International Political Economy
IR	International Relations
IT	Information Technology
KPI	Key Performance Indicator
NATO	North Atlantic Treaty Organisation
NGO/s	non-government organisation/s
NHS	National Health Service
NPG	New Public Governance
NPM	New Public Management
OECD	Organisation for Economic Cooperation & Development
PASs	Policy advisory systems
SRA	Strategic Relational Approach
TNC	Transnational Corporation
UK	United Kingdom
UN	United Nations
UNFCCC	United Nations Framework Convention on Climate Change
US	United States
WTO	World Trade Organisation

Notes on authors

Kate Crowley is Associate Professor of Public and Environmental Policy at the University of Tasmania. She is widely published on green politics and environmental policy, and has chaired a number of policy advisory councils. Recent edited collections include *Minority Government: The Liberal Green Experience in Tasmania* (2012) and *Environmental Policy Failure: The Australian Story* (2012) with Ken Walker, and *Policy Analysis in Australia* (2015) with Brian W. Head.

Brian W. Head is Professor of Policy Analysis at the University of Queensland. He has also held a number of senior roles in government. He is widely published on public policy, public management, social issues, and environmental policy. He has won funding for projects on research utilisation, wicked problems, policy innovation, natural resources issues, and social program evaluation. He is co-editor with Kate Crowley of *Policy Analysis in Australia* (2015).

Adrian Kay is Professor of Politics and Public Policy at Swansea University and an Honorary Professor at the Crawford School of Public Policy, Australian National University. He is a past President of the Australian Political Studies Association and has held Chairs in Australia, the UK and Asia. He was a member of the UK government's European Fast Stream for several years and has worked for the EU Commission in Brussels. He researches international and public policy, focusing on public health, and Islam in public administration.

Jenny Stewart is a Visiting Fellow in the School of Business, UNSW Canberra, where she was previously Professor of Public Policy. She has published across a wide range of practical and theoretical policy problems and issues, including environmental governance, the role of engagement in policymaking and policy learning. Her most recent book-length scholarly publication is *Public Policy Values*.

Preface

Re-thinking the policy sciences after the 'governance turn' – identifying and creating a (more) capable state

Michael Howlett

This book is premised on the idea that good policymaking requires a capable state and the observation that much contemporary policy literature is not helping achieve this goal. Among the many causes of this problem is singled out what might be called 'the Governance turn' in policy studies in recent decades. This turn is blamed for having led to an epistemological and practice-oriented dead-end in policy studies by replacing more traditional and time-honoured ways of thinking about the state with abstract ideas about the merits of enhanced participatory processes. By continually promoting the advantages of collaboration and co-production over state-based goods and service delivery, it is argued, this approach has de-politicised many aspects of contemporary policy studies and contributed as well in the failure of governments meeting many current policy challenges.

The differences between a policy-oriented approach and those that have focused more on governing are clear. 'Governing' is what governments do, that is, controlling the allocation of resources in society and providing a set of rules and institutions setting out 'who gets what, where, when, and how' in society. A policy orientation towards better governing thus highlights the kinds of resources and capacities governments have in meeting policy challenges, as well as what it is that makes policy formulation and implementation efficient and effective. 'Governance', on the other hand, is a term used to describe the mode of government coordination exercised over social actors in the governing process. Viewed from a policy perspective, the 'Governance' turn has been all about establishing, promoting and supporting a specific type of relationship between government and non-government actors in the governmental and policy processes, one which is horizontal or 'plurilateral' rather than a more traditional vertical or 'hierarchical'. Rather than focus on the attainment of policy ends, it instead is focused almost exclusively on the processes through which that delivery occurs.

In itself this is not a terminal issue and such an arrangement may well be preferable in certain areas of state activity such as education or health care which require a great deal of social support and activity if training and wellness goals are to be achieved. However, when adherents of the governance approach reject structured state-controlled hierarchical arrangements, *a priori*, in favour of more plurilateral or society-driven ones, the governance approach to policymaking contributes to the hollowing out of the state and to the promotion of governing processes that are unsuited to many sectors and areas of policy activity. Such arrangements, the book argues, fail to deal with many basic aspects of policy-making behaviour so that proponents of governance reforms generate prescriptions and plans that are often infeasible if not downright damaging to the attainment of policy goals.

This preference for plurilateral processes is not an inherent part of the Governance turn but is nevertheless clear in many writings on the subject. But as the chapters in the book attest, 'governance' is more than a one-dimensional concept. Many permutations and combinations of possible governance arrangements exist depending not only on the hierarchical or plurilateral nature of state-societal arrangements present, but also upon other factors such as the extent to which these arrangements have been institutionalised, the manner in which they reflect existing arrangements of political power and the types of instruments states have deployed in the past.

Many proponents of plurilateral governance simply expect new, less-hierarchical governance arrangements based on collaborative principles to shift all policy practices away from those associated with traditional hierarchical governing: formal institutions, coercive power relations and the use of substantive policy tools. These are expected to veer towards more informal institutions, non-coercive relationships of power and a marked preference for procedural instruments and soft law, but this has not happened in practice. As the chapters in the book suggest, such an approach to thinking about the roles of states and societies in policymaking has nevertheless de-emphasised the study of traditional state-based activities such as law-making and bureaucracy-based public service delivery and favoured participatory tools and principles, and has failed to take into account the different capabilities of civil society, corporate or state actors to influence each other and the formulation and attainment of policy ends.

As the authors note, a clearer view of governance would examine the many possible variations in governance types and their impact on outcomes. That is, the relationships between policymaking and governance systems should not simply be assumed but need to be anaylsed much more carefully than has occurred to date. As this book underscores, the de-politicisation of the study of policymaking, which has occurred under the governance umbrella, poses a conundrum for policy studies, just as it does for policy practice. It is paradoxical as well, in the sense that both pleas and plans for enhanced participation and collaboration are often thoroughly immersed and embedded in Foucauldian-type critiques of bureaucratic power, while at the same time prescriptions for ever more collaboration fail to address, and often completely ignore, issues around differentials in state and corporate power which disadvantage social groups and actors, and make plurilateral arrangements problematic in many sectors and policy domains.

The chapters in the book detail how this limited view of governance has generated many alternatives and prescriptions for policy processes and actions that are misguided, unrealistic or infeasible. Significantly, however, it goes further in stressing the need to both better understand the reality of the policy-making environment and to improve its theorisation. The solution proposed by the authors for re-orienting policy studies and practices entails a return to some of the basics of policymaking and policy studies before the governance turn, re-examining the actions of societal and state actors, and especially the state, through a capacity lens, putting governance modes and the kinds of relations existing between actors into clearer perspective.

This highlights the significance of the second major theme of the book: that of the need for policy studies to more closely examine the nature of policy capacity and how it can be enhanced to result in more effective policymaking and policy delivery. To simply argue that having adequate policy capacity is a necessary pre-condition for policy success is inadequate, and the book also notes the many disagreements in the policy literature about the detailed conceptual and definitional aspects of the subject. These, it argues, like the Governance turn, have hindered both efforts at better understanding and diagnosis, and improved practice.

To this end, the authors urge scholars and practitioners alike to define policy capacity as the set of competences and capabilities necessary to perform key policy functions: a combination of skills and resources affecting the ability of governments to make intelligent choices; to scan the environment and set strategic directions; to weigh and assess the implications of policy alternatives; and to make appropriate use of knowledge in policymaking. Needed competences are analytical, operational and political in nature and need to be assessed at the individual, organisational and system resource levels. And policy failures can be seen to result from imbalanced attention to, or achievement of, these different components of policy capacity, a fact that the governance approach generally ignores.

In making this case, the book constructs a strong case that building and attaining the capacities required to formulate and implement better policies is a difficult but not impossible task. More research and better understanding of this important component of policymaking is needed, it is concluded, if the policy sciences are to transcend the limits and false promises of the governance turn and policy studies are to be re-oriented towards a more promising path to improved theory and practice.

Michael Howlett
Department of Political Science
Simon Fraser University
May 2019

References

Howlett, M., Rayner, J. and Tollefson, C. (2009) 'From government to governance in forest planning? Lesson from the case of the British Columbia Great Bear Rainforest Initiative', *Forest Policy and Economics*, 11: 383–91.

Wu, X., Ramesh, M. and Howlett, M. (2015) 'Policy capacity: a conceptual framework for understanding policy competences and capabilities', *Policy and Society*, 34(3–4): 165–71.

1

Reconsidering policy – *our agenda*

Introduction

Policy studies are in a rut. While policy problems have grown in complexity, decision makers and policy analysts have struggled to develop models and frameworks to assist both understanding and action (Kay, 2006). The need for better theories about the policy process – systemic but also empirically grounded – has been evident to many observers. Since the 1980s, the scholarly development of new approaches to policy studies has been mainly through deeper engagement with particular aspects of the policy process. For example, scholars have fruitfully explored the topics of policy design, policy implementation and how policy agendas are changed through political debate.

New theoretical approaches have proliferated, most of which were abstracted from deep empirical observation of US policy developments and institutional patterns. Cairney and Heikkila identified eight such theories, or theoretical lenses, each focusing in different ways on actors, institutions, networks, ideas or beliefs, context and events (Cairney and Heikkila, 2014). However, despite the best of intentions, it has not been possible to combine such lenses and insights to form an integrated contemporary approach to policy studies that would offer an assured basis for building knowledge (Pierre and Peters, 2000).

Despite the analytical eclecticism that therefore characterises much of policy studies, some important progress has been made. The critique (from policy studies) of 'traditional' policy analysis has brought a focus on the need for a more nuanced epistemology, one that acknowledges that policymaking should not be seen in purely instrumental or technocratic terms. Normative questions of value and goals of social progress have been reintroduced to scholarship as well as an acute awareness of the contested nature of policy problems themselves. Indeed, as the work by Bacchi and others reveals, what makes some set of social conditions a 'public policy' problem are its political features. Further still, the way a problem is represented and defined paves the way for a favoured set of policy solutions.

However, even with this relativistic streak, policy studies did not develop as a fully fledged 'critical' discipline, except in the sense used in discourse analysis. In the real world, policy-related debates became dichotomised. The right, for example, has been focused on the economy, the left on problems of identity politics, human rights and equity (Béland, 2017). For the left, there was a loss of connection with many working-class voters as social democratic parties have faltered in many of their post-war heartlands. For the right, the apparent triumph of competitive capitalism obscured the fundamental social importance of values, of community, of place and of belonging. More broadly, the decline of the Cold War in the 1990s led to US military overreach, widening instability and state breakdown, particularly in the Middle East.

It seems ironic that, just as politics in both the global and domestic spheres was again taking more partisan forms, policy studies itself became more inward-looking, and less interested in politics and practice than in the past. A more pronounced tendency for 'spectator' theories of the policy process became evident along with less ambition to assist policymakers grappling with questions of what to do in a complex, uncertain and ambiguous world (Ansell and Geyer, 2017). For a school that started with Lasswell as an aspirational science with real world effects, why did policy studies become more academic and descriptivist? While a sceptical stance towards policy rationality has left us with an increased ability to identify the limitations of much policy discourse and clipped the analytical wings of the policy sciences, some threads in contemporary policy studies offer little help for those looking for better ways of defining problems and developing imaginative possibilities for policy action and a better future.

At the same time as conceptual proliferation in policy studies and approaches has occurred, there have been major changes in the perceived role of government and in the nature of the task of governing. Many of these changes and the ideas driving them emanated from economic analysis, which, from the 1970s onward, tended to dominate wide fields of applied public policy, with profound consequences for both politics and the state. Increasingly, governments in developed countries (and elsewhere) have outsourced and privatised many of their activities, under the influence of economic value assumptions. Reflecting this change in the prominence of socio-economic forces, and in some ways going beyond it, many policy scholars have become less interested in explaining public policymaking and more interested in documenting the changing patterns of 'governance'.

Governance, understood as the practices and rules for deliberation, decision and accountability, has proved a very fertile and popular field of inquiry. Insofar as governance has impacted the study of public policy, it has directed attention to the broad social and organisational arrangements through which policy is articulated and managed, rather than the more traditional focus on the processes, institutions and contexts, which determine public policy formation and policy success. Indeed, the rise of governance is associated with the assumption that governing is now largely accomplished by negotiation among networks comprising a diverse array of organisations and institutions (Klijn and Koppenjan, 2015).

This is the basis for the 'governance narrative'. Traditionally the governmental institutions (the state) were seen as providing authoritative direction and control, but this has been superseded by perceived changes in the institutional order that we now label as governance. This was the assumption, for example, of the widely cited book about the UK by Rhodes (1997). Yet, as more recent scholarship has pointed out (Chapter 4), there has been no historical documentation provided to demonstrate that the UK used to be governed simply by authoritative direction within public bureaucracies in a pre-governance era. Provocatively, we may ask, in a book reconsidering public policy, whether the governance literature inspired by Rhodes has actually served to conflate a normative account of how complex societies should be governed with an historical account of changes in how societies are actually governed.

We argue that this overdevelopment of 'governance' themes emerged partly as a result of the reform and revitalisation of public administration associated with the changes initiated through the rise of New Public Management (NPM) practices. The 'policy' dimensions of these organisational changes were widely critiqued (and opposed) at the time by scholars who pointed out the deficiencies of their underlying rationale, namely, public choice theory (for example, Self, 1993). From an empirical point of view, however, what was interesting was the production of widespread and variegated effects of reforms under the NPM label, rather than identifying a coherent intellectual underpinning. As a form of institutionalism, 'governance' had some advantages, not least of which that it enabled scholars to view change through a broad organisational lens, rather than through the uncertain parameters of the complex world of policy itself.

We concede readily that 'governance' leaves plenty of room for the role of the state, including acknowledging the importance of state capacity. Indeed, the governance perspective very usefully shows us some features of an adaptive state, one that reflects the impacts of neo-liberalism and the complexities of modern business and informational organisation. However, it has failed to engage substantially with the big political economy questions underlying the state's battles to contain the massive disruptive forces of late capitalism, and the surging financial flows that have defied conventional nationally bounded analysis. There were also some normative consequences of emphasising governance over state authority. Governance modes such as networks might emerge (or be devised) without adequate understandings of the policy and managerial requirements of the issue fields (Howlett and Ramesh, 2016).

After 50 years of effort, it would seem that an impasse has been reached in policy studies. If public policy analysis has moved away from stressing the importance of institutions in its search for better scientific evidence and more sophisticated techniques, governance seems to have lost its connection with politics, power, interests and ideas – the lifeblood of any active polity. In an era that is wrestling with increasing policy demands, can we revive the problem-solving optimism of previous generations of policy studies scholarship, tempered with a realistic acknowledgement of the constrained capacities of states to deliver better outcomes?

Why bother with public policy studies?

An alternative to our hopeful agenda is the viewpoint that 'public policy' as an orientating focus of scholarship has lost direction. As a concept it exhibits a notorious fuzziness, while many decades of research have been unable to pinpoint clear ways of 'doing' policy better, or of greatly improving chances of success. At the same time, those whose job is to 'do' policy within government continue to see the policy process in terms of authoritative and instrumental decision-making, whereas scholars see policy-related activities as interactive, continuing and process-oriented within challenging contexts. Perhaps despairing of ever reconciling these views, policy scholarship has tended to become more esoteric. It has taken either a post-positivist turn, seeing policy debates as types of social construction, or it has become embroiled in very abstract depictions of process, often without a clear empirical connection with the more familiar worlds of politics, the economy and interests.

Despite all this, we believe that public policy remains our best way of describing what governments actually do, rather than what they say they do, and why that difference is important for social outcomes and a better world. Politics and electoral rhetoric may be all consuming for media commentators, but it is what happens 'on the ground' that is crucial. Our argument does not diminish the importance of politics

– indeed, it is the tendency for governance research to depoliticise policy that we would wish to correct (see Painter and Pierre, 2005, for example). We appreciate that actual policy decisions always have to be made with the future in mind and in the context of uncertainty, yet policy studies have often tended to avoid this either by relying on historical analysis of institutional development, or by focusing on the analysis of how institutions have constraining effects in the present. The book is animated by the conviction that useful knowledge in policy studies comes from attention to the wider political context of policymaking.

Policies remain the hard currency of politics. Contenders for electoral support offer promises that will deliver benefits for various groups – a stronger economy, better roads, hospitals, more jobs and greater environmental protection, for example. At the very least, these policy promises are part of the necessary camouflage of the machinations of power. Promises are sometimes unrealistic and may eventually break on the cold stones of reality. We are also well aware that a purely bureaucratic policy process would become rigid without the lively renewal of politics, and that the persistent energy and agenda-setting actions of interest lobbies, community groups and policy advocates keep alive the tension between what is demanded and what is really needed.

Although disruptive of the policy process, political contestation has the great virtues of shaking up consensus and generating surprises. There is a common tendency, even in democracies, for elites to be cut off from the societies they try to lead. The lived experience of policy outcomes – the actual and perceived results of change – may on occasion rock the complacency of received wisdom. As we saw with the Brexit vote of 2016 and the election of Donald Trump to the US Presidency in the same year, 'the system' that had delivered prosperity for some was exposed as being deeply fractured and widely perceived as unfair. The Pandora's box of complex and divisive policy choices that has resulted presents an ongoing series of challenges.

We see the study of public policy as critical to political science and government studies, spanning as it does the crucial space between the political world, society and its diverse wants and needs. In reconsidering the policy studies agenda, we reconceptualise the nature of the relationship between complexity, governance and the state and its impact upon policy capacity. We argue that public policy is directly related to issues of state capacity that are often overlooked, underplayed or de-contextualised by constructivist, interpretivist and governance-based approaches, and that the key role of the state and public authority should be confirmed within policy studies.

Bringing the state back in

Policy studies should be refocused on state capacity and the roles of politics, policy and institutions in building capacity to engender positive change. These are roles, we argue, that successive decades of literatures on governance and public policy have tended to downplay, or to treat them as residual features of the policy system or as background context. How can policy studies approach this refocusing? We suggest it is necessary to rediscover and redevelop some lost (or at least overlooked) traditions in political science that relate directly to state action. While theories of the state relate to power relations, rather than to policy directly, the policy dimension can be discerned through the responses of states and their agencies to changing domestic and international conditions. These latent traditions in political science support several important theoretical perspectives that assist our ambition to move policy studies beyond description and critique, towards supporting efforts for imagining alternative futures and developing policy capacity for thinking holistically and systemically. Three theoretical lenses suggest themselves as provocations in reconsidering policy studies: political economy; mobilisation of interests; and regulatory forms and capacities.

Political economy

Traditional political economy drew our attention to the relationship between politics, the state and power. States were structurally bound to methods and relations of production both nationally and (increasingly) internationally. The best way to understand policy as the 'mobilisation of bias' was to ask who benefits ('cui bono'). Estimates of the distribution of costs and benefits from any particular set of policy interventions would provide the foundation for an analysis of the politics of those policy interventions. Canadian and Australian scholars, for example, contributed to this tradition by analysing the position of these states in the international trade system, with their dependence on resource exporting, as ways of highlighting a range of policy problems in political economy that endure today (Crough and Wheelwright, 1982; Marchak, 1985; Mercer and Marden, 2006).

In the broader sense, analyses of the 'capitalist' state in the 1970s uncovered the sources of the loss of legitimacy and the state's propensity to suffer from fiscal crises (O'Connor, 1973; Habermas, 1975). The Global Financial Crisis (GFC) in 2008 and its aftermath have revived many of the concerns dissected by O'Connor and others four decades previously. However, these enduring analyses of the 1970s and 1980s overlooked many other influences on the behaviour of states. Globalisation seemed to signal the end of the nation-state as the primary locus of economic policymaking. In practice, however, states in a globalising world proved more versatile than structuralist models suggested (Kay, 2006). States morphed and changed, but some analysts failed to recognise this adaptability, such as some later Marxist writings that tended to overemphasise class-based domination of state structures and functions (see Jessop, 2016: 91–2). In the empirical sense, the concept of 'the state' began to seem a little dated, and recognition of 'the state' faltered in academic writings from around the 1990s. But states operated in different ways, exercised their power in different ways. Some survived well, others less so.

According to neo-liberal principles of good governance, the Chinese state, for example, should have self-destructed given its lack of a recognisable rule of law. However, while Chinese economic policies continued to defy easy classification within the Washington consensus textbook, they have become the template for much policymaking in the developing world. States might have also devised policies that misused or overestimated their own power (for example, the Organization of the Petroleum Exporting Countries (OPEC) oil cartel, or the US incursion in Iraq), but it is also widely acknowledged that states have incurred considerable risks in choosing to subordinate their power to transnational structures (for example, recent tensions within the EU). In an increasingly complex world, nation states have needed policies that transcended borders, while building and maintaining a viable political consensus for doing this. Our academic interest in policy therefore transcends borders.

Policy and interests

The relationship of policy to interests, through the state, was the staple fare of traditional policy analysis through the 1970s and 1980s. The extent to which particular states might be regarded as 'pluralist' or 'corporatist' formed a backdrop to a broad comparativist literature, which flourished in particular from the 1980s through to the 1990s (see, for example, Katzenstein, 1984; Castles, 1993).

Interests themselves seemed to grow more diffuse in the eyes of scholars in this period. Iron triangles gave way eventually to policy networks, policy subsystems, and even issue networks (Chapter 3). These classifications, however, proved difficult to operationalise empirically. In writing about specific policy fields (for example, environmental, health, education policy), it remained essential to identify and explore the relevant interests. This way of looking at policy remains central in the discussion of specific policy fields, but in the broader sense, the behaviour of interest groups in a globalising, more complex world began to receive less attention.

This is unfortunate, as the power of interests to shape national and sub-national policy choices directly, through political influence, donations and public-private revolving door relations, and to bypass the 'reach' of international policy-making institutions, has arguably never been greater. The failure of the global community to act successfully to reduce greenhouse gas emissions and to avert the onset of dangerous climate change are testimony to this. Furthermore, the dysfunctional features of the US political system are widely seen as undermining the capacity of governments to effect much needed change. Here we see the policy world repeatedly paralysed or derailed in terms of effecting change. Evidence of policy incapacity and frailty draws attention to the importance of policy capacity and state capacity; and further justifies a reconsidering of policy theory and analysis.

Policy, politics and regulation

The work of Lowi (1972) drew systematic attention to the reciprocal relationship between politics and policy. While policy has remained the child of interests, and of political leaders and parties seeking election, policy also created its own politics, according to the extent to which extant policy types created 'visible' incentives for action. Regulatory policy domains could be particularly potent, as interests mobilised to pre-empt, to counter, to reinforce or to dismantle the decisions of previous administrations, as well as attempted to set the agenda for new regulation. These features are obvious in debates, for example, over gun control in the US.

Regulatory theory, through the work of Braithwaite and others, showed the 'cat and mouse' behavioural dimension of prescriptive policy settings (Ayres and Braithwaite, 1992). For example, moves to regulate the insurance industry, or to minimise tax evasion, have engendered game-like relationships between regulatory bodies and those who were supposed to be regulated. In this context, ideas (or ideals) about collaborative forms of regulatory governance seemed to meet a need for a more nuanced perspective, transcending traditional 'command and control' approaches.

The growing importance of environmental issues over recent decades reinforced this trend towards regulatory pluralism and experimenting with policy mixes. There have been many studies pointing to the need for a varied menu of environmental governance tools and approaches, involving appropriate mixes of scale and participation. However, increasingly, 'regulation' studies more narrowly have become the domain of economic analysis on the one hand, and legal analysis on the other, rather than of multi-disciplinary policy studies. Climate change policy analysis, while eliciting a huge literature in a broad range of disciplines, has remained uneasily moored between governance, political science and environmental studies.

Yet the state remains crucial here. The need to regulate for the protection of environmental assets has produced a moving frontier of conflict, with states able to exercise power in some cases, and not in others. US regulators were in a position to expose deceptive conduct by companies such as Volkswagen in relation to air quality standards for vehicles. At the same time, pollution and the externalities generated by rich countries were increasingly exported to low-cost countries or communities where firms did not have to abide by high-quality environmental restrictions. Climate change policy in the global sense has foundered on the structural inequalities and perceived unfairness of international processes underlying the Kyoto Protocol and Paris Accord.

As production patterns have continued to be globalised, powerful states continue to be able to assert their interests in particular ways (for example, through trade deals). In OECD countries, the regulatory state has expanded domestically in areas such as employment rights and occupational health and safety. Nevertheless the objects of regulation retained their structural power ('jobs and growth') with mobile capital increasingly able to relocate to less demanding jurisdictions. The demands for better policy in this complex world, both from within and without the state, should form the context of policy inquiry – the places where scholarship needs to shed more light.

Organisation of the book

If it is accepted that the study of public policy needs revitalising, including taking more account of the matters we have described, the challenge becomes one of analytical approach. In the chapters that follow we develop the practice of 'reconsidering' key aspects of public policy analysis. By reconsidering, we mean two activities: firstly, revisiting and adding to those key concepts or practices that have been prominent in the past but have in some cases faded; and secondly, further developing concepts that have not become fully established on the research agenda. Our objects of reconsideration are of two types:

- firstly, themes relating to what we call 'deep' policy: policy systems; institutions, the state and borders; and
- secondly, policy-in-action: information, advice, implementation and policy change.

Through these eight perspectives, each developed as a chapter of this book, we have produced a melded approach to policy, which we call systemic institutionalism. We define this approach as one that provides a broad analytic perspective that links policy with governance (implemented action) on the one hand, and the state (structured authority) on the other. By identifying research agendas based on these insights, we suggest how real world issues might be substantively addressed, in particular more complex and challenging issues, through examples that bring out the 'policy' (the history and potential for collective public action) in the system.

Through this combination of abstraction and example, we hope we have surmounted the continuing dilemma of public policy studies: how to remain empirically relevant, while avoiding 'adjectival' policy case studies that may acknowledge the politics, but that subsume or neglect the state. In 'reconsidering' public policy, we believe we have also gone some way towards addressing the paradoxical nature of policy – that as we attempt to understand it, so (both as a distinctive activity and a mode of activity) it seems to disappear into its own constituent parts.

In summary, we suggest that making public policy scholarship more relevant requires an understanding, not just of policy development and selected policy-related themes, but a broader engagement with structure, process and system: as a way of depicting not just the formation of policy, but also its modes of action in the world. Doing this involves building on earlier iterations of policy thought and relating them not only to the complexity of current policy problems, but also to the immense technological and political changes that have occurred in the 21st century.

2

Reconsidering *policy systems*

Introduction

The term 'system' is widely used in the policy sciences to denote a field of interest characterised by multiple, interconnected actors (for example, education system, health system, policy subsystem, and so on). In this reconsideration, we argue for the development and use of systems thinking as a way of expanding our understanding of the relationships through which policies achieve their effects. Systems-based analysis provides an important means for bringing together policy and governance.

This type of thinking is far from mechanistic: indeed in focusing on human action in multiple contexts, it moves beyond reductionism to more nuanced notions of cause and effect (Chapman, 2004). A common response to policy failure, for example, is to tighten control, while more significant causes, such as failures of leadership, funding or communication may be neglected. While systems thinking in the policy sciences is not new (Stewart and Ayres, 2001), after a promising start, policy analysis has failed to provide a clear rationale and structure for the use of this mode of analysis, whether the purpose be prescriptive (analysis 'for' policy), or descriptive (analysis 'of' policy). A reconsideration is timely.

We make two general claims for the approach: firstly, systems thinking is likely to be particularly productive where policy problems defy conventional solutions and unintended consequences are rife. In these situations, systems thinking has the ability to move beyond the specifics of each problem to identify and depict underlying complexity; secondly, in the governance era, sites of policy-relevant action are more likely than in the past to lie outside the formal boundaries of government, and to require complex interactions among stakeholders. The long-running difficulty of implementation – relating policy intentions to effective action 'on the ground' – is exacerbated (Chapter 8). In these situations, systems thinking helps the policy analyst to find associations and linkages that might otherwise be hard to discern.

Specifically, when we apply systems thinking:

- we think about context, the political and institutional setting of the policy in question;
- we think about scope – what's in, what's out; who's in, who's out;
- we think about actors (both stakeholders and organisations);
- we think about interconnections between actors (flows of information, money and influence);
- we think about interconnections between systems – problems observed in one system may be caused by developments in another;
- we think about the ways in which actors change systems (complex adaptive systems) and what this may mean for policy intentions;
- we think about feedback, and its implications for regulatory controls; and
- we think about the nature of change itself, because systems are interacting constantly both with themselves and with their environment.

This chapter traces the trajectory of systems thinking in the policy sciences, draws in themes from complexity science and concludes with practical examples of applications.

The evolution of systems thinking in the policy sciences

The classic definition of a system encompasses 'a set of inter-related elements, each of which is related directly or indirectly to every other element, and no subset of which is unrelated to any other subset'. In addition, systems have a relationship with their environment, such that changes in the environment will cause a change in the system under consideration (Ackoff and Emery, 1972: 380–1; Rittel and Webber, 1973: 159).

Systems thinking has a long, somewhat convoluted history in the policy sciences. Our starting point is the work of David Easton, encapsulated in his *A Systems Analysis of Political Life* (Easton, 1965). Easton was the first theorist to use a systems approach to produce a general theory of politics. Public policies (authoritative decisions) were seen as 'outputs' of the system, which, in satisfying a sufficient number of the demands imposed by citizens, created a stable environment of support for the regime. As Easton himself had made clear, this work was intentionally abstract and theoretical in character. It was his hope that these qualities would assist the advance of the discipline by enunciating a theory broad enough to draw together previously fragmented approaches based on the analysis of specific actors (such as political parties or interest groups) (Easton, 1957).

While influential, however, Easton's theory did not shape the empirical trajectory of the policy sciences in the following decades. Analysis 'of' policy tended to be structural-functionalist in the tradition most broadly articulated by Talcott Parsons. Analysis 'for' policy followed the positivist path of Lasswell. However, from the point of view of intellectual history rather than direct influence, we would argue that Easton's systems-based approach to the question of political legitimacy overlapped with a growing interest in the sustainability of capitalist states, the subject of a broad spectrum of work appearing in the 1970s and 1980s. Seeing state support – and survival – in systems terms provided innovative ways of thinking about the structural problems of the capitalist state.

The state in crisis

In the 1970s a number of theorists used a Marxist, or neo-Marxist critique, to analyse what they saw as enduring deficits of the capitalist state. These theorists included the early Habermas (Habermas, 1975) and – from a more identifiably public policy perspective – James O'Connor (O'Connor, 1973).

While not overtly 'systems' thinkers in the Eastonian sense, Habermas and O'Connor identified the importance of the connection between loyalty to the state and the outputs (policies) of the state. Legitimation and accumulation were the state's necessary goals. For O'Connor in particular, the contradictions between the two imposed conflicting policy requirements on governments. The resulting vulnerability of the capitalist state was emphasised – although in practice, as events in the 1980s proved, it was nominally socialist states that were to prove the more vulnerable. However, the sense of 'crisis', or at least of inadequacy of conventional policymaking, persisted.

Unless public expectations could be more constrained, governments would become 'overloaded' by the intractability and breadth of the demands placed upon them (King, 1975). As King himself noted, referring to the recent work of LaPorte, the degree of complexity with which governments were required to deal was increasing (LaPorte, 1975). The discovery (or re-discovery) of complexity in the 2000s, underlines the importance of this strand of systems thinking.

The work of Luhmann

From the early 1970s, Luhmann's exploration of societal differentiation (which he saw in terms of the development of new systems of thought and action) opened up fresh horizons for systems thinking. Despite its theoretical scope and density, Luhmann's work derived initially from his practical experience in public administration. Famously, Luhmann did not share Habermas's critical perspective on capitalism. In depicting the political world in systems terms, Luhmann drew attention to the deeply problematic notion of 'steering'. How could a system be 'steered' without in some sense being conscious of itself?

Luhmann's work on self-steering (*autopoiesis*) was a significant attempt to deal with this issue. Human systems must be systems of communicative order (Luhmann, 1993). Therefore, if we can include reflexivity (the way in which communicative order is constructed for participants in a particular system), in our understanding of social systems in general, we have a means for understanding the relationship between system boundaries and the work the system must do. As Brans and Rossbach put it, Luhmann's *oeuvre* rests on, and develops, 'an epistemology capable of dealing with ... self-reference' (Brans and Rossbach, 1997: 418).

While it may seem esoteric, this is an important result for the relationship between politics, policy and public administration. Luhmann's point is that these are subsystems that are not (and cannot be) fully 'closed', therefore there can be no clear separation between politics, policy and public administration. The state is inherently fragile, and the task of steering, particularly where authority is dispersed, is always contested. While a 'governance' perspective seems very compatible with this view, it is clear that governance is not, in itself, a systems-based concept in the Luhmann sense. We return to this point in our discussion of the episteme of system.

Systems modelling and 'soft systems'

Beginning in the 1970s and continuing for several decades, the leading edge of systems thinking in the policy sciences concerned the use of systems models for planning and decision-making purposes (Forrester, 1970; 1992), and in problem definition in a range of contexts (Checkland and Haynes, 1994). Forrester showed that policies should be understood as structures setting relations between parts of urban systems, which mutually influenced each other over time (urban 'dynamics'). Failure to understand the nature of the policy setting and the interconnections within it meant that many planning policies failed to work, or even more often, produced results that were counterproductive (Forrester, 1970). By the early 1990s, systems-proponents were insistent on the need for policymakers to become systems thinkers (de Greene, 1993: 14). Policymakers did not need to be model-builders: the systems perspective could be operationalised in many ways.

Advocates pointed out that systems thinking did not necessarily entail a quantitative or even mechanistic approach. The concept of a 'soft system' stressed the contingent nature of problem-solving, in situations in which problem definition was difficult. Principally associated with the work of Peter Checkland, a 'soft' systems methodology was one based on identifying human activity systems. It was a tool for thinking about issues, rather than a hard and fast, or mechanistic approach, for resolving them. As Checkland put it, 'all problematical human situations can be thought of as situations in which people are trying to define and take useful purposeful action' (Checkland and Haynes, 1994: 192).

Since its first enunciation, soft-systems methodology has continued to be employed in the analysis of policy problems, largely as a decision-support technique (see, for example, Antunes, et al, 2016). Structuring policy problems from the perspective of the actors within them, gave a specific way of resolving, or at least clarifying debates, about the nature of these problems. Versions of soft-systems thinking have also been used as a way of understanding change and innovation in specific policy settings, most notably in the health sector (Atun, 2012).

Despite these kinds of applications, however, policy analysts did not 'convert' to systems thinking to the extent that its advocates in the 1990s hoped. In part, this may have been because de Greene and others gave systems thinking too demanding a character. Indeed de Greene himself took the view that 'true' systems thinking required a level of cognitive sophistication that not everyone possessed. 'Systems thinking, *when it does develop*, emerges from a long period of personal experiences and interactions and testing of one's own mental models' (de Greene, 1993: 14). If systems thinkers were, in a sense, the authors of their own research method, it was difficult to see how proficiency in the art could be inculcated or sustained.

Systems thinking in policy studies

We turn now to policy studies: the study of the processes and structures through which policy is made. While systems thinking, in the sense advocated by de Greene and others, was not explicitly employed in policy studies, the term 'system' has been heavily used to denote sets of relationships between actors, and between actors and the state, in the context of policymaking. Two applications of this idea are recorded here. The policy 'subsystem' proved analytically useful in identifying the location of specific types of policy work. The subsystem had an imagined boundary but also, within that boundary, a recognisable structure and associated processes. In this overview we also include models of the policy process (such as the policy cycle) that include systems features, such as a feedback component.

Policy subsystems

The policy subsystem literature, as initially developed, was intended to delineate situations where interests were closely aligned with government, to the extent that specific sub-governments could be discerned. These sub-governments were most evident where interests were clearly defined and well organised. In the US in particular, the term 'iron triangles' was employed to denote the three vertices of government agencies, congressional committees and interests (Howlett and Ramesh, 1995: 125).

But there were many areas where the relationships were more diffuse and the connections of mutual dependence less pronounced. Policy was made, or at least discussed, in meaningful ways, in many more places and instances than more rigid frameworks supposed (Jordan, 1990). In systems terms, the sectors concerned were less tightly coupled. Writers imagined a continuum, from arrangements that were based on more stable dependency relationships, to those that were much more fluid. As governments were themselves seen to become more diffuse, the idea of policy 'networks' replaced that of 'systems' or 'subsystems'. This mode of thinking made it possible to discern the potential and 'reach' of governments in new ways (see, for example, Considine et al, 2009).

Policy cycle

The idea that public policy develops through identifiable stages has a long history, appearing in standard textbooks from the early 1970s. The policy cycle, which provided a more 'joined-up' approach, came a little later. As an intellectual tool, the policy cycle has had a chequered career, seen by some as a valuable teaching tool, but criticised by others as being too simplistic to be of much use in understanding how policy is formed (Colebatch, 2006a). Academic opinion, in particular, would favour a much broader view of the kinds of processes that inform policymaking. The policy cycle does, however, have a number of 'systems' characteristics. As a kind of 'ideal-type' teaching model

(McCool, 1995: 169), the policy cycle alerts students to the existence of distinct phases or types of decision-making. Moreover, as a 'cycle', it encapsulates the idea of policy management via feedback.

The evaluation phase of the cycle takes into account the effects of the policy, and feeds them forward into the design phase. The problem is that, in the real world of policy and program evaluation, we know that this connection is very muted (Stewart and Jarvie, 2015). We would argue, however, that the flaws of the policy cycle are not those of systems thinking, but of systems thinking too simplistically applied. If we are interested in analysis 'for' policy, comparing what has been achieved with what was intended seems both logically attractive and systemically informed. It is, perhaps, the rather daunting concept of 'evaluation' that defeats this purpose. Learning, with its pedigree in organisational systems thinking, would seem to be a more satisfying formulation, in that it focuses attention on possibilities for ongoing improvement rather than on summative judgement. Practitioners have found a learning perspective to be an effective antidote to over-reliance on 'command and control' (Chapman, 2004).

In terms of the development of policy studies, system-related concepts continue to have relevance in the age of governance. The policy subsystem has morphed into an appreciation of networks and network analysis. The policy cycle continues to inform understandings of both the limits of evaluation and the potential of learning. In practical terms, however, it is important to acknowledge that the development of ever-more complex models of the systems that policy must affect, can lead to a reversion to the 'top-down' approach. To balance this tendency, a more nuanced understanding of complexity itself is needed.

Making sense of complexity

As defined by Axelrod, 'a system is complex when there are strong interactions among its elements, so that current events heavily influence the probabilities of many kinds of later events' (Axelrod and Cohen, 2000: 7). A complex *adaptive* system contains agents within it who are seeking to pursue strategies, which, in turn, will affect others, and also the context in which others operate.

The concept is easiest to understand at the organisational level. Any organisation with inter-linkages within it, has the capacity to evolve, that is, for decisions taken in one part to impact on others, in ways that are difficult to predict from the outset. Regarded in this way, an organisation will be difficult to control, but this does not mean that positive outcomes may not ensue from purposeful action.

From a policy perspective the central concern is that when we apply pressure to organisations or relationships, they will adapt in ways that are both self-seeking and self-organising. The trick, from the point of view of policy design, is to know when this kind of complexity imposes limits, and when it can be used as an asset. The instinctive policy response to many issues (imprison all terrorists; stop prices rising by introducing price control) ignores the fact that agents will adapt in their own ways. Creating a situation (such as a consultative scenario, or a market), which utilises adaptive capacities to positive ends, may be the only productive means to address this type of policy problem.

Tipping points

Some aspects of system behaviour are not regular or predictable and do not develop in a linear way. A system may be close to 'tipping' (about to undergo rapid change) without that fact being obvious. Or the potential to 'tip' may be widely signalled (as in commentary on 'overheated' housing markets), without a precise timing being evident. Some systems (such as poorly regulated markets for risk) may be particularly prone to sudden implosions. Others (such as some natural ecosystems) may give clear evidence of localised tipping points, without providing decision makers with sufficient incentives to act.

Comparing systems that do – and don't – tip may provide valuable lessons for future policy. For example, after the onset of the Global Financial Crisis (GFC) in 2008, the Australian and Canadian banking sectors proved less vulnerable than those in the UK and the US, because their particular (less competitive) structure gave bankers less incentive to make risky lending decisions. In forming a policy response, therefore, redoubling regulation over banking may be a less useful starting point than clearly identifying the origins of risk-taking behaviours.

'Tipping' may be a consequence of previous policy programs, or omissions. Policies designed to encourage transformation of complex systems need to be compatible with those systems, a tall order for simplistic, binary, combative politics. Responses to climate change show some of the disruptive consequences that can emerge in finely tuned energy markets. In Australia, renewable energy targets initially created a flourishing green industry of wind turbines and solar panels. But without a workable price on carbon, the privatised national energy market lacked any overall direction to guide investment. In the absence of alternative mechanisms of coordination, market-oriented policies proved destabilising, leading (in a summer of extreme weather turbulence) to shortfalls in electricity production at critical times.

Resilience

The concept of resilience is intuitively attractive, although difficult to define precisely (Reid and Botterill, 2013). From an ecological perspective, Walker and Salt define resilience in terms of the ability of a system to absorb disturbance, while retaining essentially the same structure, function and feedbacks – to retain its identity (Walker and Salt, 2012). Other perspectives stress the ability of resilient systems to adapt to change, even to self-transform (Grigg et al, 2012).

For policy analysts and practitioners, resilience (in both positive and negative senses) has proved a useful concept in understanding the effects of policy and management interventions in large-scale social-ecological systems. Allison and Hobbs, for example, were able to show how, over time, counterproductive farming practices could become so entrenched they were resistant ('resilient') to policy initiatives aimed at change. In the West Australian wheat-belt, practices that impoverished the soil had become 'locked-in' to the extent that policies aimed at reducing land-clearing had only superficial impacts (Allison and Hobbs, 2004).

On the other hand, resilience (as a policy perspective in itself) suggests an enhanced capacity to respond to crisis or challenge. In the wake of devastating forest fires in California and in other states of the US, ecologists have proposed a new framework of response, which matches an understanding of the urban-forest interface with community attributes and institutional flexibilities (Abrams et al, 2015).

In policy terms, we are talking about 'designing in' attributes of resilience. Empirical work suggests that these may rest on not pushing too hard against boundaries, allowing flexibility for the future (see, for example, Rabe, 2016). But not every policy sphere will be amenable to this approach, and trade-offs will be inevitable.

An emphasis on learning and innovation at appropriate ecological scales has been held to imply polycentric or decentralised governance (Dovers, 2005). If, overall, we are dealing with a 'system of systems', complexity-oriented governance implies policies that establish or facilitate systems that enable good responses to evolve. It will be just too difficult to apply policies 'from the top'. The state works from within systems, rather than directing, in more complex circumstances.

Regulatory apparatus, for example, may have been more emphatic when production was more monopolistic in character. However, a lack of competition generates considerable inefficiencies, a situation which the widespread de-regulation of (for example) information and communication technologies was intended to remedy. Experience has shown that complexity-informed governance must be regarded as a balancing act. The ability of a sector to perform well emerges from many decentralised market-based decisions (Bauer, 2004). Rather than being unwanted, emergent attributes in a polycentric environment may be positive, if planned for (or at least allowed for). The challenge for governance is to retain the light touch that complexity demands, without sacrificing the capacity to identify and respond to undesirable behaviours when they arise.

Complexity in policy studies

By the early 2000s, policy studies had begun to incorporate ideas about complexity, but as we would expect, in ways that were eclectic, rather than following any particular line. Cairney, (2012a: 346) describes a 'small literature using the language of complexity to describe complex policy systems and a larger literature identifying complexity themes'. Empirical studies, employing complexity thinking to illuminate actual policy events, have been rare. Those that have been done, have used complexity as a heuristic (an exploratory device), rather than as a definitive form of analysis.

For example, Rhodes's work on housing policy used a Complex Adaptive Systems (CAS) framework to show the importance, in designing policy, of understanding agents' decision-making schema (Rhodes, 2007). Eppel et al's 2011 study employs three extended examples to illustrate the application of complexity principles such as non-linearity, feedback, self-organisation and sensitivity to initial conditions. Risks related to 'top-down' interventions that ignore or overlook these factors are specifically highlighted (Eppel et al, 2011).

Reflecting the uncertainty associated with complex systems, a growing body of work has taken its rise from implementation studies (Chapter 8). From this perspective, implementation consists of the working-out of self-organising subsystems (Butler and Allen, 2008; Trenholm and Ferlie, 2013), and/or (in the design sense) of aligning flexible ways of working with the interconnectedness of problems (Jarvie and Stewart, 2011).

These studies confirm that the consequences of particular interventions may go well beyond the original intentions of policymakers, with (probably) negative implications for 'top-down' implementation approaches (Tenbensel, 2013: 183). From the perspective of policy design, the scope for the application of rationalist approaches (which suppose the discernment of clear-cut cause and effect connections) becomes much more limited.

Even where the behavioural logic of an intervention is clear, the decision to respond may rest on many factors other than those of straight rationality. Patton gives the example of a research program whose objective was to demonstrate the advantages of screening and then treating police officers for obstructive sleep apnoea. Patton shows that the decision to become involved in the program rests on many factors, such as each officer's network of relationships, rather than simply on an individual appraisal of costs and benefits (Patton, 2011: 117–19). Allied with insights from behavioural economics, a system perspective draws attention to these modalities.

But where, exactly, is the value-added? There has been some scepticism from policy scholars. Summarising developments in the health policy field, Tenbensel writes of 'a relatively novel conceptual repertoire', rather than a clear methodological advance (Tenbensel, 2015: 381). In a critical review of policy developments in relation to climate change, Wellstead et al criticise complexity-based systems thinking as overlooking the 'system' of government itself. If governments are conceptualised as a black box in an adaptation mechanism, they argue, this is scarcely helpful to policymakers. Moving forward requires 'moving beyond the abstractions inherent in contemporary system-led complexity theory and instead seeking to incorporate knowledge of formulation and implementation into complexity-inspired models of political and policy interaction' (Wellstead et al, 2015: 406).

We would agree that institutionally informed mapping helps policymakers understand more about the meso-level variables (institutions, elites, the shape of networks, and so on) that shape problem-responses. If this work is well done, an important component of policy is made explicit, not least because government is complex in itself. Any given problem can be found to have many impinging pieces of legislation, applied through a large number of administering agencies.

If, for example, we wish to identify adaptive capacities, in relation to climate change, we can identify a particular threat (for example, sea level rise) and consider which parts of the governance system would be most immediately impacted. For most countries, it is the local level of government that controls planning permissions, and to which citizens would go for assistance. The bigger system, of course, is both national and supra-national (Corfee-Morlot et al, 2011).

Another approach is to use systems thinking to characterise responsive governance in situations of complexity. The work of Duit and Galaz suggests the need for trade-offs between principles of exploitation and those of exploration. But finding appropriate principles for doing this in multilevel systems is not easy: 'Designing governance systems that simultaneously produce high levels of collective action and learning often means overriding basic institutional features such as path dependency and stickiness—a feat that is not likely to be accomplished easily and without conflict' (Duit and Galaz, 2008).

From a policy science perspective, some general principles for working with complexity have been put forward. We should choose policy instruments that are themselves adaptive, rather than those that seek to impose a particular current view of the world: opportunities for learning based on experimentation and measurement will be of particular importance (Busenberg, 2004). Assumptions about rational action should give way to a more nuanced understanding of interactions between citizens and government – 'nuzzle' rather than 'nudge' (Room, 2016). Policy actors may themselves hasten processes of adaptive evolution by problem-solving in ways that counteract dominant institutional forms (Tenbensel, 2018).

What these advances might mean for policy scholars in more generic terms, however, remains unclear. Overall, it would be fair to conclude that policy studies have noted complexity without embracing it. In the next section, we explore ways in which this frontier might be productively expanded.

The *episteme* of system

What kind of knowledge is generated when we bring together the concept of 'system' and that of 'public policy'? Are systems somehow real, or do they exist only as we attempt to discern them? What is the status of the knowledge that a systems perspective brings us? Checkland and Haynes (1994) stress that it is 'systems thinking' that we need. From this perspective, systems are a metaphor, rather than a model. But if this is so, how do we know whether we are conceptualising our systems well, or badly?

The ultimate test is whether the application of systems thinking adds value to the work of policy analysis. Practitioners advise that a systems perspective avoids the traps inherent in 'linear' policy analysis, where the policy intent is seen as tightly bound to the necessary action. For example, linear policy thinkers may suggest that the best way to deal with crime is to increase prison terms, without considering the ensuing effects on (for example) prison capacity. Building more roads may seem to be the answer to traffic congestion, but often leads to even greater congestion, as more drivers are attracted to using their cars. We do systems thinking well if delineating the represented system brings us closer to understanding the problem we are dealing with.

At a deeper level, however, we need to address the phenomenology of systems thinking. The relationship between the 'Life-world' and our perception of it, becomes a particularly pressing problem. What is the scope for directed or planned change, given that we as humans can operate on the world only by representing aspects of it to ourselves? Where are 'we' in the systems we create? Are policies 'in' the systems we discern, or are they to be understood as operating 'on' these systems?

One approach to this problem is to revisit the work of Luhmann, who envisaged communicative systems as becoming functionally distinct and therefore self-steering via a process of closure. Moving on from this essentially sociological perspective, 'policy' might be thought of, at least potentially, as a way of taking advantage of this self-steering capacity. At the same time, the steering capacities of states (from which policies must emanate) are compromised in a world of proliferating functional systems (Esmark, 2011: 101).

Considerable effort has been applied to understanding what this conundrum might mean for policy capacity (see Crozier, 2010). Crozier uses systems theory to characterise an interactive shift in the nature of policymaking, in a world of dispersed governance. As he puts it, 'In the earlier policy chain model, communication was understood to inform and explain policy, whereas in the new patterns of governance 'communication' itself seems to make policy' (Crozier, 2008: 6). The proliferant nature of modern governance is facilitated by developments in communication, which, in breaking open the recursive properties of previously 'closed' systems, has implications for both policy and politics. This use of systems theory highlights, as well as extends, the importance of the policy/politics relationship in these circumstances.

Interestingly, our attempt here to reconcile governance with systems theory points up quite strongly the contrast between governance and the policy perspective. From this perspective, 'governance' is not self-steering, but is itself an emergent property of a continually changing institutional system. The boundaries of the 'state' become more fluid and less assured, necessitating steering choices (policies) that, paradoxically, may need to acknowledge steering limitations in order to be effective (Chapter 4).

In Chapter 7 we explore the communicative dimensions of this reinterpretation of public policy. In the remainder of this chapter, we consider the implications, for both the understanding and making of policy, of systems thinking as a form of social action and analysis.

As policy thinkers, we are interested in human action systems, to use Checkland's term, operating in particular contexts. In human action systems, relationships between people are expressed in terms of mutually understood objectives and ways of doing things (Checkland and Haynes, 1994). A policy perspective that derives from systems thinking understands the analytical consequences – and opportunities – of this type of interconnection. In the next section, we suggest how these principles might be applied, through the use of practical examples derived from recent policy history.

Applications of systems thinking – an overview

Application 1: boundaries and points of intervention

If one of the key insights of systems thinking is interconnection, where do we draw the boundary around our field of interest? Boundaries of complex systems are open, fluid and socially constructed – therefore, working across these boundaries requires an understanding as to how they have been constructed by human social processes (Eppel et al, 2011: 52; Chapter 5).

There are many examples of policy analysis transcending its immediate context. While practice may have lagged, policy thinking about the determinants of health, for example, has gone much further than a focus on the availability of hospitals and pharmaceuticals. The links are articulated between health and poverty, between disease and nutrition; between disease and lifestyle and between lifestyle and the built form of cities (see Chapter 5, Reconsidering Borders).

How do we create modes of decision-making that reflect this reality? For example, if one of the key links between poverty and ill health is poor diet, how might this be addressed? Conventional policy instruments may lack penetration, or may in themselves discriminate against poor people (for example, taxing soft drinks is often recommended but may simply antagonise and further impoverish consumers without changing behaviour).

Particular institutional contexts may suggest particular responses. In the UK for example, free school lunches are provided to all children in the first three years of primary school. Celebrity chef Jamie Oliver decided to teach school meals-makers how to cook better and more nutritionally. The trial site school remains an exemplar of the new approach. However, Oliver himself said he had 'failed', to the extent that poorer folk still regarded eating healthy meals as something that only 'posh' folk did (Furness, 2015).

Systems thinking suggests some tools for traversing this apparent gulf between desired outcomes and underlying realities. The boundary of the policy field, for example, considered systemically, might well be particular communities, and the policy-means a community engagement strategy speaking to parents as well as children. But of course, such an endeavour would require more resources, in terms of time, money and expertise, than most governments would be prepared to allocate.

Another example of rethinking boundaries is road congestion. Modern technologies allow policymakers to impose congestion-pricing charges on the users of particular roads, either in general, or at particular times. Markets are responsive mechanisms, and (in the case of congestion pricing) if the price is set correctly, markets will allocate the road-resource efficiently (that is, so that the number of road users is such that the marginal social cost of the trip equals the marginal benefit) (Parry, 2008). Ironically, though, due to its probable political unpopularity, a strong government is required to implement a price-based policy.

When we think about transport as a complex adaptive system, however, we have a far less structured scenario, in which our spatial 'boundary' becomes the city itself, and our time boundary also extends outwards. We may think about why and how people move about. What influences their choices? What do they tell us about these choices? What public services are involved? What is the adaptive capacity of these services?

In any given city, transport choices are shaped by many factors, including the density of settlement and relationships between where people live and work. We know that people will use public transport if it is seen as fast, reliable and reasonably priced. But we also know that most of us prefer to use privately owned motor vehicles whenever convenient. Changing social trends and concerns about personal security may even have accentuated private motor-vehicle use. In many rich (but fearful) cities, parents prefer to drive their young children to school, rather than have them use public transport, or ride a bike. In addition, parents' choice of school may mean the local school is bypassed, ruling out the walk-to-school option. But this increased complexity may itself be a trigger for discussing a range of possible interventions. One approach to alleviating traffic congestion, for example, might be to encourage more parents to walk with their child to school.

Our examples show that change-interventions (which are what most policies are) need not operate at the level of the 'big' system to be effective. Jamie's program to improve nutrition achieved noteworthy success by focusing on the practical. Skilful understanding of boundaries may take us beyond the initial site (but not far beyond it), or may suggest micro-changes which over time will have much bigger effects in terms of achieving policy outcomes in complex circumstances.

Application 2 regulation: feedback and control

Regulators are constantly trying to 'control' certain behaviours (for example, by collecting tax, or controlling flows of people). Yet the policy action itself changes the behaviour of those affected by it. As a result, public policies are part of a cycle of action and reaction, with frequent episodes of failure. Australian policy towards international students is a good example of a regulatory system that lacked the feedback mechanisms needed for effective control.

International education has become one of Australia's largest export industries (Dodd, 2016). A major component relates to the vocational education sector (trade-training). Traditionally, colleges of technical and further education (TAFE) were the main providers of this form of training. Since the industry was deregulated, numerous private colleges have sprung up, offering courses to international students keen to gain a useful qualification. Student visas have also permitted them to work. A further provision, for those who continued to work, allowed access to another visa type connecting the vocational education students and the skilled migration stream, which offered the prospect of permanent residency. Not surprisingly, there was a surge in applications for these courses.

Problems soon appeared. Many of the private colleges offered little or no value for money. Unscrupulous employers preyed on many of the students, who were prepared to work for very little and for longer hours than their visas allowed. Unions first alerted governments to this situation. Even so, it took several years for the loophole to be closed. By 2017, many colleges were switching attention to the domestic market, encouraging students with little prospect of completing a course to enrol. The Australian Skills Quality Authority (designed to audit the burgeoning industry) announced in its 2015–16 Annual Report that it was adopting a risk management approach to its work (ASQA, 2016), meaning that it planned to give more attention to colleges with particular characteristics, rather than running the same 'compliance ruler' over all of them.

There are many ways of characterising this type of policy issue. The transition from regulation to deregulation to reregulation is a familiar one. From a systems perspective, we can see the policy itself as seeking to influence a complex adaptive system, in the sense that policy instruments impact upon stakeholders, who then move to preserve their advantage. If there is a reasonably quick feedback loop (in this case, from unions to the Labor government), then there is the possibility for regulatory policy change (such as restricting access to the transitional visa category).

We can go further. Administrators are engaged in values balancing (Thacher and Rein, 2004). There is a need to attract fee-paying students, but also a need to ensure they do not undermine the general skilled migration stream, which is strictly capped, and for which applicants are rigorously vetted. In this situation, administrators become de facto policymakers. A growing body of work attests to the importance of implementers as 'values-balancers' in public policy (Steenhuisen and van Eeten, 2008; Chapter 8).

We would also suggest that a CAS approach gives a fresh perspective on what should be done (that is, on policy design). In regulating vocational colleges, we wish to take actions that will bring about desired, rather than undesired, responses from stakeholders. Mixing policy instruments in appropriate ways – using the 'scalpel' rather than the 'blunt instrument' – will be important (Howlett, 2008). Shutting down shonky operators sends a clear signal to the rest. But managing an adaptive system needs information inputs that are fast, clear and reliable. Consultative mechanisms play a part. But an adaptive system requires something more: experienced field officers who know what they are doing and who can (with the necessary delegations) make decisions on the spot. Public servants scrutinising performance information from their desks may not be seeing the most important parts of the picture.

Note that this way of working requires new models of bureaucratic functioning, which in many respects go against the longstanding fashion for centralised agencies to contract out as many activities as possible. Effective policy requires public agencies to be able to act in dispersed, networked ways when they need to (APSC, 2007). We return to this issue in Chapter 7.

Application 3: exploring multiple pathways: implications for comparative public policy

Although not often invoked in policy contexts, one of the most useful perceptions of systems thinking is that of equifinality (multiple pathways to similar final states). This is the idea, first enunciated in the context of general systems theory, that open systems, despite quite different starting points, can evolve to achieve a similar end-state. The concept was adapted by organisation scientists, to explain the perceived fact that organisations, in similar circumstances, could achieve similar outcomes using different structural and strategic mechanisms (Gresov and Drazin, 1997). Interpreted in this way, the principle of equifinality suggested a flexible menu of strategic choices in management design (Child, 1972).

The same principle can be extended to public policy analysis, and to comparative public policy in particular. Hoard, for example, in recent work on the role of gender policy expertise, employed a comparative analysis that brought out the role of multiple causal effects in producing equivalent results (Hoard, 2015). Earlier work on industry policy came to similar conclusions (Stewart, 1994). A system with institutional structures that looked quite dissimilar might in fact produce an equivalent result, because one part of the system compensated for another.

To find the 'common thread' running across a range of successful countries required attention to both the constraining and enabling impacts of context. The industry policies of a small country such as New Zealand, for example, differ from those employed in a much larger economy such as Japan's. These differences do not mean that one country is right and the other wrong, simply that public action in the form of industry policy necessarily takes different forms in a smaller country.

Appropriate conceptualisation of outcomes is essential to bring out these factors. For example, jurisdictions may achieve housing security quite differently. Some may invest in public housing, others in tax incentives for home ownership. Conversely, systems that look similar in terms of their institutions may in fact produce quite different outcomes, given different contextual factors. A trade policy that worked for Canada, for example, would not necessarily work for Australia because of Canada's crucial contextual differences – such as the presence of the US as a near neighbour. Work on policy success implicitly allows for these 'deep' commonalities. Equally, context may account for variation in the outcomes of seemingly similar implementation approaches (Johns, 2006). In learning from others, therefore, understanding contextual differences will be critical in drawing the right lessons. Potentially, systems analysis helps us to draw the right lessons by showing the precise parameters of equivalent policies – that is, how and in what circumstances different means achieve similar ends. But much work remains to be done in this area (Moon et al, 2017: 18).

Application 4: state legitimacy and adaptation

We have seen that there is a useful connection between literatures dealing with state legitimacy and state capacity, and systems thinking. One of the key issues in development-assistance policy is that of fragile states, defined as 'those that are unable to meet [their] population's expectations or manage changes in expectations and capacity through the political process' (Organisation for Economic Cooperation and Development) (OECD), 2008). Multi-country perspectives suggest that fragility is often aligned with poor governance. The World Bank assesses countries across 16 criteria, including a cluster specifically related to public management and public institutions (World Bank Fragile and Conflict-Affected Countries Group, nd). 'Governance' variables typically include measures of accountability; political stability, government effectiveness, regulatory quality, rule of law and control of corruption.

However, systems thinking would suggest ways in which policy may address these seemingly intractable situations. There are many examples of states that appear to be in crisis – that is, overwhelmed by change to the point where institutions begin to break down. Poor public policies and poor institutions are often at the heart of these problems. Venezuela, for example, implemented generous policies in the Chavez era, but found they were no longer viable when national income (almost entirely based on oil) fell.

Easton's simple model of the political system suggests that without adequate adjustment mechanisms, the stability of the state may be under threat. Interestingly, however, the many governance problems associated with state fragility are no longer considered an insuperable barrier to effective aid. Provided the aid objective is chosen with an eye to the specific problem situation, success rates are comparable for both fragile and resilient states. Rather than a rigid picture of inadequacy, researchers are becoming more attuned to the possibilities of identifying smaller systems that are more easily influenced. 'Donors should narrow their resources on a few specific sectors that correspond to core functions of the state, to help foster its legitimacy based on demonstrable performance and to strengthen citizen-state and citizen-citizen trust' (Chandy, 2011).

In terms of our discussion in this chapter, a failed or faulty state may manifest itself through poor or inadequate governance. An appreciation of the possibilities of complexity allows the boundary of consideration to be drawn wider (to encompass the state as a whole) but also more specifically (to allow for more specific policies). The CAS framework suggests that, given uncertain outcomes, a modest intervention that 'joins up' valued activities and characteristics, will be preferable to a macro approach that seeks to address entrenched governance problems, such as corruption. This avenue, based on modest augmentation of performance-based legitimacy (where good outcomes, no matter how small the improvement, are rewarded), would appear to be one of the most promising for the future.

The four types of application considered here illustrate the versatility of systems thinking – through it, we access scales of governance at the macro (state), meso (regulatory) and micro (community) levels. Moreover, by focusing on boundaries and their implications within a given level, it becomes possible to consider sites for policy intervention that range outside the nominal range of policy thinking, thereby acknowledging the dispersed nature of the governance landscape. Systems-based analysis represents an important mode for bringing together policy and governance.

Conclusions

We have seen how the word 'system' has continued to dominate the business of writing about policy, but as a way of designating a field of interest, or of describing distinctive activities at a particular subsystem level, rather than as an analytic approach. In policy studies, systems-terms have proved useful as a form of structured description. The concept of policy 'subsystems' drew attention to the inter-relationships that were seen to underpin the activity of policymaking. Subsystems could also be classified according to their number and type of participants, ranging from those that were relatively closed, to more open issue networks. The nature of the policies under consideration (particularly their technical content) was seen to be paramount in shaping the degree of 'open-ness' of the system.

Despite these advances, it would be fair to say that the language and perspectives of systems thinking have never been harmonised with those of the policymaker, or of the policy analyst. Systems thinking is difficult to grasp, and may often be counter-intuitive. Social, political and economic systems are so messy and so complex that simplifying them to the extent required to make models tractable, limits (or overstates) their practical usefulness.

Even for systems enthusiasts, it has been difficult to answer the question: why go to all the additional trouble? The stance of policy studies has been shaped by its disciplinary parentage in political science. Public policies have been seen to emerge from fairly well understood situations and scenarios – from interest group activity, and political utility. Institutional analysis confirms the longevity of agency roles, values and interconnections. Empirical policy writing, in recounting the 'story' of public policy in any field, employs familiar tropes and emphases. There seems, on the face of it, no reason to add to the methodological menu, particularly if we are concerned with analysis 'of' policy.

On the other hand, we also know that the policy world has changed. Since the early 2000s, there has been an upsurge in complexity-related thinking (with or without an explicit systems aspect) via the discourse of 'wicked problems' and to some degree through the adaptive management literature. It has been shown that changes in the structures and processes of governance have both contributed to, and been affected by, these requirements.

Our perspective is that complexity and systems thinking go hand in hand. Far from being abstract or esoteric, systems thinking can provide fresh perspectives on age-old problems of state legitimacy and governance. A system is not – or should not be – a mysterious or overly abstract entity. From a practical policy perspective, systems are sets of relationships created to achieve various purposes. When we create (or change) a public policy, we create (or change) the structures, flows and accountabilities that link actors in a system.

At the meso-level, there is much to be gained by thinking about policies as complex adaptive systems – that is, as constantly changing flows of actions and values. When we do this, we understand the status quo (often overlooked or neglected in practical policy analysis) much better. We can usually see what the consequences of certain actions might be (or alternatively, from an ex-post perspective) using the changes that have occurred, to see more clearly what the underlying system is actually about.

The key implication of complexity science for policy does not lie in greater complexity of policy itself. It is subtler than that. It is an acknowledgement that there may be useful capacities available that are difficult to identify. There may also be threats that have implications for the design of our institutions. There may be relatively simple things that we can do, that will positively affect a complex system. Or perhaps systems that are more complicated than they need to be should be simplified. Bureaucracies that do not talk to each other may need to be re-engineered. In other words, useful points of intervention may be quite 'other' than those we imagine.

Because so much policy is reactive, there will be many instances where policy is seen to have failed. Far from being pessimistic, this acknowledgement should give us hope, if we can learn to make use of complexity, rather than being defeated by it. To quote Axelrod and Cohen, 'Rather than undermining the value of complexity thinking as a way of thinking about social systems, an appreciation of how Complex Adaptive Systems can fail provides valuable guidance for the design and management of complex systems' (Axelrod and Cohen, 2000: 31). Where uncertainty is endemic, public policies that are informed by these insights have a vital role to play.

3

Reconsidering *institutions*

> The development of modern political science and public policy has tended to neglect the fact that politics and policymaking take place in the context of institutions.
> (Parsons, 1995: 223)

Introduction

Institutions have always been fundamental to the study of public policy, as constraining, enabling and structuring settings and influences upon policy actors and outcomes. Institutions endure, whether as the formal structures of politics and policymaking, or informal influences, routines and processes. Institutions, both formal and informal, shape policy, but they are also shaped by it. They exist within political, economic and societal contexts, and are themselves subject to overt and covert power and influence that may or may not induce change. There are many varying approaches to explaining this, and to explaining the ongoing role that institutions play in politics, society and policymaking (Rhodes et al, 2008). We see institutions as critical to understanding public policy because, as policy theory and policy challenges have advanced in complexity, so too have institutions and institutional theory kept pace through constant reinvention. We reconsider institutions here from the policy perspective with an interest in the evolution of the theory, the dynamics of institutions and institutional change in the governance era, and the problem-solving, policy-shaping role of institutions in contemporary times.

Although institutions are now central to the study of public policy, the focus upon them has shifted over time. They have been, variously, central to analysis, marginalised in analysis and, more recently, rediscovered as central, but in more complex, networked circumstances. The seminal work of 'rediscovering institutions', or rediscovering their study as central in political analysis, in reaction to the behaviourism and rational choice approaches, was March and Olsen's (1983; 1989). Prior to that, March and Olsen saw the discipline of political science as having been led astray by pluralistic depictions of politics as entirely society dependent, neglecting, at least in the US, the role, and the changing role, of the state (Peters, 2012). New institutional analysis is focused on understanding and improving political systems, with an emphasis upon how institutions 'fashion, enable and constrain political actors' (March and Olsen, 2006: 4). However, its many variants have emerged in part in an effort to capture, not only the constraining features of institutions, but also the norms, values, behaviour and narratives by which institutions themselves are constituted, shaped, influenced and changed (Lowdnes, 2010: 60).

Our interest is in how this renewed focus on institutions relates to contemporary policymaking in the addressing of highly complex, wicked problems such as homelessness, indigenous disadvantage or global climate change, that require connected, systemic solutions. Institutions have long been recognised as playing a significant role, for example, in policy success or failure, as highlighted by Pressman and Wildavsky's (1984) study of federalism and implementation failure (Chapter 8). Similarly, Skocpol's (1985) state-centric analysis highlights the role of the state as an institution in shaping public policy, both as the consequence of the actions of various bureaucratic and political actors, and of the distinctive structuring and organisation of the state. There is less emphasis in political studies, however, on the impact of policy in terms of its shaping of institutions. Institutions affect policy in various ways, but politics, power, policy and implementation are also important in effecting change, including institutional change. Monetary policy change in the 1980s, for instance, and responses to the Global Financial Crisis (GFC), both led to institutional change across many jurisdictions, although similar circumstances provoked both similar and differing institutional responses.

Arguably there is a parallel between the economic, social and environmental challenges to the problem-solving capacity of Western liberal democracies over the last 50 years and the significant changes over that time in institutions and institutional analysis. The rise of new institutionalism may represent one symptom of growing complexity in problems and policymaking. Institutional analysis, prior to the Western liberal democratising period of the 1960s–1970s (Heclo, 2006: 731), was more bounded, narrowly preoccupied with historical and descriptive research in the formal-legal sense. This tradition persists today, Rhodes argues, in analysis of 'the historical evolution of formal-legal institutions' and of the 'ideas embedded in them' and thus in 'the interplay of ideas and institutions' (Rhodes, 2008a: 103). Nevertheless, from the 1970s more opening and engaging socio-political contexts prompted theorists to identify a 'society-centric behaviourism' (Eulau, 1963; Rhodes, 1995: 42) drawing attention to the role of agency in politics, policy, society and institutional change.

The literature suggests that behaviourism flourished while institutionalism languished until March and Olsen's revival that reflected, in part, an interest in constraints on the state as a result of neo-liberal structural change (Chapter 4). Institutions and institutional theory have changed remarkably over the last 50 years. Both are relevant to contemporary policymaking. From the policy studies perspective, and in particular where institutions are seen to fail, policy, politics and power can be seen as driving change in the hope of building more effective institutions as a means of addressing challenging problems. The utility of the institutional approach is, however, complicated by the fragmentation of its theory, with some dismissing it on these grounds, and others arguing against the validity of its endless variants, or reconciling the newer and more traditional approaches. However, institutions are important for problem-solving, with institutional failure offering valuable lessons, and so the institutional approach is an important component of policy analysis, illuminating in some circumstances, but certainly less so in others. Appropriate, effective institutions in both the traditional and new institutional sense remain a concern for policymakers.

In this chapter, we therefore argue that institutions are fundamental to the study of policy and policy capacity, despite varying opinions about how to study them, and about the relative influences of institutions and agency, or purposive action, upon outcomes. This chapter reviews a complex and shifting landscape in terms of approaches to the study of institutions, and considers how governance and systems theory and approaches in particular have recast the significance of institutional analysis for policy studies, in theory and practice. We follow the trajectory of institutional theory; we reconsider institutions in the context of networks and systems in the governance era; and we reflect on institutions and the shaping of policy today. Furthermore, we argue that institutionalism is significant for understanding policy, not least because, as public problems have advanced in complexity, so has institutionalism in order to better depict their circumstances and explain outcomes.

Why institutions matter

Policy studies routinely find that institutions matter. When Western institutions were being challenged by democratising influences, it was partly because they were seen by a new generation of activists as 'instruments of social control' that harboured 'racism, sexism, consumerism, militarism' (Heclo, 2006: 731–2). Depictions of institutions as 'iron cages' were nuanced over the following decades. Conceptions of institutions as formal structures became augmented by a view of institutions as less formal, influenced and shaped by power, people, politics and processes (Hay and Wincott, 1998). Not only were institutions parliaments, executives and judiciaries, then, but also the result or reflection of, for example, values, ideas, attitudes and activism. The former endure certainly, but attention was increasingly drawn to the manner in which they may evolve and change, not least as a response to powerful influences and public pressure. Institutions matter then for drawing attention to the context in which actors strive to address complex problems, at the organisational, political and structural level of the state, and at the social level of interactions, behaviour, politics, power and practice.

Differing institutional contexts matter. Weaver and Rockman (1993) investigate the significance of differing UK-style parliamentary and US-style separation of power contexts in a range of countries across a range of policy areas including energy, the environment and trade. They see differing institutional constraints as impacting attributes of decision-making and therefore, in cascading fashion, impacting policy-making capabilities, policy choices and policy outcomes. Their analysis shows that institutional contexts generate differing policy risks and opportunities in differing circumstances. While they find that institutions matter to policy success or failure, they do not identify the most efficacious settings or recommended change for the most desired policy outcome. Rather they find that common issues exist across different contexts, and there may be, for example, a common network governance response to the same complex problems in varying settings.

Studies show that institutions matter to policy outcomes. As a means of generating lessons for best practice, Benoit (2003), for instance, considers why similar systems in similar circumstances adopt different policy responses to the issue of illicit drugs. While many focus on the deviance aspects of drug policy, she argues that 'drug policy is a product of the legislative process, and its variations, too, are shaped by the ways in which institutions mediate the fortunes of policy agendas' (Benoit, 2003: 270). International institutions matter (Chapter 5) in the framing of domestic climate policy over recent decades, in terms of initial agenda setting, in terms of aspiration setting and in terms of monitoring, accountability and pressing for effective change. Furthermore, '[i]nternational norms can shape or redefine domestic interests, enable policies in conformity with those norms, and create normative pressures for change by linking with extant domestic and foreign policy norms' (Bernstein, 2002: 203). Such norms have been the impetus for multilevelled institutional climate policy responses.

Institutions matter because they shape responses to wicked problem-solving. They matter where they are capable of recognising and addressing wicked problems; where they can adapt their skills and structures to manage them; and where they deploy the resources to address them (Australian Public Service Commission (APSC), 2007). However, the literature suggests that institutions tend conservatively towards path dependency (Kay, 2005), not only in terms of systems (constitutional, legislative, electoral, territorial, executive, and so on) but also in terms of past policies limiting future options. If current structures, laws, policies, programs and processes are to respond to wicked problems, then institutions must also foster innovative, collaborative solutions that may not have been previously deployed (Klijn and Koppenjan, 2015). There is no one optimal response to complex problems, so institutions would ideally be open to innovation, flexibility and adaptation, which may be challenging in political systems with no democratic tradition of engagement and change.

The formal-informal nuances now recognised in institutions matter in terms of more effective responses to wicked problems, and of meeting these challenges of innovation and change (Banerjee et al, 2006; Chapter 9). Given the fractured literature, there is no single explanation of informality in institutions, but there is recognition, as there is in governance theory, that some formalising of networks is characteristic of new governance practices (Bevir, 2009: 112). There is scope for future policy research that investigates this formal-informal characterisation and dynamic. Conventionally, the state and its institutions were seen as isolated, authoritative enforcers of government dictates, but they are now seen, by governance theory for instance, as more directly connected with, and responsive to, civil society (Pierre and Peters, 2000: 81–2; Chapter 4). This connectivity is of concern to policymakers as key to complex problem-solving, as reflected in Klijn and Koppenjan's (2015) studies of network responses to policy complexity, but is not entirely new, and has previously been investigated by policy communities and networks studies. The many issues of interest to future research interest include the operation of differing networks within and beyond government, the impetus for forming and formalising networks, their role, if any, in policy, their interaction and the style of their interaction with government, and the role of the state in networks.

Institutions matter then because their significance endures as sites for, and influences upon, policy shaping in increasingly complex contexts, where both governance theory and systems theory have utility, we will argue, as complementary explanations. Our reconsideration of institutions here is realist in the sense that the role of the state is taken as a given in policymaking (Heclo, 2006: 732), but reflective for its interest in the changing role of the state, policy-related behaviour and society. The reflexive, adaptive, disaggregated yet resilient liberal democratic state is proving capable of change and enhanced interactivity in contemporary times, and its differing operations in differing policy domains of varying complexity are of interest to policy researchers. Many would argue that the state has not been left behind in the governance era, but is enduring, although transformed, as Chapter 4 suggests, by new forms of engagement, collaboration, partnering, and hybrid management (Bentley and Wilsdon, 2003). The role of ongoing policy studies is to examine the state as policymaker with an awareness of its changing nature, the pressures upon institutions, and the emergence and operation of networked configurations in the management of complex policy.

Institutions and institutional analysis

The institutional literature is daunting for its complexity. The study of institutions is nevertheless fundamental to the study of politics and policy (Peters, 2011: 79), constituting much 'of what could be called early political science' (Steinmo, 2008: 118). At its most basic, institutional analysis explains institutional contexts as key to real world outcomes and the ways in which they may shape, facilitate and constrain policy. Institutional analysis had less utility traditionally with its narrow focus on formal-legal structures and processes. However, its recent iterations identify actions and agents within institutions as central to political life (Peters, 2012), and to explaining political decisions and policy (Cairney, 2012b: 70). While traditional institutional analysis failed to capture the dynamics of political and policy-based behaviour, new institutionalism has grounded theory in a balanced way by depicting institutions as both structuring political life *and* being influenced by human agency (Raedelli et al, 2012: 539). This is a robust approach to explaining policy in the governance era.

New institutionalism has also introduced more nuanced understandings of the nature of an institution itself, with wide-ranging definitions now common. Institutions are recognised as both structure and process (Peters, 2011: 81), operating in ways both *formal* (constitutional-legal) *and informal* (patterns, relationships, understandings) (Cairney, 2012b: 69). The boundaries between formal and informal institutions, and the formal-informal relations and interactions that may develop in pursuit of policy outcomes, will increasingly attract the attention of researchers. Formal institutions include governments, executives, judiciaries, in arrangements at multiple levels, while less formal institutions typically include relations, norms, processes and routines, although this distinction may vary according to circumstance (Table 3.1). New institutionalism sees institutions as: incentive structures (rational choice institutionalism), macro-historical structures and regularities (historical institutionalism), cultural norms and frames (sociological institutionalism) and meaning structures and concepts (discursive institutionalism) (Schmidt, 2010: 5).

In an applied or operational sense beyond government, institutions are:

> (T)he set of working rules that are used to determine who is eligible to make decisions in some arena, what actions are allowed or constrained, what aggregation rules will be used, what procedures must be followed, what information must or must not be provided and what payoffs will be assigned to individuals dependent on their actions. (Ostrom, 1990: 51)

Table 3.1: Hard/formal and soft/informal institutions

Hard/formal (and/or physical) institutions	Soft/informal (and/or virtual) institutions
• Structures of government, confederal/federal, federal/unitary, presidential/parliamentary, unicameral/bi-cameral, courts, departments, and so on. • Rules, laws, agencies, bodies, offices, powers, the role and reach of the judiciary, procedures [for example for referendums and citizen initiatives], and so on. • Electoral and party systems, rules of government formation, executive-legislative and public-private structures, structures of bureaucracies, and so on. • Structures, powers, systems, organisations, strategies and/or procedures beyond government and at the supranational, global level.	• Intergovernmental relations, executive-legislative and/or public-private relations, and so on. • Economic, regulatory or welfare based policy norms, models, organisations, conventions, processes, and so on. • Traditions, norms, behaviours, understanding, custom and/or practice, informal contacts, communications and/or ways of operating, and so on. • Routinisation, socialisation, mobilisation, conversation, community groups, voting coalitions, policy communities/networks, and so on.

Sources: Adapted from Pierre and Peters, 2000: 43; Cairney, 2012b: 70–4; Bevir, 2009: 110

Much institutional analysis is comparative. The influence of federalism and the separation of powers between federal and subnational governments are, for example, obvious in the shaping of policy, but also in reflecting differing values and priorities in differing contexts. Constitutions codify the rules governing federal-state powers, but may be amended by referendum, which is a formalised process itself, but may be invoked as the consequence of public pressure or values change. The recognition of the rights of indigenous peoples is one such change under varying formalised processes in the previous British colonies in Australia, New Zealand and Canada (Armitage, 1995). Policy change in Australia finally followed the 1967 referendum giving the federal government the authority to legislate in Aboriginal affairs, including establishing new institutions. While aimed at ending exploitative state and territory practices, these new institutions embodied values and engendered practices that have nevertheless failed to overcome enduring indigenous disadvantage (APSC, 2007). However, their establishment shows that policy can initiate institution building and presage change.

In an applied sense, institutional analysis often considers influences over, and constraints upon, public policy, often by comparison across domains, jurisdictions or countries. Institutional explanations may be invoked where problems are longstanding, where solutions fail, or where success offers lessons that may be replicated. Lesson drawing is a significant component of institutional analysis, in terms, for example, of the relatively more successful climate policies in leading countries in the European Union than those in the Asia-Pacific. The formal structures of the EU have facilitated leading actions by member countries to reduce emissions, while the absence of such structures in the Asia-Pacific has impeded actions there (Crowley and Nakamura, 2018). There are multilevelled influences and arrangements in climate policy from international, to regional, to domestic, local and indeed to the level of individual choice and action. This illustrates, not only the complexity of addressing this wicked problem, but also the responsiveness, adaptation and redesign that is required to match the rate of accelerating problems like climate change (Gupta et al, 2010).

Analysis of institutions is anchored in this 'real world empirical' analysis, rather than in 'grand theory' (Steinmo, 2008: 118), answering real world questions through empirical investigation, using document and case study analysis, often with historical, comparative explanations (Bevir, 2009: 110). However, the methods by which institutions have been studied have varied. The methodology of 'old institutionalism' was primarily 'thick', detailed description through historical analysis, which is recognisable in historical institutional analysis today. It was criticised for lacking rigour by behaviourists and rational choice theorists (Peters, 2012). Rhodes (1995: 48) cites Easton's concern that 'analysis of law and institutions could not explain power or policy because it did not cover all the variables'. However, behaviourists pursued more scientific methods, in order to analyse cases in terms of measurable variables, but to the neglect of the 'basic processes and mechanisms motivating politics' (Steinmo, 2008: 120–1). New institutionalism offers a middle course by recognising both the need to study factors or variables as well as policy and political differences that may be fashioned in an institutional context or as an institutional response (Raedelli et al, 2012: 545).

The many variants of new institutionalism

While new institutionalism is a broad church with many sub-variants, its theorists agree that institutions are rules, practices and narratives that structure behaviour; where they differ is in their views of 'the nature of the beings whose actions or behaviour is being structured'. Do

Table 3.2: Old, behavioural and new institutionalism

	Old institutionalism	Behavioural-rationalism	New institutionalism
Concerns	Law, legal processes, structures	Developing socialised accounts	Structured contexts for action
Emphasis	Structural/ organisational focus	People/ processes as influences	Social phenomena as influences
Description	State-centric formalism	Society-centric behaviourism	Society-state dualism
Analysis	Normative, descriptive, comparative, historical	Objective, 'scientific', methodological individualism	Empirical, objective, 'scientific', socio-structuralism
Method	Formal-legal	Rational-choice	Multiple (variant based) methods
Focus	Legal-institutional context	Behavioural-rational context	Behavioural-institutional context
Strength	Historical explanation	Recognises human agency	Emphasises agency and context
Weakness	Under-socialised analysis	Ignores structuring factors	Broad array of sub-variants

Sources: Adapted from Rhodes, 1995; Steinmo, 2008; Peters, 2012; Lowdnes and Roberts, 2013; Cairney, 2012b

human beings 'calculate the costs and benefits in the choices they face' (*rational institutionalism*); do they ask instead 'what should I do? What is appropriate?' (*sociological institutionalism*); or are they self-interested and/or rule abiding depending on the circumstances? (*historical institutionalism*) (Steinmo, 2008: 126). New institutionalism emphasises the structuring of behaviour, and therefore power and dominance, as central in analysis (Hall and Taylor, 1996) with an appreciation of norms, rules and understandings that was less emphasised in traditional accounts (Lowdnes, 1996: 183). Again there is debate (Rhodes, 1995; Rhodes et al, 2008) over the extent to which this is new, given the early work by organisational theorists (Selznick, 1948; 1957) on the role of adaptive social structures whereby 'informal organisations evolve within formal structures' (Parsons, 1995: 325; Peters, 2012: 130).

Schmidt (2010) and others (Hay, 2006) have suggested, however, that even new institutionalism underplays the significance of ideas and discourse in the rational, sociological and historical accounts. They propose a constructivist *discursive institutionalism* that is concerned with 'both the substantive content of ideas and the interactive processes of discourse in institutional contexts' (Schmidt, 2010: 1). Discursive institutionalism more overtly acknowledges ideas, and the dynamics, power and influence by which ideas gain traction, through processes of deliberation and legitimation, as platforms, programs, policies, paradigms and even philosophies that can drive change (Schmidt, 2010: 3). It emphasises the role of discursive coalitions in institutional change, while retaining new institutionalism's recognition that institutions both constrain (ensuring continuity) and facilitate (enabling change) (Schmidt, 2010: 4). Bell (2011) is not convinced that an ideas-focused institutionalism is needed to explain change when a suitably tailored historical institutionalism would do, however, the role of beliefs and the intentions of agents remain a key focus of policy research.

Among the new institutionalisms are those that emphasise connectivity, collaboration and/or networking between formal and informal institutions, ideas, processes and actors, often with an interest in complex problem-solving. Individual and community behaviour would ideally feature as a key variable in policy outcomes, then, but in the context of networked efforts, overarching strategies, services and processes employed at times by various levels of government (APSC, 2007). Network institutionalism recognises this, with institutionalisation manifest as the 'recurrent pattern of behavioural interaction or exchange between individuals or organisations', with government and non-government networks as critical variables. It assumes: 1) a relational perspective; 2) complexity with overlapping, cross-cutting linkages; 3) that networks are both resources and constraints; and 4) that networks mobilise and influence in differentiated ways (Ansell, 2008: 75–6). By this account, networks vary markedly, in terms of formality and intentionality, being both deliberately and inadvertently structured, and varying in terms of efficacy or capacity, and behaviour types.

While institutional theory has already evolved significantly, its many variants and sub-variants are less daunting and disconcerting if, as Rhodes suggests, the 'individual ingredients' of institutional analysis 'are (seen as) as old as the hills' (1997: 79). What matters is that, despite their differences, the variants of institutionalism are complementary and that, in combination, they offer a robust account of policy continuity and change (Peters, 2012). New institutional theory has played a significant role in reconciling structural and behavioural accounts, but it has also introduced a distinctive emphasis upon institutions as: rules not organisations; informal as well as formal; dynamic as well as stabilising; embodying values and power; and contextually embedded (Lowdnes, 2018: 59–63). Network institutionalism (Ansell, 2008), which emphasises connectivity and complexity, has utility in terms of analysing complex challenges, crises and responses, as do governance and systems-based accounts of the broader policy environment and political contexts.

Governance, networks, systems dynamics

The rise of new institutionalism roughly parallels the rise of governance theory (Bevir, 2009: 112), and for us suggests that both theories are responses to changing policy contexts, including more complex circumstances. We are also interested in the manner in which governance theory, with its emphasis on decentralised, networked and collaborative organisation beyond the state, necessitates a reconsideration of institutions, institutional analysis, policy shaping, problem-solving and change. While institutions have always been considered central in the analysis of differing political systems, with distinctive policy systems operating within them, governance theory has highlighted the significance of policy systems and networks across boundaries and beyond government (see Bodin and Crona, 2009). Furthermore, network governance theory and network institutionalism draw their emphases from the earlier policy network and policy community approaches that emphasise connectivity at the subsystem and policy domain level (Marsh and Rhodes, 1992). While structural and systemic contexts are rightly not seen to wholly determine policy, given the insights of the behaviourism and the influence of actors and actions (Eulau, 1963), they are nevertheless significant.

Governance today is understood as more than the act of governing (Rhodes, 1997; Chapter 1). Notions of governments as rulers have been redefined to reflect the emergence of more collaborative processes, with formal routines increasingly augmented by informal processes (Osborne and Gaebler, 1992). The study of governing process is now concerned with the governing of interactivity both within and beyond state boundaries, the control government retains and the legitimacy of societal inclusion and action (Kjaer, 2004). Governance theorists reconceptualise institutions as impacted by this broader change. While this change has occurred, institutions have also remained embedded in, and impacted by, various types of more static systems – ideational, political, economic and spatially multilevelled from local to global – with transboundary impacts (Chapter 5). Policy is shaped by systems and structures that are 'relatively fixed and difficult but not impossible to break down' (Cairney, 2012b: 111) and that may shape structures, systems and subsystems in turn. Ideas, actors and institutions interact in subsystems, within and beyond government, that vary from structured to less so; and the study of subsystems is prominent in governance and institutional analysis (Freeman and Stevens, 1987).

Governance and institutions

There is considerable overlap therefore between governance and institutional theory. Depictions of changed, more networked, collaborative and deliberative policy processes in the governance era have also influenced the interpretation of institutions. Institutions are now seen as embedded in changing circumstances and impacted by various types of systems at varying levels from local to global in geographic and policy terms. Formal institutions, the structures of government, rules, bodies, powers, systems and strategies remain significant, but operate more reflexively in response both to heightened public expectations and their own changed capacity. Informal institutions now have greater policy influence and capacity in the more open, deliberative and connected governance era. Both governance theory and institutionalism account for formal institutions, but acknowledge the rise of informal institutions and the dynamics and implications of the interactions between them. Governance theory is more focused on networks than the state, but both governance and institutional theorists see the state as more collaborative because the 'conventional institutions of government' can no longer provide 'effective steering of their own' (Peters, 2011: 79; Chapter 4).

Governance and institutional theory are also focused upon change in an era of disaggregated institutionalism with challenges for conceptions of, and the operation of, the state. Lowdnes echoes network governance when she suggests that, since the 1990s, 'the pace of change in the governance and delivery of public services provides part of the rationale for a continuing focus on institutions' (Lowdnes, 1996: 181). Network theory recognises this too with policy seen to increasingly emerge 'from the interaction between government and other networked organisations' (Rhodes, 1995: 53). This is not to deny the traditionally 'long-term pattern of mutual state-society influence' (Peters, 2012: 10), however, and that state-society engagement, both traditional and newer, will fluctuate (Pollitt and Bouckaert, 2017). The modern state is nevertheless proving institutionally inventive in more fiscally constrained and policy challenging times (Chapter 4). The network institutionalism that has resulted is adaptive and inventive, for melding the informal institutional aspects of a network with the stable, recurrent features of formal organisation (Ansell, 2008). The result, as governance theory suggests, is the state working closely with social actors and networks, for example, in order to build broad-based resilience to natural disasters (Adger et al, 2005). Indeed, we can map networked governance against disaster preparedness and see the relevance of institution building and change.

We learn that strong state action informed by strong political leadership is imperative in order to establish strong institutions with appropriate warning systems and early responses to crisis. But building longer-term resilience is seen as a key to building preparedness. Adger et al (2005) describe this in novel institutional and systems-based terms. They advocate a *social-ecological system* built upon institutional (formal or hard features) and individual stakeholder memories (informal or soft features), the 'social' drawing on 'reservoirs of practices, knowledge, values, and worldviews', and the 'ecological' on observations of 'biological legacies that persist after disturbance' (Adger et al, 2005: 1037). Such an institution would be 'knowledgeable, prepared, and responsive', with formal and informal, authoritative, adaptive and collaborative features, incorporating robust governance, collectivity and diversity. Multilevel networks would develop social capital, support governance frameworks, and share formal-informal authority (Adger et al, 2005: 1037). This hybridised networked disaster preparedness response aims in principle to integrate well-designed systems-based features with more open, connected governance processes (see also Bellamy et al, 2017: 416).

'New' network governance

The formal institution of the contemporary state is therefore augmented at times by informal, 'soft' processes, like networking, collaboration or steering (Sullivan and Skelcher, 2002; Lowdnes and Roberts, 2013: 3, citing Rhodes, 1997). The impetus for this augmentation is varied but relates not only to crises, but also to the state struggling in general to resolve complex problems without connectivity and collaboration (Ferlie et al, 2011), within government in terms of joined-up processes, and beyond. Networked government is also seen in contrary terms as both a response to neo-liberal downsizing and the need to rebuild capacity, and a response to overload with the need to establish manageable issue networks (Cairney, 2012b: 181–2; Peters, 2011: 81). It is also considered a solution to wicked problems, because networking combines the resources and problem-solving capacities of the government, non-government and community sectors (Head and Crowley, 2015; Klijn and Koppenjan, 2015; APSC, 2007; Crowley, 2004). Classically new governance sees policy emerging and being deployed in collaborative fashion 'from the interactions between government and other networked organisations' (Rhodes, 1995: 53). As a neo-liberal ideologically driven exercise, this has transformed delivery, in areas like 'community care, education, housing and crime control' where a reduced role by government was sought by the UK's Thatcher government (Kjaer, 2004: 37).

Again there is ample scope for investigating the claims of new governance and network institutionalism. In terms of focus, it follows much research on the changing nature of state-society relations in terms of pluralism, elitism, subsystems, agenda formation and policy community theory. In terms of policy processes and outcomes, there is an extensive implementation literature (Chapter 8) with its focus on policy delivery, integration, coordination and partnering, and the study of exercises in collaborative governance (Klijn and Koppenjan, 2015: 234). The claims of new governance and network institutionalism could be tested. To what extent is collaboration actually new, for example? Is it a universal trend, or specific to particular types of domains, issues or circumstances? Is it a fluctuating trend, enhanced perhaps by periods of economic constraint? Are the capacity and influence of networks overstated? Are they steered by the state (Bell and Hindmoor, 2009)? Are there common and differing network features, and if so when and why? And do networks cohere in their intentions and operations, or do observers attribute coherence to them?

Systems theory and new institutionalism

New institutionalism places more emphasis on formal political and policy structures than does new governance theory, although the emphasis depends upon the variant of theory in question and the policy examples under discussion. Broader contexts and systems are significant to policy processes and outcomes (Hofferbert, 1974). We see systems theory (Chapter 2) as relevant here for spanning the macro (historical, geographic, demographic, economic, social, technological and institutional) context of problem-solving (Cairney, 2012b: 114; Simeon, 1976), and the more immediate detail of systematic policy design. Although the structural content of problem-solving is regarded as highly significant, systems theorists can be seen as deterministic (Kickert, 1993), and although policy design is highly regarded, systematic design can be criticised as overly mechanistic and uber-rational (Everett, 2003). Systems and systematic analysis are nevertheless crucial to problem-solving, indeed to wicked problem-solving, as argued by Rittel and Webber (1973) who describe the change from closed policy systems to opening, and interacting, systemic networks as crucial to policy outcomes in complex circumstances. Indeed they saw the addressing, if not resolving of wicked problems as dependent on deliberative processes generated by large and interconnected systems linked to social processes in ways that are increasingly complex. This is the language of network institutionalism (Klijn and Koppenjan, 2015).

As well as conceptual overlap, there are useful resonances between governance, networks and systems theory when reconsidered from the institutionalist perspective. While institutional theory is now distinguished by multiple, and ever increasing, variants, we see the commonalities between these as important, and an indication of the common context of, and issues involved in, complex problem-solving. The various nuances in depictions of each theory, often expressed in terms of 'old', 'new', 'formal', 'informal', 'synthesised', or 'disaggregated' variants, offer flexibility in analysis (see Lowdnes, 1996). The distinction between 'hard' (concrete, descriptive) and 'soft' (abstract, interpretive) versions of institutions (Table 3.1), is common to both institutional and systems theory (Luhman, 2013: 39). Common observations of the changing state are also useful for identifying both a hollowed state capacity (by governance theory) and, conversely a state strengthening through networked policy domains (by network institutionalism). Meanwhile, the question as to 'What do institutions do in terms of shaping policy?' becomes ever more interesting, as institutions are seen both to retain and relinquish power by structuring *and* devolving policy in contemporary times.

Policy shaping, problem-solving and institutions

Institutions have a policy shaping, problem-solving role. In terms of policy framing, they facilitate and thwart policy change in ways that are critical for complex problems, with institutional operation and design directly influencing policy outcomes (Radaelli et al, 2012: 538). However, as we have seen, new institutionalism also acknowledges the importance of broader political and policy systems in shaping governance, as well as the influence of conflict, norms and values in both resisting and facilitating change (Pierre and Peters, 2000: 43–4). Contestation, norms and values do this in several ways. They construct the issues that enter the policy agenda; they shape assumptions for accepting or rejecting change; and they operate as discursive weapons in battles for reform (Béland, 2009). Norm-based policy shaping has long been recognised, and recognised as contentious at times within liberal democracies, for example in terms of social and environmental conflicts within civil society over recent decades. However, contestation of policy norms is now also part of governance-based collaborations, partnerships, joining up and networking that augment state capacity and the resolution of more challenging problems. These themes of complexity, capacity, values and change are critical to our view of the role of institutional analysis in real world problem-solving.

Real world problem orientation?

The appeal of institutional analysis has always been its real world orientation. Institutional scholars have always been interested in real world outcomes, and 'the ways in which institutions shape political outcomes' (Steinmo, 2008: 121), however much the tools and approaches they employ have varied. This is because politics and policymaking takes place in institutional contexts (Parsons, 1995: 223), with definitions of institutions today more likely to acknowledge more expansive contexts, as Hall (1986) does and policy itself acknowledged as an institution shaping influence. Not only do institutional contexts shape and determine the conduct of policymaking, but, as Hall has shown, 'institutions do not exist in isolation from the wider relationship of state to society', nor can 'a state-society approach' fail to account for 'specific historical experiences' (Parsons, 1995: 334). While policy shaping is not a well-understood concept in terms of process or outcomes, behavioural, comparative, normative and historical explanations can provide complementary accounts that illustrate the significance of choices, authority and interactions (Peters, 2011: 81). Institutional context 'structures policy choices', 'the menu of choices' (Peters, 2012: 124), 'who participates' in policy processes, and 'their strategic behaviour' (Steinmo, 2008: 123–4), noting that, conversely, policy itself and its implementation also shapes institution building and delivery processes.

The utility of institutionalism in real world analysis is clear in empirical research, for example in the relative policy shaping powers of health care professionals in various countries. In Immergut's (1990) comparative study the limits of the influence of health care professionals on the design of health care policy are explored, and institutional and actor veto points to the extent of this power are established. The differences between jurisdictions are instructive. Some 'have overcome professional opposition to introduce both national health insurance programs and substantial restrictions on the economic activities of physicians. In other nations, by contrast, medical protests have blocked government efforts to introduce national health insurance as well as controls on doctors' fees' (Immergut, 1990: 392). The study moves beyond the political-administrative system as a unit of analysis, and the maxim that similar systems will 'produce more or less the same outcome across (different) policies' (Radaelli et al, 2012: 541), to find that legislative and political battles were also responsible for significant policy divergence that was otherwise unexpected. In differing policy domains, however, differing political-administrative systems can be just as likely to produce similar policies, offering lessons about structural, behavioural and indeed policy influences upon outcomes (Weaver and Rockman, 1993).

Complexity, capacity, values, change

Complexity is implicated in policy shaping with extensive referencing in the literature to Rittel and Weber (1973) and drawing more often than not, especially in environmental policy analysis, upon governance and networked-based responses (Crowley and Head, 2017b). However, we have seen, from both state-centric and systems-based perspectives, the key role that the state, politics and civil society play not only in terms of contextual influences but also in terms of directing and shaping policy. Crises such as the GFC, natural disasters, terrorism and climate change emphasise the need for strong states and resilient institutions, despite the complex, at times contentious, circumstances of such crises and the need for adaptive policy responses. The policy connectivity, highlighted by governance and networked-based responses, is inadequate, unless seen as situated, as it is by state-centric and systems-based perspectives, within critical national and international contexts. Institutions, in turn, are not only representative of the attitudes and values by which they are constituted, but are the mechanisms for transferring or shaping those values into policy, and so are deeply implicated, with the state, in issues of legitimacy that are of concern to us in this book.

Institutional theory suggests that the quality of public policy relates directly to state capacity (Steinmo, 2008), however, governance theory implies that capacity must be reconceived as the ability to establish connections and adapt to change (Pierre and Peters, 2000) to withstand crises, for example. Policy change, for example major reforms required to address a wicked problem, has always been seen as difficult to achieve in the absence of a crisis or exogenous shock to shake path dependency (Schmidt, 2010: 5; Chapter 9). Part of the state's adaptive response to complexity and crisis (Gupta et al, 2010) is in its fostering of networked institutionalism (Ostrom, 1990; Adger et al, 2005; Klijn and Koppenjan, 2015) within and beyond the state. And many theorists see the state as enhanced, not diminished, by its adaptive capacity (Bentley and Wilsdon, 2003). Indeed, paralleling transformation of the state has been the adaptation of liberal democratic institutions into more contemporary governance-based configurations (Sullivan and Skelcher, 2002), recognisable still as institutions but evolving into more effective policy managers (Chapter 8). However, for institutions to change (Clemens and Cook, 1999) there must be a rethinking of, or contestation over, the ideas, values and norms by which they are constituted, by which they determine policy priorities, processes and practices, and by which they deploy power and influence (Douglas, 1986; Heclo, 2006).

Policy innovation and constraint

The circumstances for policy shaping and problem-solving today are much changed to those of the 1960s and 1970s, with more open and engaged institutional contexts, more prominent deployment of policy networks and a new social media-driven societal reflexivity and connectivity. The same basic structures and processes of government likely endure, in terms, for example, of federal or unitary government and parliamentary or presidential systems, while many of their processes have changed. More significant change prompted by institutional failure, and that impacts policymaking, is rare, but can be seen in New Zealand's shift to multi-party governance. This has seen policy innovation result from the consensus-based coalition politics that is now necessary in order to exercise government. This change was a political response to public discontent with the previous majoritarian system (Shaw and Eichbaum, 2011). Policy experimentation continues under the current Labor-New Zealand First minority government, which is supported by the Greens in return for their holding ministerial portfolios, albeit outside of cabinet. It is too early to judge the efficacy of this arrangement, but worth noting that it delivers both government and policy payoffs for government supporters under a novel 'contract parliamentarian' (Bale and Bergman, 2006) arrangement.

New Zealand also provides an interesting study of the impacts of enhanced financial internationalisation since the 1970s upon domestic policy capacity and the market liberalisation experimentation in a response that shaped policy and institutions from the 1980s (Schwartz, 1994). These pressures were common across advanced industrialised countries, effectively wresting control of their economies away from their governments, some of which responded not only in terms of market-based policy experimentation, but also with regime change. Schwartz identifies 'Thatcherism' as the most notable response with its 'ambitious project to restructure British politics permanently by restructuring the institutional fabric of the state' (Schwartz, 1994: 528). However, four small states, Australia, Denmark, New Zealand and Sweden, with, at the time, left-leaning governments, were all facing institutional failure as a result of 'declining international competitiveness and rising fiscal deficits' with substantial foreign and public debts (Schwartz, 1994: 530). The drastic policy and organisational restructuring actions that all they took in response, despite the resistance that each jurisdiction encountered, showed that liberal democratic states are indeed capable of crisis-driven, ideational change that can fundamentally remake established institutions and traditions.

Complex social and environmental problems are, however, more insidious and contested than a debt crisis or a financial crisis, with the implications of action or inaction less clear and calculable. Some of these problems manifest at times as a crisis, requiring swift state intervention but at the same time presenting no clear, uncontested or likely effective and immediate policy response. There are limitations as to what institutionalism can offer in these instances without a broad focus on state capacity, preparedness, priorities, resourcefulness and politics, for example. And yet institutional reinvention, renewal and rebuilding are acknowledged as key to addressing and building resilience to crisis over the longer term (Birkland, 2007), after the 2005 Hurricane Katrina, for example. The shaping of coastal policy is a prime example of how significant, widespread and contested problem-solving approaches to the impacts of climate change can be and the importance of lesson learning. Around 38 per cent of the global population – 2.5 billion people – live within 100 kilometres of the coast (Barbier, 2015), so this is a global problem managed at the national-subnational level but in the context of multilevelled formal and informal institutionalised efforts to address climate change.

Conclusions

Institutions can be neglected in process- or behaviour-based accounts of public policy in particular, while the fracturing of institutional theory is not only daunting in its own right, but at times sees institutional approaches used as a 'stalking horse' for broader intellectual debates (Lowdnes and Roberts, 2013: 199). Nevertheless, the complexion and operation of institutions have changed significantly with changes in state capacity in recent decades, and with network-based institutionalism (Ansell, 2008) in particular now recognised as a prominent means of addressing policy crises and complexity. This networking exhibits governance-based, systemic characteristics within and beyond the state, at various levels and in various policy domains from domestic to international, in ways that challenge traditional notions of both isolated institutions and an autonomous state (Peters, 2012).

While recognising this change and reconsidering its implications, we have argued that institutions and the state context remain fundamental to the study of public policy and policy capacity, and to arguments about the relative influence of structure and agency in policy outcomes. The literature shows that institutionalism remains a significant means of understanding public policy, not least because, as policy challenges and theory have advanced in complexity, so has institutionalism been found wanting and reinvented itself in response. Governance theory, and its identification of networked and collaborative organisation beyond the state, also offers a reconsideration of institutions, and institutional analysis, for its depictions of the transformed state, which we argue, remains central to the policy and broader political system.

There is much to be learned, we have suggested, from reconsidering the shifts in institutional theory, the advent of more networked ways of delivering policy, and the implications for public policy shaping and delivery. The relevance of doing this is evident in the 'institutions matter' literature that has flourished with broad and varying examinations of the traditional and non-traditional ways in which institutions shape public policy. We have seen that conventional comparative analysis continues to find that institutional contexts impact upon policymaking and are implicated in policy success and failure, sometimes in similar fashion despite differing circumstances. We have also seen that conflict, norms and values can reshape or redefine domestic and international policy and institutional settings, suggesting that institutional origins, design and change, should be the focus of future research.

When we reconsider the trajectory of institutional analysis, as others do in attempting to make sense of a complex literature, it is clear that institutions are now broadly recognising as straddling a formal/traditional to informal/novel dimension. Examinations of the formal structures of government, rules, organisation and powers, are now complemented by examinations of less formal but routinised and influential relations, norms, behaviours and socialisation. It is now acknowledged that not only do institutions shape, constrain and endure in the traditional sense, but also that they facilitate, enable and change as new institutionalism suggests. We have seen the trajectory of institutional theory – from 'traditional' to 'behaviourist' to 'new' – both asserted and contested, but with Rhodes (2008a) seeing continuity and Peters (2012) seeing complementarity in an increasingly complex literature.

Having reconsidered institutional analysis and how it has evolved, we find that, of all its variants, network institutionalism, which draws upon earlier policy network and policy community approaches (Marsh and Rhodes, 1992), has particular utility for understanding complex policy. It is a state-centric theory, but, in its recent iterations (Klijn and Koppenjan, 2015), has resonance with both governance-based analysis and systems theory, with its focus on connectivity and interaction within and beyond government. Moreover, system-like, network-based approaches have long been recognised as best suited to addressing complex, wicked problems (Rittel and Webber, 1973), as long as they are depicted within broader contexts that account for the role and influence of the state. This remains true today. There is clearly resonance between new institutionalism, governance theory and network theory, but we argue for the acknowledgement of the importance of institutions in terms of their structural and systemic contexts, with an appreciation of the adaptive capacity of the state.

4

Reconsidering *the state*

Why the state matters

There is a longstanding, varied and occasionally unruly academic literature on how, why and the extent to which the state should be central to the study of public policy. Much of policy studies accepts the idea of the state as the modern equivalent of the sovereign ruler; a set of enduring political institutions which enjoy a monopoly of formal, legal authority over an organised political community marked by clear territorial borders. In this historical analogy, public policy is the democratically endorsed roadmap or guide for the use of state power to improve, for example, social welfare. Within this taken for granted view, there are two counterpoints in public policy analysis; in broad terms, state-centred and society-centred perspectives, which disagree markedly on the extent to which the state has autonomy, is an organisation with agency, or is essentially a clearing house for outside forces from the market and civil society. The purpose of this chapter is not to reach some resolution of these two positions or stand on one side or the other in terms of their ability to deal with complexity. Instead, we argue that a reconsideration of the state in terms of policy studies for the governance era needs to reflect both perspectives and draw on the blurring of state-society boundaries as a central feature in what is 'public' in public policy. In a complementary argument to that presented in Bell and Hindmoor (2009), we advance a claim about the enduring power of the state in policy studies; both as a set of public institutions and organisational arrangements, and an analytical concept to describe the foundations of a polity and sources of authority in policymaking. Building on notions of a policy-making system elaborated in Chapter 2, we reconsider the position of the state in policy studies by investigating the interactions and inter-dependency between the state and society rather than in making a binary choice between state-centred and society-centred governance. We follow Sellers (2011) who argues that scholars should converge around a broadly similar line of inquiry: that society provides crucial elements of support for a state to be effective, and that a state is critical to collective action in society. Among its many meanings, governance labels a variety of ways in which society is not simply acted upon by the state, but actively shapes the actions of and outcomes of state activity (Peters and Pierre, 1998).

The core argument of the chapter is that policy studies can prosper by drawing on both perspectives to improve its ability to apprehend the position of the state in dilemmas of contemporary policymaking. In most important respects, debates about state autonomy in policy studies have mirrored shifting political economy debates in advanced industrial democracies. The expansion of the scope and scale of the state in the 20th century and the various political backlashes this expansion triggered provides the backdrop narrative to much of contemporary policy studies. Investigating the relationships between the state and society is an essential component of policy studies, although one often neglected as the state is assumed into the background context to policymaking without a map from theories of the state into the conventional concerns of policy studies.

As Chapter 2 of the book has elaborated, the study of the state has been linked, at least indirectly, to the development of the systems approach in policy studies. Systems thinking encourages a view of a dynamic interdependence between the state and society, characterised by tensions, disruptions, discontinuities crises as well as periods of relative stability in forms of the state where politics temporarily finds an accommodation between the use of state power and social demands. Importantly for reconsidering the state, systems thinking does not imply that there are forces to produce a balance of state power and social demands or that any equilibrium in the state–society system will be stable over time.

The most elementary form of a state is the Hobbesian state. This cornerstone of liberal political theory refers to the development of an organised political community to provide basic physical security against the threat of violence amid widespread wars in the 17th century (Gray, 1993). This points to the importance of the symbiotic relationship between the state, civil society and markets in driving change rather than examining the relative strength or weakness of the state in isolation. Gray (1993) argues that a Hobbesian analysis warns that the contemporary state can overreach, become too large and claim an unwarranted authority over parts of civil society and markets. The expansion in the coverage of the notion of security in the 20th century is a case in point; where states struggle with the dilemma of providing national security using legitimate authority as modern societies expand the range of demands to include economic, social as well as cultural security (Rosenau, 2004).

The rise and fall of the Keynesian Welfare State illustrates the relationship between the state and economy. This term is widely used to label the period of state development in advanced industrial societies between 1945 and 1980. This notion was developed conceptually to label changes in the state that were the corollary of economic policy changes. The policy problem Keynesianism identified was the failure of laissez-faire policy prescriptions, grounded beliefs in free trade and the self-correcting qualities of capitalism, to prevent and alleviate permanent slumps in the macro economy. Instead, the Keynesian Welfare State places state action at the heart of economic and social policymaking, state changes were subordinate to economy and social policy shifts which required successful planning and efficient bureaucratic organisation for the delivery of public services according to the needs of all citizens.

A set of economic crises in the 1970s marked a turning point in policymaking, as neo-liberalism as a political project was launched with its stated ambition to 'roll back' the state. In retrospect, this was never consistent enough in its influence across time and space to qualify as a full reversal of the Keynesian Welfare State (Pierson, 1994). Indeed, even in the neo-liberal heartlands, the state never really withered. For example, Margaret Thatcher left office in 1990 with the proportion of public spending in GDP the same as it had been in 1980. Across the Organisation for Economic Cooperation and Development (OECD), there is limited empirical evidence for the shrinking state thesis since 1980 (Castles, 2007). The size of the state, measured as a proportion of national income, is constant over time and a striking feature of the political economy of neo-liberalism.

This political economy scale of analysis, however, disguises changes in how the state is organised and run. An important driver of contemporary policy change results from rethinking about the nature of the state, its objectives and its capacities. Such rethinking itself is linked to different trajectories of economic, social and political change; variously, growing complexity, individualism and fluid identities, growing middle class and a decline in deference to formal authority. For governance as an analytical framework, Thatcherism and its cognate political projects were about changing the way the public sector operated, bureaucracies were dismantled and forms of competition and choice incorporated into the policy-maker toolkit. Different ideas about the management, organisation and delivery of public policy has spawned a whole set of labels for a changing state in the era of governance: for example, New Public Management (NPM), the hollowed-out state, the enabling state, the competition state, the market state.

Even after a decade of austerity in advanced industrial democracies after the Global Financial Crisis (GFC), the role of the state remains in flux. There appears to be a consensus on the size of the state; for example, like Thatcher, David Cameron left office in 2016 with public spending accounting for roughly the same share of UK national income as he had inherited despite placing austerity at the centrepiece of his political mission when taking office. In a study of a previous era of austerity and conservative government, Pierson (1994) found that the welfare state remained resilient despite a political discourse about its dismantling. Instead, so much of social expenditure within the public finances is already locked in. However, this stable measurement of the size of the state conceals ongoing arguments about the role and purpose of the state and the deeper transformative impacts of neo-liberalism as well as the emergence of hybrid political economies that vary policy sector by policy sector.

Crisis, resilience and the state

Crises and recessions, although often identified as ushering in new forms of governance and indicating a weakening of the state, have provided many opportunities for states to discover new roles, to restore and reclaim legitimacy as well as produce novel sources of authority (Le Gales and King, 2017). Crises tend to lead to a myriad of fresh policy interventions with the consequence of changing the scope, size and capacity of the state. This claim can be advanced without any presumption that these policy interventions are successful or represent progress. Instead, it is an open analytical claim that the state remains the centre of the action for policy studies scholarship even in crisis situations. There are discontinuities and crises involving different state forms linked to the failure to support contemporary policy capacity, but episodic tumults cannot be interpreted straightforwardly as a weakened state, far less wholesale abandonment of the state as the principal means of organising territorial political communities. For example, the crisis of the Weberian state is a parallel narrative to the decline of the Keynesian Welfare State (Kjaer, 2004). This crisis is rooted in a general critique of bureaucratic forms of organisation and, notably, their failure to support successfully top-down, command-and-control policy-making processes to manage the challenges of a more economically integrated, socially diverse and ecologically precarious world (Braithwaite, 1999; 2006; Pollitt and Bouckaert, 2004). As is widely observed, the crisis of the Weberian state has given rise to a set of new policy instruments and modes of governing but this change process does not admit a simple interpretation as a weakened or decayed state (Peters, 2001).

To understand what drives state change and its relationship to policy change, brief reference to the established and ongoing debate about the ontology of the state is required (Hay, 2005; 2014). Hay (2014) suggests the most useful analytical approach is to act 'as if' the state was a real thing while also being open to its socially constructed nature. Indeed, this is probably the only way the concept of state can enjoy a degree of external validity and be used in comparative research. For policy studies, the key is to work around the ontological queasiness that characterises many political science approaches to the state and employ the concept usefully to mean the same thing over time and through cross-national sections. In policy studies, there is a wide, if not deep, consensus that the state consists of interdependent but relatively differentiated institutions, which are somewhat fragmented and operate autonomously. Whatever changes in forms of the state, which are witnessed, the enduring feature of the state is the generation of legitimacy and authority in the policy-making system. Even where the state is implicated in policy failure or system-wide political economy crisis, it is this requirement for legitimacy and authority that drives adaptation and innovation rather the abandonment of the state.

For example, in GFC terms, the state was the only part of the financial system that had access to the necessary capital to provide adequate short- and medium-term support to capital markets. The idea of 'free banking' in which market forces control the provision of banking services remains an abstraction; instead the free economy has always needed a central bank to protect commercial banks, and the state to serve as a 'lender of last resort'. The banking system and the state are co-dependent; especially so during a crisis. This is because the private banking system holds a public monopoly on creating money. Although the banking system creates money through the process of making loans it is backed by the state; it is the state that allows private banks to say that the deposits they are creating in the process are equivalent to real money. Post-GFC this has not changed nor has monetary policy's focus on price stability despite great policy innovation in which the state had to guarantee all bank deposits and interbank transactions in several European countries. This extraordinary policy intervention came with the condition that banks – after the acute crisis phase was over – would face greater regulatory scrutiny. Although it is moot whether regulators have become bolder than in the past in challenging the political power of the financial services industry and its general preference for deregulation or 'light touch' regulation, this case can be taken as illustrative of state-resilience in a crisis.

Even though the substantive policy challenge is different, questions of state-resilience similarly permeate environmental policymaking. That we live in uncertain times seems incontrovertible; a standard refrain is that fast-moving, fluid and turbulent political-economic, social and technological changes make any stable parametric assumption for policymaking hazardous. Adaptive governance has emerged in response to these conditions for policymaking in natural resources management (Ostrom, 1990, 2010; Rijke et al, 2012). Although sharing the diagnosis of the failings of the Weberian state, the resilience of the state remains a central feature of analyses of adaptive governance; an extension of the governance framework that stresses learning and adaptation rather than prediction and control in multi-layered and polycentric governance without a unified or central authority. Yet adaptive governance continues to hold to the idea of state as the resilient element of public authority that is the building block of policy innovation, the thing that both authorises action and does the acting in the interests of environmental management (Rijke et al, 2012).

This chapter develops the argument that we should reconsider the state in terms of a growth of hybridity of policy arrangements and structures, rather than the straightforward substitution of market-based policy instruments for bureaucratic-based ones associated with a permanent move in its boundary with society. This diversity and lack of isomorphism makes it difficult to generalise claims about the state in public policy but helps avoid 'big' versus 'small' or 'strong' versus 'weak' dualisms about the state. Instead, the acknowledgement of rich, complex and diverse policy arrangements sustains an analytical version of governance in which the state matters and its authority a central means of governing.

This chapter has three main sections and a conclusion. The first section summarises briefly the main themes from the literatures on the state in governance, and extracts the question of metagovernance as critical for policy studies. Moving on from this macro-scale perspective on the state, the second section investigates the policy-level implications of changing state-society relationships over time. The third section presents future directions in policy studies that emanate from the reconsideration of the state in the first two sections.

The state in the concept of governance

Central to the concept of governance as laid out in the book is the observation of change in the pattern and exercise of state authority. This is often, and not always helpfully, reduced to identifying a historical trajectory from government to governance from the late 1970s. This is described as a shift from a hierarchical and bureaucratic state to governance in and through networks by the Anglo-governance school (Marinetto, 2003). This seam of work attributes a growing complexity and fragmentation in state activity to a set of deliberate policy reforms in the 1980s, such that the state increasingly has come to depend on other organisations to implement policy and achieve its objectives. In this networked governance diagnosis, state power had been deconcentrated, hollowed out and dispersed among a significant array of functionally distinct networks composed of hybrid mixtures of public, voluntary and private organisations with whom the remaining 'central' state then had to interact in order to make public policy.

An important question for those who see governance as a historical epoch, rather than analytical framework, is the extent that this is simply an Anglo sphere story and more strongly a UK story. Of course, the UK is an important and influential case for the comparative study of public sector reform, but it cannot simply be assumed as typical of all states. Although Rhodes, (1997; 2011) never sought to generalise from this one case to broader analyses of governance, it has become an influential strand of thinking on the state, governance and policymaking. As Perri 6 (2015) argues, and Rhodes (2011) acknowledges, it was never a historically accurate account of state change even in the UK. The UK state as conceived by Rhodes (1997) was ephemeral and a time-specific function of the Second World War and the introduction of the final pieces of welfare state by the Labour government elected in 1945.

Aside from historical critics, scholars investigating the portability of the Anglo-governance school typically focus conceptually on the argument the state has been hollowed out. For example, Pierre and Peters (2000) argue that any shift to network governance may have the unintended consequence of increasing the capacity of the state to make public policy. Command-and-control policy instruments may be replaced by softer ones that serve to steer society, but capacity has not obviously been diminished. Some argue that the state has not been hollowed out but instead maintained its capacity to govern through new mixes of policy instruments such as markets and networks and deploying indirect instruments of control (Peters, 2001).

This insight provided the basis for a second important tranche of governance literature that focused on metagovernance, or the governance of the constituent elements of the state (Jessop, 2008; 2016). Metagovernance is an umbrella concept that serves as a label for the roles of the state and its favoured policy instruments in networked governance. Given that governing is distributed among various private, voluntary and public actors, and that power and authority are more decentralised and fragmented among a plurality of networks, the role of the state has shifted from the direct governance of society to the 'metagovernance' of the several modes of intervention and from command and control through bureaucracy to the indirect steering of relatively autonomous stakeholders.

Metagovernance is a useful concept in highlighting the continuing role of the state in coordination with governance networks and the use of negotiation, diplomacy and more informal modes of steering society. It is now commonplace to observe that the state steers and regulates actors within networks rather than rowing as in the direct provision of public services through state bureaucracies (Osborne and Gaebler, 1992). Such non-state organisations undertake much of the work of governing: implementing policy, delivering public services and at times regulating themselves. The state governs the organisations that in turn govern society, hence the oft-quoted label of the governance of governance. Although the state sets the political-administrative borders for different spatial scales of policymaking; as Chapter 5 notes, states remain the principal expression of territorial political communities, even if these are 'imagined communities' (Anderson, 1983) the boundaries of a state express a nation as a practical polity that makes public policy. While there are stateless nations, and multi-national states, for the most part national identity is the basis for much of public policymaking; it sets out who 'we' are as well as the starting point for what 'we' owe each other.

There are several modes of metagovernance, or policy means, through which the state can steer social actors involved in governance. We do not present a typology of policy instruments here but suggest an indicative list to establish the link from metagovernance to policy studies. First, in regulatory terms the state can set the 'rules of the game' for other actors and then leave them to do what they will within those rules but ensuring they work 'in the shadow of hierarchy' (Héritier and Lehmkuhl, 2008). Relatedly, the state has available several policy options to redesign markets, reregulate sectors, or introduce constitutional change. There are other policy means of metagovernance associated closely with critical strands of policy studies where the state can try to steer other actors using narratives, rhetoric and storytelling. It can organise dialogues, foster meanings, beliefs and identities among the relevant actors, and influence what actors think and do. More conventionally, using Hood's (1983) framework, the state can steer by the way in which it distributes resources using policy instruments, such as money (treasure) and authority. Further still, the state can play a boundary spanning role to alter the balance between actors in a network, act as a court of appeal when conflict arises, rebalance the mix of governing structures as well as step in when network governance fails.

The changing state and its implications for policy studies

The centrality of the state in policy studies is a theme of the book, but this chapter reconsiders the concept and practice of a changing state in the context of policy studies. We argue that the two most promising lines of inquiry seek to connect the state as a level of analysis with insights into variations in policy sectors. On this basis, we identify two approaches for investigation: first, the Strategic Relational Approach (SRA) in state theory and second, the recent and still emerging literature on the New Public Governance (NPG).

The SRA shares concerns with the NPG in questions of state adaptation and resilience, as well as a common set of assumptions about a plural state, with multiple interdependent actors as well as a pluralist state, where multiple groups use their power to bargain in the policy process. Whereas the SRA is a more macro-level perspective derived from a longstanding political economy tradition with a stress on the power of capital, the recently minted NPG concept from within public management seeks to develop – through its emphasis on inter-organisational relationships and governance processes – firm foundations for insights into state-resilience and adaptation. Here the NPG tends to identify the power of elites and bureaucracies as state actors in public policymaking.

NPG approaches, implicitly more than explicitly, in advancing arguments about the plural state and the pluralist state (Osborne, 2010) connect to the SRA seam of political economy work. In both lines of inquiry, the state shapes, and is shapedby those within its many parts as well as those outside in civil society and the economy. The idea of the state having many forms and operating across different spheres and sectors (profit, not for profit and governmental) is the undergirding logic of NPG (Osborne, 2010), as well as the foundation of Jessop's SRA to the state and its power, as it affects capacity to make policy successfully.

Both the SRA and NPG raise questions about what enables and constrains policy systems (Chapter 1). The core argument of the chapter is that public policy is connected vitally to issues of state capacity. At the broad contextual level of the state, we contend that its shifting nature is a more useful starting point for policy scholars rather than attempting to verify claims of its decline or weakening. The idea of the state, as well as its practice, may well have changed significantly in the governance era, but this should not be diagnosed as the withering of the state but instead as multiple changes in its form and scope. This conjecture has implications for the study of public policy and the practical endeavour of building policy capacity; rather than a quality derived from expertise, bureaucratic administrative processing capability and organisation of delivery system we argue it is rather something that resides in the nature of state-society relations.

Although the SRA is most closely associated with the work of Jessop (1990; 2006; 2008; 2016) it has been developed in the hands of others (Hay, 2005; 2014; Hay and Lister, 2006; Hay and Farrall, 2014) and elsewhere, in a related but cultural political economy turn, in works by Clarke (2004; 2005), Newman (2005) and Newman and Clarke (2009). The NPG is associated with Osborne (2010). Both seams of work support the underpinning theme of the chapter: the role of the state should be acknowledged in policy studies as contributing influentially to policy capacity. In turn, the demand to generate policy capacity is relevant to the state. The study of the state and its development is longstanding and predates the policy sciences and policy studies. Further, whereas public policy may be an unambiguously modern concept for a modern practice, the state has its origin, as Chapter 5 on borders discusses, in the mutual recognition of boundaries of respective territories by nomadic peoples and was critical to the ancients in the earliest city-states. The changing form of the state is both a contemporary and historical question; present in the history of feudal states, of the absolutist early modern states, and then subsequently in the development of the Westphalian system before the Keynesian Welfare State and the contemporary concerns of policy studies.

Jessop (2016) describes the difficulties that confront theories of the state, or scholarly attempts to use the state as an analytical construct. Theories of the state tend to bypass public policy, regarding policy outputs as the residual of state change explained by another, most often 'bigger', factor. For our purposes of reconsideration, it is precisely its polymorphic and dynamic nature that allows us to cast light on how we should study public policy. The state varies in form across space, the same territorial state varies in form over time, and further, any disaggregation of the state at a certain place and time reveals its internal variety. This internal variety is well established in the study of public policy with its important comparative research program based on sector categories such as the policy subsystems and policy instrument mixes or packages.

For example, as regulatory scholarship has burgeoned over the last 20 or more years, so it has become a mainstream part of thinking about policy processes and governance. States still redistribute and distribute (tax and transfer, tax and allocate), they also still organise to provide certain services but they also regulate; it may well now be the major part of state activity but undoubtedly this is what has, and still is, changed most about the state and public policy in recent decades (Ayres and Braithwaite, 1992; Braithwaite, 1999; 2006).

One of the main contributions of regulatory scholarship to policy studies has been in breaking down the classical political economy distinction of the state and market as separate spheres. This blurring of state and society has given impetus to policy studies and succeeded in providing fertile conditions to reconsider public policy instruments beyond a governance typology of markets, hierarchies and association as modes of economic coordination to see also networks, information, experimentation and learning as key features. These do not lend themselves easily to treatment as separate spheres such as market or the state. All are combined in varying proportions in all governing arrangements.

Regulatory scholarship shifts policy scholarship away from questions about whether the state is getting bigger or smaller measured in some proportion of GDP and instead supplants questions such as what is the role of public policy in sustaining a public domain against diagnoses of increasing competition? Are there public roles for private interests and how might we insist on them in public policy? What capability does the state possess in regulating in an open economy era?

This surge in regulatory scholarship has its origins in longstanding arguments about the feasibility and desirability of a large, capable state. There is a significant literature on government overload and the fiscal crisis reactions (Parsons, 1982). While some of this came from the Left (Newman and Clarke, 2009), others – and arguably more influentially – were on the Right (Buchanan, 1988). This latter counter-reaction has had several versions in terms of political movements and eventually found its way into 'steering not rowing' mantras of governance and the position that we outline in this chapter that states still matter but in different sort of ways.

Alongside debates about whether the state acts autonomous of society or is a clearing house for elite interests in society, New Right and public choice critiques by different schools of the 'big state' also deal with apparatus questions and the changing nature of control (or governing) in modern states. Critical in this is the Héritier and Lehmkuhl (2008) analysis that almost all of these new modes of control under the governance rubric operate in 'the shadow of hierarchy'. While different and novel forms of governance may well be redrawing and blurring inherited divides between the public and private, the state remains as sole entity capable of managing the balance among all these novel forms and activities at the policy problem level. This metagovernance backstop remains an essential, enduring function of the state even in the midst of significant change.

The leading problem of the SRA to the state is common to many political economy analyses of the state : there is a tendency for them to produce insights for 'spectators' of state change rather than provide much practical wisdom and distil useful statecraft for policy studies. The relationship between states and societies is bi-directional and mutually constitutive. From this insight comes the need to link state change with economic and social change. In turn, we can begin to locate possible sources of policy capacity within an ongoing process of state change.

To treat the state as a single starting point for the analysis of relations between government and society, however, requires the aggregation of patterns of institutions and informal practices that will inevitably tend to reduce and level out the important diversity that is familiar to students of policy studies. Existing contemporary states encompass dozens of institutionally distinct policy sectors with highly diverse organisational architectures, including: delivery of welfare services, environmental regulation, macroeconomic management, and foreign policy as well as trade policy.

There is vertical as well as sectoral diversity in states. The multiple institutional jurisdictions with some amount of autonomy in most contemporary states range from the nationally elected leaders at the peak, the core executive, to the local officers who deliver local services. Alongside this vertical diversity, there is also territorial diversity. Configurations of policies, institutions and actors may be assembled in distinctive ways in one region or local area than in another.

In the governance era, it is the imagined dichotomy between state and society that has withered rather than the state itself decaying. In many areas of policy, sector-specific regimes have given rise to separate spheres of relations between society and official stakeholders.

For example, the expansion of environmental and consumer regulation has mobilised both expert groups and interests representing diffuse and activist citizens as well as business groups representing corporate interests. Further, policymakers have also engaged a third sector of non-state organisations like non-profits and charities in the delivery of social services and a variety of public-private partnerships (Sullivan and Skelcher, 2002). Other new participatory mechanisms have provided for public and stakeholder participation in policy, opportunities for citizens and groups representing interests have expanded in a wide range of contexts, from environmental impact procedures to public hearings, to new freedom of information rights to challenge state action (Chapters 6 and 7).

Privatisation of natural monopolies brought requirements for new regulatory regimes in which public policy objectives were inserted into regulations designed to compensate for deficiencies in unregulated markets with non-competitive structures (Vickers and Yarrow, 1991). Decentralisation of important policies and other decisions has opened new local channels of state-society relations, manifest in multilevel governance themes. Debates about state fragmentation and polycentricity in a range of policy sectors have revolved around efforts to incorporate regional and local participation in arrangements to conserve ecosystems or implement environmental policy (Ostrom, 2011; Rijke et al, 2012), or to pursue local social and economic agendas (Ostrom and Cox, 2010). State regulation has itself taken new, more flexible forms that also deploy market mechanisms for public policy goals. For example, cap-and-trade systems that allow market exchange of rights to emit carbon dioxide, taxes that impose penalties on carbon emissions, and voluntary green certification systems are used widely as means to accomplish policy ends more effectively as well as more efficiently than direct state control.

Future directions for policy studies after reconsidering the state

At the beginning of the chapter state-society relationships were divided into two counterpointed perspectives. On the one hand, these accounts have differed in whether they adopt as their primary unit of analysis the lens of elite level policymaking within the state itself, or a fundamental unit of ordinary citizens, groups or organisations in society; the public in public policy. As we have argued through the chapter these two accounts are increasingly blurred as state-society relationships no longer observe a clear demarcation. These two accounts are best seen as contrasts rather than opposites, distinguished by whether they tend to favour the 'top-down' view of actors and institutions at the top of either state in policymaking, or a 'bottom-up' perspective of those in direct receipt of public policy or on the 'front line' of organisations delivering services to the public.

In this vein, the substance of policy problems matters along with associated interests and institutions. While these contribute to variety across different policy sectors, the top-down perspective relies on structuralist traditions of a state autonomous from society. In contrast, as Chapter 8 on implementation sets out, the bottom-up focus on the lived experience of citizens affected by public policy as well as front-line workers is a longstanding theme of policy studies. Here the society and the state are interlocked in different relationships of co-production. This is a key point in reconsidering the state for policy studies as there is now an established literature relating to co-production of social services, as well as in the responsive regulation field.

The institutionalist work on public management reform continues to stress the centrality of organisations or their leaders in adopting innovations (Barzelay and Gallego, 2006; Pollit, 2008). Similarly, approaches to regulation such as that of Ayres and Braithwaite (1992) look to firm and society dynamics, but analyse them from the standpoint of the strategies of elite policymakers. As Pierson (1993) puts it, in an echo of Lindblom (1959; 1979), how does policy create politics? Even as these accounts shift the focus of empirical inquiry beyond the circle of elite policymakers, the analytical focus remains top-down explanations from the central, core of the state into markets and civil society.

With the array of shifts in the state and state-society relations, however, it has become increasingly clear that this top-down perspective fails to capture a large component of the state and what it does. In an era of increasingly complex state activity, an expanding line of research has incorporated a disaggregated conception of the state and its relations with society. Accounts adopting a bottom-up approach to state-society relations that remains centred on the state itself have sought to reconceptualise relationships within the state in ways that capture these additional dimensions.

Chapter 8 describes how the study of implementation started from the perspective of higher-level policymakers but developed subsequently to analyse the variety of political, economic and social conditions at the local level that are crucial to the success or failure of policy (Pressman and Wildavsky, 1984; McConnell, 2010a; 2010b). Accounts of multilevel governance have gone a step further to view 'the state' as organisational apparatus and policy implementation and delivery mechanisms (Daniell and Kay, 2017). Work in this vein demonstrates that lower as well as higher levels in the hierarchy of a state play important roles in policy and governance, and analyses the interplay between levels. Marks and Hooghe's (2004) comparative analysis of two different varieties of multilevel governance, for instance, highlights contrasts between models based on functional divisions between policy sectors and on hierarchies of territorial divisions between general purpose governments.

As noted at different points in the chapter, the shifts in state and public policymaking have tended to be driven by changes in the political economy through time. For example, a mainstay of regional development policy in the EU has been a search for competitive advantage through and in policymaking. The concept of institutional competitiveness has emerged in the varieties of capitalism literatures (Blyth, 2002; Campbell, 2004; Crouch, 2004; Campbell and Hall, 2015)) to refer to socio-economic success as a result of the competitive advantages that firms derive from operating within a particular set of institutions and policy-settings. The institutional basis for successfully coordinating labour markets and vocational training programs at the regional level are often seen as key underlying mechanisms in institutional competitiveness and unlock the puzzle of how high taxes and state spending seem in certain contexts to enhance socio-economic performance even as the dominant discourse of the effects on globalisation on public policy is a regulatory 'race to the bottom' as environmental, labour and consumer protection standards are lowered by pressures for competitiveness.

There is substantial work that suggests that the spread of political economy ideas about policy and the ways it should be crafted has been one of the most powerful drivers of the institutional, economic and social changes that have blurred the state-society boundary (Hall, 1993; Blyth, 2002). An increasingly professionalised, internationalised class of policy experts has diffused such ideas as 'fast policy', rapidly circulating plans and prescriptions for innovations in state-society relations such as the new public management, anti-poverty social policy and local participatory experiments (Peck and Theodore, 2015).

This chapter has sketched an account of the changing nature of state-society relations as a central feature in reconsidering the state. This account highlights the blurring of the boundary between the state and society, arguing that these are mutually constitutive and best thought of as a system rather than a set of linear cause-and-effect relationships. This inquiry suggests several promising lines for future inquiry in policy studies.

Comparative public policy at the sectoral level

As governance arrangements place growing emphasis on responsiveness and the effectiveness of policy, the observation that 'policy shapes politics' has taken on added significance in sequencing accounts of policy change over time (Mahoney, 2000). In comparative public policy, the notion of a policy style is an established cluster concept that refers to the culture, conventions, norms and history of policy-making process in a particular sector. Howlett and Lindquist (2004) chart how this line of research has moved from looking at variation in policy styles at the national level to investigating variation in styles at the policy sector level. The Policy Agenda Project of research over the last 25 years has produced extensive empirical work on the sector-specific characteristics of different agenda dynamics (John, 2016). Work has now started investigating the difference that these agendas make for the involvement of different types of state actors and society interests in processes of policymaking (Heinelt et al, 2005; Sellers and Kwak, 2010).

Although cross-national comparative studies focusing on a single domain of policy within different countries such as social policy, environmental policy or economic policy are relatively common, work that investigates the relationships between sectoral and national institutional differences for state-society relationships remain underdeveloped in policy theory terms. This is an area of future research that will help scholars tack between macro perspectives of the state and its change over time within a national political system to meso-level perspectives on variety in state-society relationships at the sectoral level. Such a 'meso-level' comparative research agenda is technically demanding, but certainly an important future direction in empirical research and empirically based theory in policy studies. Such multi-dimensional analysis may contribute to elaborating dimensions of policy capacity, which are relevant, both to design thinking and implementation planning in policy studies.

Policymaking across multilevel architectures

Along with processes of governance themselves, patterns of state-society relations have also increasingly organised around places. As theorists of 'joined-up' governments in the UK (Pollitt, 2003) or 'administrative conjunction' in the US (Frederickson, 1999), have noted, policy problems are often territorially concentrated. For example, efforts to conserve ecosystems have frequently centred on coordinated governance arrangements among a variety of stakeholders concerned with a particular region (Layzer, 2008). Similarly, urban governance often takes its shape from an array of state and society organised at the territorial scale of a city or city-region. The governance of city regions often occurs through various intergovernmental and state-society channels, including multiple levels of government and diverse sectors of policy with a common focus on the region (Sellers, 2011). Within UK social policy, the notion of place-based poverty has been influential during the last decade and a half in inspiring a series of novel policy interventions coordinated and targeted at micro-scales of neighbourhoods and housing estates with low levels of socio-economic status.

Analyses of how the politics of novel territorial formations across different levels within the state, and the role that society elements play in local governance as well as in higher-level policy, promises to cast new light on a dimension that has increasingly become a focus of governance (Marks and Hooghe, 2004). Multilevel governance scholarship often stresses the fluidity of state-society relationships and the critical role of coalition-building across the state-society divide. However, the object of empirical analysis in this fertile research program remains on political actors occupying formal institutional roles in the state and the extent to which they can make and implement public policy successfully.

There remains a relative lack of research in policy studies where groups, individuals and institutions beyond the state comprise the main analytical focus, either as a potentially decisive influence on policy processes and outcomes or as the main concern for purposes of understanding the consequences of governance (Daniell and Kay, 2017). Although there is a burgeoning but separate field of non-for-profit research which has yet to be cross-pollenated successfully with policy studies traditions. As state-centric approaches have increasingly acknowledged the importance of society, so society-centric approaches generally include state actors and institutions as an important element in their explanations. In these latter accounts, however, the state remains a disaggregated, multilevel contingent set of institutions open to influence from outside the formal boundaries of the state at all levels. There is important research in policy studies work to be done that investigates the networks of organisations and interests at multiple levels, and which has increasingly been employed to account for patterns of governance, incorporate participation by governments at a variety of levels and informal dynamics of interaction.

Policy feedback

An emerging, but still underdeveloped, seam of work looks at improving the processes of public policymaking as a means to better governance. This line of inquiry advocates more systematic attention to outcomes from policy and their backward mapping to the reproduction and reinforcement of the policy or its gradual undermining and reversal in direction. The study of policy feedback processes to subsequent policy decisions, the detailed elaboration of negative and positive loops, has the potential to deepen understandings of state-society relations (Mahoney, 2000). A body of scholarship in historical institutionalism, (Chapter 3), has begun to develop better understanding of the ways in which policies may unleash effects on societal forces that then work to either reinforce, or undermine, the original policy trigger. As set out in Chapter 2 on systems, shifts in society interests and movements over time are often a consequence of the feedback effects from earlier policies and institutions (Pierson, 1993). Tracing the causal chains between policy and politics in this way, such as between changing settlement patterns and public opinion about policy can illuminate underlying connections between state action and society change.

Conclusions

Even amid growing complexity in the policy-making challenge, the state endures as a central feature of policy analysis. A system thinking approach from Chapter 2 assists the investigation of the SRA and NPG as theories of the state that reveal the continued salience of the need to generate policy capacity in state-society relationships. The irony that state power is required for state restructuring and the disassembly of the Weberian state, or what the literature often characterises as weakening state alongside a shift to governance, is important to appreciate.

Both SRA and NPG encourage policy scholarship to see the relationship between state and society as one of dynamic interdependence in which attempting to gain leverage on observed changes in policy-making terms without bringing 'the state in' is as partial and incomplete as exclusively statist accounts of the policy process. Without recognition of the dynamic interdependence of the state and society, studies of individual policy successes and failure will miss the full set of drivers in the development or diminution of policy capacity.

The notable advantages for policy studies of a sustained engagement with theories of the state such as the SRA approach is to adumbrate power at a structural level with common characteristics but with different consequences which vary across policy sectors within a state. There are always advantages and disadvantages to any scholarly strategy of aggregation or disaggregation in the study of a phenomenon; the field of policy studies has tended to aim for meso-level ground which brings advantages in terms of fine-grained accounts in which different forms of agency are foregrounded in accounts of change but has also sometimes missed out on the useful benefits from stepping to the more coarse-grained level of state–society analysis. Controlled comparison research designs which used an aggregated state perspective alongside detailed cross-sectoral policy analysis would help investigate how differential power relationships are playing out and understand emergent themes in the zeitgeist which are employed politically to glue policy packages together. For example, policy about the gig economy, the precariat or the squeezed middle; or, on another dimension of power, novel policy instruments for the culturally insecure; or perhaps innovations in the roles of democratic expert. This has implications for the ability of policy studies to say something about tides of political ideology, which focus on the overall contours of the state–society boundary and the role of various forms of power in shaping policy outputs and outcomes.

Theories of the state help support the investigation of policy capacity for a complex world in terms of broader concerns of legitimacy and authority and not something exclusively derived from sector-specific policy analysis. Studying patterns of policy instruments involving users, citizens and stakeholders as actors in policy development through collaborative platforms, events and design challenges will help match patterns of state change and policy change. It helps push the study of governance beyond closed policy communities, and shifting policy roles of those with insider status and shared expert knowledge, to something potentially transformative in the relationship between state and society. It places questions about the resilience of the state and its ability to generate new sources of authority in crisis moments into broader public domains beyond official bureaucracy; and highlights issues of participation and deliberation in policy-making processes, and the extent to which they support openness to learning about ends as well as means, increase capacity for risk management, and give permission for failure and course correction as well as policy experimentation. These novel policy practices have all emerged in different arenas, authorised and enacted by the state, to cope with the complexity challenge.

5

Reconsidering *borders*

Why borders matter

A recurrent theme in this volume is that the world in which public policy actors seek to move towards their preferred futures is an increasingly complex one. One dimension of this increasing complexity in policymaking is in the relationship between the territorial scale of existing political and administrative jurisdictions, such as nation states on a map, and the scale of major policy problems. From clean rivers, to population health, to migration, to crime, to macroeconomic management, to climate change, there are a series of contemporary policy challenges, which are so large in scale that they cross national borders. The problem of borders in public policy is easily stated in the abstract: these are an increasing number of important policy challenges that cannot be solved by the policy actions of states within their own borders. However, the consequences for complex problem-solving are less straightforward to identify. Hence the reconsideration of borders in this chapter and investigation of policy capacity for collective action across borders, at the international and national levels, and involving governments, private interests as well as civil society.

From the perspective of policy practice, borders may be open or closed to varying degrees to encourage or prevent flows of goods, services, capital and people. They can be reshaped as increasingly hard or soft to pursue policy objectives and goals in terms of economic growth, social development outcomes and security. From the analytic perspective, the challenge of framing transnational policymaking in those policy sectors where actors and ideas operate across, and beyond borders, to shape agendas, policy content and modes of governing, is an active and burgeoning seam of public policy scholarship (Skogstad, 2011).

Wimmer and Schiller (2002) present a wide-ranging critique of methodological nationalism in the social sciences, teasing out the effects on scholarship of the assumption that a system of nation states is the natural order of the world. As with any methodology, assumptions are required about the nature of the world being studied, or in other terms, an ontology needs to be adopted about borders. The criticism that methodological nationalism acts as a brake on policy scholarship inevitably involves some claim about the changing nature of borders in the study of public policy (Stone, 2008; Callaghan, 2010). In turn, fresh assumptions about borders impact on the usefulness of existing policy studies frameworks, theories and models for supporting claims about cross-border policymaking. In a strong challenge to policy studies in these terms, Stone (2008) argues that there are now multiple and diffuse sources of sovereignty at the global level, where mixed hybrids public and private spheres of governance facilitate increasingly transnational forms of politics, alongside weaker and more porous national borders in establishing national administrative jurisdictions within which actual policymaking takes place. Further, these real world developments require methodological advances in the contemporary policy studies in which new concepts are formed, the parameters of state action are revisited and the trajectory of policy capacity redrawn.

One plausible starting point for dating the modern era in terms of academic scholarship is Fukuyama's (1992) claim about the end of history, in which humanity after 1989 had entered a new era of market liberal ideology, economic integration and a borderless, or in Thomas Friedman's term 'flat' world (Friedman, 1999). This mode of historical thinking was the conventional backdrop to the debates about governance that emerged in the 1990s that inspire this book. In this trope, the nation state is increasingly hollowed out and various forms of transnational or global governance emerge as putative replacements.

Whatever the residual influence of this view in certain transnational policy networks, it is moot as a description of political change over the last 40 or so years. A multitude of overlapping and contradictory factors seem to be playing out in the economic globalisation project rather than some widespread and unidirectional shift to a borderless world. The outcome of this following combination is unknowable: the rise of religion and nationalism, Russia's decision not to join the West and instead to chart an imperial course, America's partial abnegation of its roles as global superpower, the Chinese model of empire especially in Africa and the geopolitical struggles over material resources. These have real consequences for understanding borders in policy-making terms; their complexity, interconnections with territorial scale and governance. Burridge et al (2017) argue this pushes scholarship towards apprehending the polymorphic nature of borders, in which they take on a variety of mutually non-exclusive forms at the same time. There is no single 'line on the map' border, hard or soft, a single policy instrument to be set up or down, but rather a myriad of different borders that are highly contingent on the policy-making context. In policy studies terms, some instruments do end at the border – formal administrative instruments or tax collecting powers, for example – whereas nodality instruments and organisation instruments can operate transnationally in intergovernmental as well as other fora.

It is not the purpose of the chapter to take an empirical position on the relative strength and weaknesses of nation state borders in contemporary policymaking. Rather it is to investigate how policy studies may reconsider its core concepts in terms of borders without presupposing a 1990s' narrative of collapsing national borders in the wake of the end of the Cold War (see, for example, Friedman, 1999). Policy studies is not alone in the dilemma of borders in a globalising world; although International Relations (IR) scholars and legal thinkers historically have offered many arguments about desirable models of relations between states, typically they assume a border demarcating the domestic from foreign affairs. In much of contemporary social theory there is a stress on the multiplication and intersection section of political identities decoupled from places marked by borders (Bauman, 2000); while there remains a strand of liberal political theory that assumes the existence of territorially bounded communities, whose borders can be neatly delineated from those of other communities. Rawls (1993), for example, assumes the presence of borders demarcating self-contained communities capable of collective reasoning about the requirements justice.

The challenge is to articulate what it means to reconsider borders and then rethink scale in policy studies. There are earlier precedents for such reconsideration in cognate fields. For example, International Political Economy (IPE) was founded in the 1970s and 1980s on an active blurring of the domestic-international, and continues to sit at the margins of both policy studies and IR literatures on something called global public policy (Coleman, 2012). Furthermore, even Stone's influential critique relies on borders to make an analytical distinction between national policy processes and those which operate at the global level: 'global policy processes are distinguishable from national and intergovernmental processes but remain interconnected' (Stone, 2008: 34).

The dominant line of inquiry in global policy studies draws an analogy with trends in governance at the national level. The claim that policy studies needs to move away from the state-centric perspectives on governance applies a fortiori in the cross-border domain and embraces a full set of global governance actors (Coen and Pegram, 2015). By extension, this argument sees national borders demarcating boundaries between sovereign governments as increasingly less relevant to policy analysis (Reinicke, 1998; Stone, 2008; Cerny, 2010; Coleman, 2012).

We are sceptical of this perspective and argue instead for a more nuanced approach in which borders vary in their scope and depth by policy sector. This approach reveals that public action by governmental authorities remains the central unit of analysis of policymaking across borders. In turn, policy studies can translate and adapt its existing conceptual frameworks for cross-border policy rather than having to freight neologisms for that purpose. The first part of the chapter aims to elaborate the relationships between borders, governance and public policy. The next part seeks to unpack the idea of cross-border policymaking into different types. The implications of globalisation for the concepts of global policy processes and global policy design are canvassed separately before a final section considers the future of cross-border policy studies in terms of potentially useful exchanges between the concept of a boundary spanning policy regime (Jochim and May, 2010; May and Jochim, 2013) and political economy scholarship on the shifting territorial patterns of policy problems.

Borders, global governance and policy studies

Among the many competing diagnoses of globalisation, there is a shared view that it involves changes in the spatial and temporal contours of human activity where a rapid acceleration in the temporality of many important forms of human activity has consequences for the significance of borders and for policymaking within the territory they demarcate. The necessity to connect geographical locations in physical terms is reduced as distance or space undergoes compression – the world gets smaller – and changes in the temporality of human activity inevitably produced altered experiences of space. The core question is how and why this should affect our consideration of borders in public policy. For example, as Chapter 6 spells out, the borders of nation states are porous in terms of the flow of information, and opportunities for policy comparison, learning and transfer as well as policy disruption have expanded.

Almost all theories of globalisation employ a version of a standard metaphor that borders are increasingly porous or permeable compared to previous eras. Our starting point is, to stretch the metaphor, they have not been washed away or dissolved. They remain in place and, as leading realist IR scholar Krasner (2016) describes, there is a lack of plausible alternatives to a system of national states as the way to organise cross-border public policy. We argue that while an understanding of cross-border activities as sources of policy problems reminds us that there is no such thing as a global government it also reveals the profound weaknesses of transnational governance mechanisms that operate beyond nation states. However ineffective, it is nevertheless international policy coordination by states that should be the baseline of transnational policy studies.

A plausible defence of methodological nationalism may be mounted around the enduring centrality of nation states and their territorial borders in policymaking even as they constitute or operate within various governance arrangements. Such global governance structures often lack the effectiveness, legitimacy and accountability of territorial nation states. Indeed, the Stone critique, though oft-repeated, does seem to be premised on a conventional wisdom about globalisation that appears possibly anachronistic. Analysis by the Peterson Institute for International Economics (2016) showed how international trade and capital flows have stagnated since the Global Financial Crisis (GFC) amid a steady rise of protectionist measures. This reassertion of national economic border controls is concatenated with popular demands in many countries for tighter borders to control the flow of people.

To avoid the risk that the metaphor of national and global levels becomes reified as fixed territorial scales, it is relevant to consider how much of the policymaking for global policy questions happens at the global level. The statement that health policy is no longer exclusively national may well be true; but its insight may be limited if most of direct 'policymaking' remains at the domestic level (even if in developing countries with substantial external support). For example, there is increasing global cooperation in global health policy over time, and crucially, much economic policy coordination with a direct impact on a health policy problem is organised at the global level. However, many determinants of global health remain inextricably bound to domestic policy processes: economics, trade, environment, development, labour regulations, social protections, welfare states and security. Decisions taken in these areas have huge implications for the health of people all around the world, but are frequently not understood as being 'health policy', still less consciously 'global health policy'.

As sovereign borders shift in their policy significance, so the number of actors involved in transnational governance is growing, as are the ways in which they interact and the roles they take on. These can range from hierarchical arrangements, through hybrid arrangements where state actors still possess the shadow of hierarchy, through to network-based and market-based arrangements. It may be that transnational policy problems have transnational solutions; or solutions available via intergovernmental arrangements. A transnational solution may be obtainable exclusively via non-state links. These can involve transboundary multinational actors (private market actors and/or third-sector and non-governmental organisations (NGO) actors), or cross-border links between actors whose spheres of influence remain defined by state borders.

The literature on global governance as a field is on the cusp of its third generation. Coen and Pegram (2015: 417) call for fresh scholarship 'distinguished by a concern for the complexity and dynamism of global public policymaking'. In their account, the intellectual history of global governance is variegated and mixed, with an IR-inspired first generation motivated by normative concerns and imaginative projects about better ways to organise global public policy, and a second generation consisting of contributions from EU scholarship, international legal studies and more international political economists.

The call for a third generation is based on the need to focus on policy challenges where national interests do not align and where externalities impact on a territorial scale far beyond policy capacity of individual member states. This analytical move has entailed orientating analysis away from design towards studies of capacity for policy action across borders and the role of factors such as incentives, networks, dynamics of preference formation, expertise and epistemic communities, the allocation of political authority among competing global governance actors. We develop the argument in this chapter that, while these remain relevant factors, they are better approached from a policy studies perspective through the notion of boundary spanning policy regimes rather than global public policy.

In parallel with the global governance literature, the call for a reconsideration of borders and their permeability is increasingly evident in policy studies (Stone, 2008; Kim, et al, 2014; Stone and Ladi, 2015). It is moot the extent to which these demands have met with any satisfactory answers even as the tendency for domestic policy problems, in sectors outside the economic or conventional foreign affairs, to spill over into the international arena has highlighted the need for cooperative and cross-border policy efforts at the regional and multilateral level.

There is a well-developed literature which investigates how globalisation has produced transnational policy actors in domestic policymaking such as multinational corporations (MNCs) and international organisations (IOs) that exert their influence over domestic policy outcomes by establishing international regulatory standards and pressuring policymakers to comply. This is probably where the literature in policy studies has made its most evident move in the direction of grasping policymaking across sovereign borders by drawing on a catalogue of already existing concepts and categories for analysis policy networks (Rhodes, 2008b), epistemic communities (Haas, 1992), and policy subsystems (Howlett and Ramesh, 2005). However, this reframing exercise remains nascent, and most of the adaptation is ad hoc and case-specific. As elaborated in the critique by Stone (2008), there is a manifest lack of conceptual development for the circumstances of cross-border policymaking.

Borders and policymaking

For ease of exposition, cross-border policymaking can be unpacked into four basic categories.

Transnational policy solutions

In this category, there is a supranational level of authority. Illustrative examples include some of the institutions of the European Union, for example the European Commission and the European Court of Justice. But we can also distinguish between these examples, where the supranational authority has a legally binding relationship with the national (territorially sovereign-based) actors and those where the relationship is not defined in such legal terms. An example here would be the Dispute Settlement Procedure of the World Trade Organisation (WTO), which relies on inter-subjective agreement between WTO signatories for compliance.

Intergovernmental policy solutions

In this category, there will be examples where countries negotiate directly with each other to deliver policy outcomes and solutions to problems. In cases with larger numbers of countries, however, a supranational organising structure may facilitate intergovernmental engagement. Following on from the last example, such a situation exists under the WTO umbrella for multilateral trade liberalisation talks. That said, the authority rests with the national parties. As the WTO has described itself on its website, it is effectively the table around which the WTO member countries sit and negotiate.

Transnational state-non-state policy solutions

This category is the one in which we are particularly interested. In this category, states engage with non-state actors but, crucially, they do so beyond their sovereign borders. As a result they lack sovereign authority over those non-state actors – indeed, they even lack a shadow of hierarchy. As a result, states thus become de facto non-state actors. An example here is to be found in EU biofuels sustainability criteria, where the European Commission must work collaboratively with non-state actors in countries around the world, from the private and third sectors, to deliver on the sustainability dimensions of EU biofuels policies. But, lacking even the shadow of hierarchy, they have no way to force/enforce participation in and compliance with a state's domestic policy.

Transnational private actor solutions

In this category, we have a multitude of possible examples where private actors – firms, third-sector actors/NGOs – collaborate on solutions to problems. Examples here include the networks on which Fairtrade, the Forest Stewardship Council, the Marine Stewardship Council, the Roundtable on Sustainable Palm Oil and many others are built. The process of economic globalisation is driving the emergence transboundary policy problems. State actors are having to find novel ways of engaging with private sector actors in order to build the requisite policy capacity to address successfully contemporary cross-border challenges. The relationship between state and non-state actors represents a new and emerging form of governance transnationally with implications for cross-border policymaking.

Global public policy

When it comes to the idea of 'global policy', most definitions still tend to identify government as the central agent and executor of public decisions, notwithstanding the waves of literature in the study of the theory and practice of global governance that suggest a scene of greater complexity. Conventional literatures in policy studies, as well as in public administration, tend to play down the degree to which states shared their sovereignty with market actors to secure policy outcomes. Indeed, corporations and non-state actors are often authorised to act on behalf of the state in a range of ways. For some, the agency of states in public policy should now be judged as much by the qualitative as opposed to simply the quantitative nature of their sovereignty; especially as large market actors, increasingly acting politically as well as economically, become sources of private authority independently (Cutler, 2003).

Further, governments and IOs design and deliver policy in partnerships with business, philanthropy and expert groups; coalitions of non-state political and social actors generally, seeking to take forward their own group interests and concerns. In such contexts, policy activity does not conform to the standard distinction of simply 'public' or 'private' (Stone, 2008). It occurs across domains such that international decision-making, policy implementation and regulation are fractured between public officials, private stakeholders and communities of scientific experts. Multiple quasi-public transnational policy communities exercise growing power and authority over cross-national problems in many issue-areas: trade, finance, environment, energy, regional integration, migration, disease, water, crime and others. Thus Stone (2008: 20) offers a definition of global policy studies as:

> a set of overlapping but disjointed processes of public-private deliberation and cooperation among both official state-based and IOs with non-state actors around establishing common norms and policy agendas for securing the delivery of global public goods or ameliorating transnational problems. (Stone, 2008)

The notion of policy studies that is 'global' or 'transnational' remains unfamiliar and still in the process of detailed specification (Coleman, 2012). Moreover, as Stone (2008) notes, global 'public' policy is not always necessarily 'public'. The post-World War II IOs (especially the UN and Bretton Woods organisations) are no longer, if indeed they ever were, the sole determinants of 'global policy'. Newer actors in addition to corporations – be they networks, private standard-setting regimes, 'global commissions' or regional fora – function independently or alongside traditional IOs in arranging policy domains.

Relatedly, there is a need to develop further ideas in public administration to study those who are not public servants but who work in the global (and regional) public domains and in tandem with various non-state actors. For example, the growing analysis of the European Commission reveals that the constitutive actors of regional policy processes and trans-regional administration are increasingly socialised differently from their state-based counterparts (see Kim et al, 2014). Where new policy spaces of public action develop, they invariably give rise to transnational teams of managers and administrators who identify with these new policy spaces rather than with sovereign states. In such emergent transnational or global policy spaces, policy studies scholarship is at a crossroad between domestic and international. Furthermore, it is not clear what rethinking policy-making scales at this crossroad imply for the existing theoretical divergence between rationalist/positivist and post-positivist approaches to the study of public policy.

For example, the investigation of IOs from a policy studies angle is still in its infancy. Contributions in Kim et al (2014) stress how in various ways public administration is beginning to develop an interest in global rule-making but without being fully engaged with the field of global governance. The working assumption of public administration and indeed IR scholarship was that IOs, or more specifically international public administrations that operate within the IOs, lacked independence and were not purposive autonomous actors and were hence not in need of deeper research. However, as Kim et al (2014) set out, there is now a growing recognition of their autonomy and influence and the fact that they are not merely simple agents of member states (Kim et al, 2014).

Within the global policy design literatures, the notion of global public goods is notable. Introduced by political economists (Higgott, 2007) in paradigmatic terms, its application to individual policy sectors is motivated directly by the claims that sovereign borders between the international and the domestic are porous. Much like the rational-post-positivist divide that had emerged in policy studies, IPE has its splits as well. The point of agreement across the divide is the need to end the analytical separation of economics from politics, and, related to the purpose of understanding borders in policymaking, and challenge false dichotomies between the domestic and international political economy.

The same traditions of rational choice theory are present in policy studies as well as formal political economy models, especially constrained optimisation and the rational actor grammar as the basis of understanding individual and collective decision-making. The constructivist strand, on the other hand, stresses the inter-subjective nature of knowledge, and alongside the interpretive strands of policy studies sees meaning in the world as constructed and variable rather than based on objective foundations. The central schism is the existence of multiple identities; the constructivists see these as militating against an objective understanding of reality whereas rationalists tend to think economic models can be developed about reality without such concerns. Constructivists privilege the 'constitutive' characteristics of knowledge, identities and norms which define not only how sociopolitical actors behave towards each other but also, more deeply, the sources of the identity of these same actors (Wendt, 1999). There are manifold sources of such identities in a world of polymorphic borders as technology allows networks to transcend the limits of geography.

However, if we see political economy as focused on a larger set of material structures that determine world order, then it is easier to see how political and economic outcomes are determined by the organisation and dynamics of the global economy, particularly the growing dominance of global finance. This awareness, especially in the light of repeated financial crises, has been accompanied by recognition of the limits of rationalism and the growing importance of institutionalist and some sociological perspectives on economic behaviour in political economy. We turn to this direction of inquiry in order to adumbrate a way forward in cross-border policy studies.

A political economy of cross-border policymaking

Some see the future of the study of public policy in a move beyond statist and national methodologies (Stone, 2008). This viewpoint has emerged in parallel to claims about the need for policy studies to work much more at the interstices of economics and politics. For example, John (2018) argues that it is time for policy studies to come closer to political economy in methodological terms: he suggests a third age of policy studies – the political economy of public policy – is taking shape. It is not straightforward, however, that the corollary of a political economy of cross-border policy is the direction suggested by Stone, namely novel concept formation for a transnational policy studies that moves beyond national states as the primary unit of analysis. Although John (2018) does not explicitly address borders, governance or shifting territorial scales of policy action, he foreshadows an engagement between policy studies and comparative political economy in which the locus of policymaking remains firmly with states. From a political economy of cross-border policy-making perspective, there is reason to cast doubt on the Stone (2008) critique as a more general claim about the role of borders in policymaking. It may well apply in certain instances, private regulation of forestry standards for example, but there are obvious policy cases where states remain powerful even where the scale of policy problems shifts with changing economic processes to spill across borders. There is intergovernmental action in a range of vital areas from security to banking regulation that determines cross-border public policy. As Chapter 4 on reconsidering the state describes, the globalisation epoch has not been associated with a general 'race to the bottom' in welfare state terms as predicted by Friedman (1999).

One corollary of the claim that policy studies are stuck in a methodological nationalist orientation is that large forces of economic globalisation are either missed or only ever partially sighted. If sovereign nation state borders are the analytical starting point for models of policymaking, then the boundary of the policy-making system, and therefore questions of legitimacy, authority and the 'publicness' of policy, becomes linked exclusively to the formal institutions of representative government. In contrast, political economy – acknowledging that in contemporary usage this term has many meanings – does not foreground national political borders in its analysis of global policy, instead privileging economic processes that may operate at multiple territorial scales of capitalism and which do not map onto democratic scales.

A political economy approach can help policy studies to model the economic processes in which policy instruments may be applied by encouraging investigation of the multiple territorial scales of capitalism that do not necessarily map onto existing political-administrative jurisdictions. It encourages new actors into studies of policymaking but also new institutions, such as the variety of trade and investment treaties that underpin flows of goods, services and capital or much of international environmental policy. Many of these institutional innovations remain intergovernmental. As we have seen, states often increase their policy capacity to act outside their territory by using non-state actors to do their work for them. Obvious examples are in the use by the US government of quasi-military and private security firms in unstable parts of the world such as Iraq. China policymakers have showcased several policy tools for exercising cross-border power in South East Asia and Africa through the use of tied aid programs, megaprojects for infrastructure development and large sovereign loans at well below international capital market rates.

States still do much direct negotiating with each other in trade and other policy fora. In the Australian case, the goal of international trade policy has been long established as freer trade but the policy means on how to pursue this have been the subject of considerable innovation, such as the Cairns Group and Asia-Pacific Economic Cooperation to advance Australia's policy interests (Capling, 2001). In the development of international economic policy, strong states tend to treat other state actors rather like interests in stakeholder analysis in the national policy sphere, in that they must be offered concessions where this is necessary, but can be ignored when they are weak. There is a normative edge to many political economy of globalisation accounts, as in discussions of the negative consequences of the 'new constitutionalism' in terms of a shrinking policy space for social policy interventions, but that is not a necessary element. The stress on this transnational context may be introduced into the field of policy studies to apprehend large-scale economic processes without necessarily importing normative debates about global justice or the ethical claims of cosmopolitism.

Policy studies have traditionally been concerned with the development and implementation of policy within states and the role of officials formally responsible for such policy. Both in political economy and policy studies, influential political actors and societal groups are not simply there to support government policy initiatives. They can and do play veto roles in the policy-making processes when government policy runs contrary to their perceived interests. Contests between key actors in state and society are a crucial component of policymaking. This is explained by students of policy studies via the use of actor-centric theoretical frameworks such as policy networks or epistemic communities. Others have chosen to focus on policy instruments rather than actors in the policy design literature that nonetheless treats state and non-state actors as policy designers with varying extents of influence over the design of substantive and procedural policy instruments.

While political economy may provide the global contextual analysis for these activities, it lacks the analytic tools of policy studies for the job of understanding cross-border policy. The fine-grained, contextual detail of decision-making under scrutiny by the policy scholar can capture the policy-making dynamics at work beyond the borders of the state. The insights that political economy and policy studies might offer the modern scholar the best option for apprehending cross-border policymaking – if their respective strengths could be harnessed collectively – have yet to be explored fully. In combination, the advantages offered by policy studies and political economy over economics is how, without minimising the importance of rationalism, they both recognise the degree to which politics can destabilise equilibrium outcomes much more than economic theory usually concedes.

Both political economy and policy studies identify processes of path dependence and sequencing as well as sharing a strong analytical commitment to the importance of institutions and the creative agency of actors – individuals, organisations, networks or classes – occupying roles in these institutions. They also share a common problematic: to describe, interpret and explain the relationship between the activities of a global market on the one hand, and the politics of national policymaking on the other. It is in the organisational elements of the study of decision-making that the strengths of policy studies analysis become most apparent. Literatures on departments, secretariats, task forces, working groups and committees are available to be used in the study of IOs, providing the kind of analysis that political economy does not.

Global policy processes

As the introductory chapter to this book elaborates, thinking in policy studies has evolved considerably over the half-century or more since the idea that 'policy' and the 'policy process' could be split into discrete elements (Colebatch, 2002). These stages of the policy process are often referred to as a policy cycle – and sometimes represented by a circular diagram with a closed loop. The significance of this lies in the idea that the policy process is unending, the 'end' of one pass through the stages represents the start of the next pass through and, in contemporary conditions of temporal compression, the tendency is to be 'always in the middle'.

As is well rehearsed, while policy cycles or stages models do not represent a theory of the policy process, they do offer a way of understanding various dimensions of the policy process, each of which may be explored in more detail through other lenses. This analytical pluralism has long been a feature of policy studies as a field. For example, Cairney (2012b) introduces the policy cycle alongside comprehensive rationality, which posits that 'elected policymakers translate their values into policy in a straightforward manner.' (Cairney, 2012b: 5). This applies to the ranking of policy preferences, with clear-cut stages for then delivering on this. By such a policy process are the benefits to society maximised.

How does this help us in our goal of trying to understand global policy processes? It offers us a framework through which we can chart different dimensions of the policy process in different territorial spaces. We can use the notion of a staged, strictly sequential process as a point of departure. If, for example, different stages are located across different territorial spaces, how might this influence the actors involved, and their roles, compared with a policy process located entirely within a single territorial space? Moreover – and, from a theoretical point of view, more significantly – how might this affect what happens when?

Peters (2015b) suggests that standard accounts of the policymaking help establish necessary and sufficient conditions for there to be a policy process, but not necessarily in a set order. Arguably, the international adds a complicating dimension to existing domestic policy process and strengthens existing critiques that suggest that there is rarely an observed set of temporally distinct stages in policymaking. For example, the elementary case of a policy process crossing a national border once suggests a limit to temporal orderliness. The first part of the process, conducted domestically by a sovereign state power, perhaps progresses through to decision-making. In an increasingly globalised world, however, perhaps implementation of the 'domestic' takes place extra-territorially. But can a policy process simply continue, sequentially, in a different territory or transnationally? Much of the international development literature suggests that the implementation of overseas development assistance policy by revisiting other policy stages – as where the interests on the ground, including recipient governments – must be engaged at the agenda-setting and decision stages to ensure aid effectiveness (World Bank, 2017). It is easy to imagine a large variety of permutations that require future policy studies scholarship to apprehend and catalogue.

New institutionalism at the transnational level: bridging the historical-sociological divide

Although implicated in the state-centric policy analysis, there is a research agenda available that looks to build relationships between the historical and sociological strands of the new institutionalism to understand transnational processes of policymaking. This line of inquiry offers the opportunity to achieve analytical purchase on situations of multiple and diffuse sources of authority, strong informal and weak formal institutions, and the role of norms and values in global public policy. Farrell and Finnemore (2016) set out several conceptual challenges for the new institutionalism to 'go global': understanding institutional effects in global policymaking without a global state; dealing with institutions that are more informal than formal (Chapter 3). They conclude their 'state of the art' chapter by suggesting a future research agenda where the historical and sociological strands of the new institutionalism reunite but without offering any clear guidance on such a unification.

We suggest one plausible avenue for policy studies in this direction is to recover the cultural theory of risk developed by Douglas and Wildavsky (1982). This research seam has other names such as neo-

Durkheimian analysis or Grid-Group theory (6, 2003). We suggest that an institutionalist research agenda seeking to build a historical-sociological synthesis along these lines would entail documenting the elementary forms of transnational policy processes and allow greater understanding of their variety. Recognising such diversity would support a research theme investigating the conditions under which stability in global policy institutions of different kinds might be sustained, or not sustained, over time.

In some policy sectors, there are loosely coupled or weakly socially integrated networks that are weakly regulated at the transnational level (for example, most of global health policy) whereas other policy processes exhibit rather tightly coupled, strongly integrated and even strongly socially (if not in every case, legally) regulated forms. For policy studies, it is important to understand why some international policy coordination takes place under a formal rule-based system and the relationship of these institutions to other forms of bonding. For example, the difference between climate policy in EU and ASEAN decision-making may be thought of in this way (Crowley and Nakamura, 2018). Alternatively, this insight may help policy studies understand why some economic policy disputes are brought under the treaty to the WTO while others are dealt with by loosely coupled negotiations.

Policymaking at NATO, for example, is rule-governed by regular reference back to the 1949 treaty and to 65 years of precedents. At the same time, NATO policymaking is conducted among members who have rather strongly integrated, tightly coupled bonds to each other in defence ranging over everything from procurement through interoperability to joint command and even intelligence sharing in some bilateral cases. Other cases are tightly bonded but weakly regulated, such as the conference of privacy regulators. Some strands of activity in the International Standards Organisation exhibit a hybrid form between weakly and strongly bonded ties with a degree of social and even quasi-legal regulation of the policy process.

This grid-group distinction permits different ways of thinking about particular transnational policy trajectories by recognising a diversity in basic ordering, there is no single global policy processes and we aim to develop an argument about the conditions under which stability of different kinds might be sustained or not sustained through rather different mechanisms. Strong bonds (group) and strong social regulation (grid) might sustain stability in some periods (stable external threat from the Soviet Union in NATO's case; the period of what Ben Bernanke called the 'great moderation' in the case of the

WTO [2004]), but might prove fragile in other periods The stability of exhaustion under conditions of strong social regulation (by a few major players) and very weak bonds, for example, which appears to characterise what little is left of international negotiations about climate change, is very different from the stability which marks the policy process within Internet Corporation for Assigned Names and Numbers (ICANN) about internet domain name policy.

This kind of approach would suggest the importance of qualifying any general claim of states as policy actors in the cross-border domain. For example, policy entrepreneurship may make sense in weakly socially integrated, weakly socially regulated settings but in others – such as the new generation of trade agreements – represent a closer approximation to a more strongly regulated international legal order in which the meaning of entrepreneurship, and scope for it, is consequently attenuated.

Policy implementation beyond the state

In Chapter 8, in terms of implementation, we set out the shifting balance of top-down and bottom-up perspectives over time and the emergence of an uneasy accommodation between the two. Peters (2015b: 98–9) identifies the recurrent dilemma: 'during implementation the social and market actors will almost certainly influence the nature of the policy as it actually goes into effect "on the ground". We should in fact expect more drift from the intentions of the framers of the legislation, and outcomes that can be compensated for by the ability to leverage the resources of the non-governmental actors involved'.

In the context of multiple and diffuse sources of sovereignty at the global level, where porous boundaries between public and private spheres of governance facilitate increasingly transnational forms of politics, this conventional implementation dilemma of policy studies looks importantly different. While diagnoses of principal-agent problems or bureaucratic slippage have proved successful across many sectors within a closed policy-making system, without a single, concentrated source of sovereignty, in an open policy-making system they lack analytical purchase. This is thrown into yet starker relief when there is no 'shadow of hierarchy' cast by a powerful state that can enforce compliance; instead, it is the relational dynamics post-public policymaking that is key to extra territorial policy implementation.

In this context of cross-border policy, the concept of non-state actors, while a useful catch-all in general terms may lose its purchase as an analytical category. This is related, in turn, to the problematic distinction between public and private authority in the transnational governance arena. Private actors, both national and transnational, participate in transnational governance regimes, but struggle to satisfy the requirements of public policy, and may fail to generate 'publicness' in their procedures and accountability mechanisms. Implementation of these sorts of post-sovereignty public policy requires collaboration, negotiation and 'soft' institutionalism.

The identification of the relevant non-state actors for policy analysis is not always straightforward. Koehn and Rosenau (2002: 106), for example, emphasise that 'as increasingly less effective national and subnational governments struggle to cope with the challenges of interdependence…the transformative efforts of civil-society networks' become more important. Other writers such as Kobrin (2009) and Doh (2011) include several other actor-types in the non-state category. As Chapter 7 on information sets out, nodality has been long acknowledged as an important policy instrument of governments. This remains so in cross-border policymaking where they can catalyse and manage interactions between domestic NGOs, international NGOs, local and transnational companies, other governments as well as IOs. In the governance arrangement under scrutiny, there is no intergovernmental policy engagement. We thus include NGOs and companies, but not other national governments. We also include IOs that, while in many cases result from intergovernmental negotiation, can also be granted authority independent of the constituent member states.

An important corollary of the foregoing is that, in this post-sovereignty category of public policy, there is no obvious point at which we can say policy is being implemented. A state can notionally begin a policy process by identifying policy aims, objectives and preferences. It can then negotiate and agree policy domestically on this basis. It must then, however, seek to shape, influence and negotiate with non-state actors, located extra-territorially in order to implement this policy. It must ensure the actors not only have the functional capabilities required, but also that their own individual private agendas accord with the policy agenda of the state. Only then can the state establish, in a network, the governing arrangements beyond the border, to help 'make' the transnational public policy that is an essential condition in the successful domestic implementation of the policy in question.

Policy studies can help apprehend these relational, collaborative systems of governance in the transnational sphere. It can help with the question: how can a state, without formal authority or real power, create relational dynamics with actors well outside its formal or effective (defined as hierarchy-based, in a traditional Westphalian setting) sphere of influence? The state is required to act as a policy entrepreneur extra-territorially, in linking different streams in windows of opportunity. Ambiguity is linked to, in this case, an absence of Westphalian sovereignty. There are no elections, hard law, tax powers; instead the dominant characteristic is institutional ambiguity and the absence of capacity to arbitrate definitively between different states. The implementation of the EU's Renewable Energy Directive in parts of South East Asia is an important case in point (Ellis-Petersen, 2018).

In reconsidering borders in policy studies, it is helpful not to reify the levels or scales of policymaking. These are metaphorical distinctions that may, in turn, lead to an analytical strategy of studying international, global and domestic policy separately. This is, of course, successful as well as valid for certain scholarly ends. However, for employing policy models extra-territorially, the metaphor of levels may be misleading. Instead, we submit that a more apposite metaphor to employ in applying policy models is not two distinct levels of policymaking, but instead a closed system, a domestic policy process, overlapping and interacting with an open transnational policy-making system. We will subsequently develop this insight using the concept of a boundary spanning policy regime introduced by Jochim and May (2010). The characteristics of policymaking across and beyond borders, where there is no dominant state or hegemon to impose its policy, remain key variables, but additionally there is a domestic policy process intertwined across various territorial scales.

The corollary is thus policy studies may be used to describe a boundary between a relatively ordered phase of domestic state-driven policy phase; and a disordered, uncertain, or random phase where the policy as agreed is taken and the state, extra-territorially, seeks to work with actors with whom policy can be implemented. These two policy processes – domestic and transnational – may be 'out of phase', such that, in stages terms, domestic implementation is potentially (or 'potentially becomes') transnational agenda setting. The policy dynamics at the transnational scale may be connected to the contingencies of domestic policy processes. A more developed cross-border policy studies requires heightened temporal sensitivity to consider alignments, moments and, here, the entrepreneurial activity of state actors in this transnational world of increasingly dense rules, norms, standards, but no global state.

Boundary spanning regimes and policy change

Jochim and May (2010) offer the concept of 'boundary spanning policy regimes' as one way of bringing together analyses of policy processes and questions of governance. In their analysis, the regime perspective facilitates investigation of policy issues that cross-conventional bureaucratic boundaries with the examples taken from domestic US policymaking. However, Peters (2015b: 18–19) expands this line of inquiry by suggesting that boundary spanning regimes may also span national sovereign borders. We suggest attention to policy regimes provides a promising means for the analysis of policymaking that spans sovereign state borders.

Jochim and May (2010: 309) are clear that compounding the established notions of boundary spanning and regimes into the concept of a boundary spanning policy regime is useful and distinguishes their work in important ways from the long-established policy subsystem literature (Howlett and Ramesh, 2005). They argue that it provides a system-wide perspective on power and authority consistent with the large debates on governance while maintaining analytical leverage on the rich contextual features of policymaking in individual sectors. May and Jochim (2013) develop further the argument for regime perspectives in policy studies as a means to understand the feedback processes of policies that shape subsequent policy legitimacy, coherence and durability. For the purposes of this chapter, there is nothing in this account of a policy regime perspective that requires the process to be contained exclusively within one sovereign border. May and Jochim (2013) argue for a regime perspective on the grounds that it provokes questions about the quality of governing arrangements and the durability of policies; in turn, serving to remind the policy studies field that these were central drivers in its development during the 1960s. While regime insights have not been entirely forgotten, they tend to be faint echoes of this 1960s literature, for example the work describing how international climate policy regimes have 'vertically disintegrated' over time (Kellow, 2012) notwithstanding their re-emergence in the shape of the 2015 Paris Accord.

While nascent boundary spanning policy regime literature is promising for the analysis of transnational policymaking, it requires significant reconsideration. Notably, the location of power and authority in the transnational domain is an analytical challenge in which the role of borders requires reconsideration. Borders are polymorphic: simultaneously demarcating the territory of the formal legal authority of different states and porous and malleable in terms of softer dimensions of power (Burridge et al, 2017).

Conclusions

In reconsidering borders in public policy, we have adopted the assumption that contemporary borders between the national and the international have many forms and vary sector by sector, but we have avoided the universal presumption that borders have withered away in the globalisation epoch. This helps to recognise the analytical challenge for policy studies: to describe, interpret and explain phenomena using existing frameworks that spill over conventional boundaries.

The chapter started with the issue of the mismatch between the spatial scale of many contemporary policy problems and the size of existing nation state jurisdictions. This can be restated as relevant sources of power and authority in many contemporary policy processes operate across sovereign borders. Using a political economy lens, we argue that many contemporary policy challenges are produced transnationally and that the policy capacity for their mitigation requires cross-border collective action for public purposes. While there is strong merit in a new political economy of cross-border policy studies, in which perspectives on power are taken on board, we still see the national state and national borders as the most helpful starting point for policy analysis. Although several works cited in the chapter hold that TNCs and transnational elites should be the locus of a global public policy studies, we are sceptical and see cross-border policy studies as a field in which conventional policy analysis can produce results with suitable adaptation and translation. To this end, we identify potential in the boundary spanning policy regime idea (Jochim and May, 2010; May and Jochim, 2013) as the basis for an expanded seam of work in cross-border policy studies. Although these authors have not intended this novel conceptual compound for cross-border policy, we argue it would enable policy scholars to get some purchase on intergovernmental fora as well as the more fluid situations of international governance such as private regulatory standards and global philanthropy that much recent scholarship has emphasised. The notion of boundary spanning pushes policy scholarship to discerning mechanisms that connect policy subsystems across national borders. The notion of epistemic communities in Haas (1992) is one such possibility, but in reconsidering public policy, there are many more possibilities in terms of institutions, information flows, regulatory systems, implementation plans and performance management.

Core concepts in the policy studies manual can all be improved by sustained engagement with phenomena that are both domestic and international in nature and that are effective and arguably legitimate but which do not have foundations in formal national political institutions. This engagement should expand the policy studies catalogue rather than demand its wholesale revision. Cross-border policy remains recognisable as public policy even in our age of uncertainty and disruption.

6

Reconsidering *advice and advisory systems*

Introduction

The provision of policy advice has underpinned governing since earliest times, however, the practice is much changed in the contemporary era. Advice and the context in which it is delivered have broadened, with more diverse sources of advice, more diverse settings for generating it and many more complex means of influencing state action. Policy advising is an activity that supports decision-making by analysing problems and proposing solutions (Halligan, 1995), however, advice has always varied, as has the preparedness of governments to listen to it. The literature has focused recently on 'policy advisory systems' (PASs) both descriptively (see Seymour-Ure, 1987; Halligan, 1995; Prasser, 2006) and in terms of their dynamics (Craft and Howlett, 2013; Craft and Halligan, 2017) and subsystems (Craft and Wilder, 2017). Advice is well understood, but PASs are less so, despite having much in common with policy networks.

We have seen in previous chapters that the modern state and its operations are complex, with policy boundaries now multi-layered, and partnering within and beyond government a more common approach to problem-solving. Policy advising needs to be understood within this context. Traditional, largely internal advising is alive and well, whether as political judgement, or impartial analysis, however, new forms of advisory activity are common. There has always been a systematic approach to the generation and uptake of advice in politico-administrative terms, but the broadening of the advisory landscape has complicated this in terms of more complex systems. However, such complexity, while challenging in traditional policy-making terms, is commonly argued to be well suited to collaborative efforts at tackling more complex problems (Scott and Baehler, 2010: 6).

There are a range of reasons for this. Firstly, wicked, or persistent, problems have long been recognised as requiring complex, deliberatively generated solutions that are appropriate in any case in an era of heightened social reflexivity. Expert knowledge alone very often does not suffice (Rittel and Webber, 1973). Secondly, liberal democratic states that have experienced neo-liberal downsizing now already augment their policy and problem-solving capacity by broadening their advisory sources. Thirdly, issues have grown more complex and their resolution has increasingly required, not only a broadened range of insight, but also the mediation of competing and contested values, beliefs and knowledge bases (Ney, 2009). And finally, the heightened connectivity of the modern state is already a significant factor in problem-solving that has complicated traditional, rational decision-making with implications for PASs.

Our interest is in how the trends in policy advice and advisory systems can be framed by the governance and systems literature in a manner that throws light upon this more complex problem-solving context. Both the governance and systems perspectives would see advice as generated by networks and systems within and beyond government, with sets of relationships of varying types created to attempt to achieve various advisory purposes. Governance practice today emphasises connectivity and recognises 'that in many situations a government is unlikely to procure satisfactory outcomes working on its own' (Scott and Baehler, 2010: 6–7). A systems perspective is complementary because it has the ability to move beyond the specifics of each problem to depict underlying complexity and to identify associations and linkages that are otherwise hard to discern (Chapter 2). The PASs literature has something to learn, we suggest, from these approaches.

There is much to be reconsidered, therefore, in terms of advice and advisory systems, including the ways in which advising has evolved into a complex set of competing relations and approaches, with tensions within and beyond the state. Our emphasis is on the need to view the shifting dynamics of advice giving as parallel to, and likely a consequence of, changes in the nature of the state from a relatively closed to a more open, connected institution. The state is less a demarcated entity and more a set of relations in the governance era (Chapter 4), and we argue that clarity about the place and role of the modern state is underemphasised in the PAS literature. It follows, we believe, that the governance literature, with its depiction of the changing state, and the systems literature, with its emphasis upon cross-relational dynamics, have utility in reconsidering PASs.

In this chapter we reconsider policy advice in several key senses. We revisit the significance of the role of policy advising, and depictions of the transformation of the practice of policy advising; we draw upon governance and policy systems frames in our reconsideration of advisory systems; and we reflect upon the place of expert advice in PASs in problem-solving today. We are particularly interested in the role of advice and advisory systems in addressing complex problems in the governance era, and in whether a more diverse advisory landscape helps or hinders the generation and transmission of policy-relevant knowledge.

Policy advising matters

Mainstream policy scholarship has increasingly focused upon the nature and varying character of policy advice, and the evolution and depictions of PASs, in terms, for example, of the role and significance of advice within policy processes and upon the determination of outcomes. Policy advice was implied as significant in the first and second stages of Lasswell's (1956) path-breaking accounting of the 'policy process' as a series of discrete stages, namely: intelligence, recommendation, prescription, invocation, application, appraisal and termination. Yet studies of policy content, process, outputs and evaluation, for the purposes of portraying either *prescriptive* models, or *descriptive* analysis (Cairney, 2012b: 32), imply rather than recognise as significant the importance of advice in policy formulation, decision-making and execution. There is rarely a separate policy advice chapter, for example, in textbooks on the policy process, however, this is not necessarily because it doesn't matter, but hopefully because it is assumed to be central or fundamental to the entire policy development process.

In recent decades, there has been an increasing focus on the place of policy advice within PASs. Weller (1987) offers an early characterisation of policy advice and advisors' varying roles in Plowden's (1987) path-breaking collection, which included Seymour-Ure's (1987) early depiction of PASs. This work was agenda setting in terms of inspiring research. Subsequently the narrow sub-field of the study of policy advisors and advice giving began to expand with empirical clarity, for example, about the roles of ministerial advisors (Maley, 2000), and relations between advisors in general and advisees (Savoie, 2003). Prince (2007), for example, saw policy advising as increasingly mattering in the novel sense of a soft, subtle craft in an environment of trade-offs, value sacrifice and hard choices, and in the context of an emergent plurality of advisory sources. Otherwise the now flourishing policy advisory scholarship is well reflected, initially in Halligan (1995), Prasser (2006), and later in work such as Craft and Howlett (2013), Craft and Wilder (2017) and in special editions of *Policy and Society* (Vol 32, 2013) and *Policy Sciences* (Vol 50, 2017).

Halligan's (1995) agenda-setting work detailed the ways in which public policy advising has been subject to the turbulence of successive public sector reforms and emerged as still mattering. Public officials and their advisory roles have been targeted, in a context of the 'increasing complexity of the policy environment' (Halligan, 1995: 138), with governments seeking greater control over the generating and dissemination of advice. Throughout these changes and despite these pressures, the public sector advisory role remains central, if more challenging and indeed more challenged. The advisory system that Halligan describes comprises advisers who operate in an 'advice system that is subject to preferences prevailing within a political system' that may be dominated by bureaucratic or political advisers and potentially influenced by external interests. Political, public service, policy and specialist advisors who are internal to government include those that have varying levels of high to low proximity to decision makers and can be more readily controlled than external or otherwise independent, for example statutory, advisors (Halligan, 1995: 141).

Politicisation has always been a factor in policy advising since the beginnings of government. Political and advisory systems, whether open or closed, have always found a place for special interests and have been open to insider and elite influence in their decision-making, with routine charges of government favouritism and neglect of impartial evidence. However, politicisation becomes more complex and is often argued to be increasing in more open PASs. Some charges of politicisation can be dismissed, Prasser (2006: 3) argues, because:

> Hierarchy, poor communication processes, department politics, and groupthink all contribute to alternate views sometimes being suppressed, ignored or just not heard through the 'babel' of advice that percolates up through any bureaucracy. (Prasser, 2006)

However, there are nevertheless increasing pressures on public administrations to provide the advice government wants, or that is the most politically expedient, rather than proffering the best, most impartial or most efficacious solutions (Weller, 2003). In extreme cases, politicians in power may, as an entirely political exercise, warn administrations against, for example, using the words 'climate change' in disaster prevention or drought management advisory settings and processes.

Policy advising matters then, as a fundamental service to government, in differing ways across differing systems and policy domains, and in increasingly more complex circumstances and with no guarantee of uptake by decision makers. But it also occurs in open, politicised and externalised circumstances and requires a reconsideration of the skills for performing it, and for managing and responding to a more diverse advisory base less directly controlled by government. Policy advising must be done differently (Smith, 2018). This is not least because managerial changes have seen a loss of policy content knowledge in public administrations, a turnover of staff, and an increase in contract staff that is robbing administrations of substantive policy learning (Prasser, 2006: 5). It is also because 'governments more and more often must develop strategies for dealing with complex, multi-faceted, multi-sectoral problems' in specific contexts where '[s]tandard issue, generic policy solutions will not suffice' (Scott and Baehler, 2010: 231). Policy brokerage is a critical skill in these circumstances with active boundary spanning work required within a complex system, and in open, and thus exposed, settings rather than entirely within government (Williams, 2002).

This increasingly dispersed policy advisory role has assumed particular significance with the heightened awareness of the need for more evidence-based policies to address increasingly complex, wicked problems in the contemporary era of changing state capacity (Head and Alford, 2015). These include: i) environmental issues, for example, the impact of global climate change and the need to achieve sustainable development and energy transitions and ii) social issues, such as homelessness, health care, indigenous welfare and affordable housing. Such issues are highly resistant to 'problem-solving' because they are not are amenable to quick fixes, simple or politicised solutions, but require big-picture thinking and innovative collaborative engagement, and policy advice from within, and well beyond, government (APSC, 2007).

Advisory sources are necessarily shifting in this context, with traditional research and expertise-based evidence sources now complemented by external, advocacy and stakeholder views in contested, mediatised and therefore political environments. The circumstances of knowledge production are now also subject to the impacts of rapid technological change and the instant sharing of information albeit of widely varying quality, veracity and provenance (Chapter 7).

We undertake this reconsideration of policy advice and advisory systems in order to emphasise the significance of advice in addressing complex problems. We see the state's capacity to deploy, receive and/or act upon expert advice as impacted by shifts in the nature of governance and thus in advice giving. Furthermore, expansive PASs are not necessarily always positive. They have unleashed a greater variety of partisan beliefs with heightened contestation of expert knowledge (Haynes, 2018) with beneficial as well as dire policy consequences. While expert advice abounds, we are suggesting that the porous, partial nature of contemporary advice giving (Prasser, 2006: 2), and the dispersed, globally impacted nature of state power, complicates its uptake. Policy challenges and options are broadly debated and contested in contemporary environments potentially with immediate political consequences or impacts upon decision-making. We are interested in how the governance and systems literature can throw light upon the politics and operations of advice giving and the prospects for evidence-informed solving of complex problems.

Policy advisory systems

The PASs literature is relatively recent (Seymour-Ure, 1987; Halligan, 1995; Prasser, 2006; Prince, 2007) and is evolving from descriptive to increasingly critical. We consider that before highlighting the positives of more open advisory systems in terms of enhanced public participation, and the negatives in terms of more complex knowledge generation. We discuss the implications for the state and state-based advisory management, before observing the manner in which PAS literature is now described as 'first' and 'second' wave with the latter focused on the policy network, domain-specific level. While the literature has been largely descriptive, both second wave and other approaches are now paying more attention to PAS dynamics, which is of interest to us in terms of complex problem-solving. In our view, the study of these dynamics would involve explicit attention to the role of the state in advisory processes and a focus on 'improving the performance of the policy advisory system' both within and beyond the state (Scott and Baehler, 2010: 229–49).

The circumstances of the broadening advisory landscape are well depicted (Prince, 2007; Craft and Howlett, 2013). There is, however, no ideal type of PAS. Halligan (1995: 140) provides the classic description of bureaucratic and political advice being offered to ministers, with advisory sources including the public service, ministerial units and central agencies, and various access points for external advice depending on the government system. The apparatus of the state (in terms of advisory units, councils and review bodies) is complemented by quasi-state and non-state advisory sources (institutes, think tanks and organisations) in country- and sector-specific political and administrative systems (Hustedt and Veit, 2017: 42; Table 6.1). Whatever the politico-administrative circumstances, political preferences, government systems and distinctive policy domains, sectors or networks will influence an advisory system (Halligan, 1995: 141–2).

PASs' use of the term 'system' is problematic, however, given that it implies a process of proffering advice, but there is little explanation of how this works. 'System' typically describes an advisory landscape, often in structurally distinctive terms, or is a euphemism for complex advice giving in contemporary times. 'System' is also used where network or community may be more appropriate. PASs are typically described as interlocking but without an explanation of their place within dispersed, complex, formal *and* informal advisory landscapes in an era of the changing state, heightened social reflexivity, and ideological contests over information. There has been empirical investigation of 'externalisation' (the increased use of external advice), and 'politicisation' (the increased use of partisan-political advice) (Craft and Howlett, 2013). There has also been emphasis on the need to review advisory management processes, in the context of enhanced externalisation and politicisation, to ensure these are robust, flexible and effective (Halligan, 1995: 162–5) and up to the task of dealing with the expanded role of consultants and lobbyists (Heinz et al, 1993).

Open advisory systems are largely uncritically welcomed. However, domain-specific studies, especially environmental studies, point to the difficulties of resolving 'messy' problems in expansive, participatory, advisory circumstances (Ney, 2009). We know from the policy network and community literature, advocacy coalition research and policy advisory studies, that some systems, networks and domains are more open than others. Most closed, for instance, may be expert, epistemic communities, and most open may be advocacy coalitions that are like-minded, or drawn, perhaps with competing views, into a policy community that is in no other way cohesive. None of this is 'good' or 'bad' for policy advising, but simply the consequence of heightened reflexivity (O'Brien et al, 1999) with citizens and organisations with competing value sets drawn now into advisory settings (Wildavsky, 1979). Public participation is welcomed, but it can be challenging in terms of its management, quality and legitimacy, causing tensions in PASs that need to be admitted.

Equally there are issues for the generation of advice. There is a significant difference, for example, between adopting enhanced participatory processes aimed at securing support for evidence-based policy, and capturing knowledge, especially from non-expert sources.

Advisory systems are not necessarily an orderly means of generating advice. Heinrichs observes that they exist in 'pluralistic knowledge societies' where knowledge is contested, between experts, but also more broadly. In such societies, advising is 'an analytical-deliberative process of knowledge compilation and knowledge assessment', with politics moderating diverging claims, values and interests (Heinrichs, 2005: 46). We can, however, look to governance literature for instances of collaborative committee, consultation, or citizen jury processes, which are aimed at generating policy consensus (Torfing and Ansell, 2017), if not evidence-based advice. If they do generate such advice, there is still the issue of how it is to improve policy and not be commandeered by political imperatives (Cash et al, 2002). Enhanced participation is welcome, but these issues of knowledge generation, engagement, contestation, politicisation and uptake are nevertheless problematic.

Advice within and beyond the state

The extent to which external advice is newly available is also arguable (Prasser, 2006: 2). Even in parliamentary Westminster systems like Australia's, government has long been advised by a 'policy advisory zoo' with 'internal sources of advice such as the public service', and a 'growing array of external advisory bodies'. There is a long tradition of advising by parliamentary committees, royal commissions and public inquiries as well as by political staff, lobbyists and consultants (Prasser, 2006: 1). There are also longstanding processes for soliciting submissions from non-government sources that inform the public record, and any inquiry recommendations that may be handed down (Stewart and Prasser, 2015). External to government there has always been an array of industry associations, think tanks, research centres, consultants, media channels and community organisations that have long provided advice from polemical to evidence-based (Table 6.1; Craft and Howlett, 2012). For a range of reasons, however, external bodies and actors are much more engaged and relied upon by policymakers today and potentially more influential within PASs (Prince, 2007).

Heightened advisory engagement is multi-faceted, in response to neo-liberal downsizing, to knowledge and capacity deficits, to heightened connectivity and social reflexivity, and to the democratisation of expertise (Maasen and Weingart, 2005). This has seen advisory sources expand and differentiate at all levels in diversified thematic fields within and beyond government (Heinrichs, 2005:

41), in varied ways in differing political, administrative and advisory systems. In Western bureaucracies, however, it is well recognised that neo-liberal reform has prompted 'debureacratisation' and the loss of the public sector's primacy and at times credibility in the provision of advice (Halligan, 1995). Internal advisors now engage in advice brokerage – sourcing external advice, liaising with networks, managing internal-external dynamics and vetting the advice given (Halligan, 1995: 160). This is adaptive governance behaviour, driven by the need for generating collaborative policy-relevant information in order to find 'the most effective and efficient solutions to policy problems' (Van Buuren and Koppenjan, 2014: 35).

So while there may always have been extensive advisory sources, the circumstances in which they are to be found have changed markedly. In turn, the liberal democratic state has adapted its policymaking to reflect the demands of the environment in which it operates, including the capacity of PASs to generate and transmit policy-relevant information (Chapter 2). This is a pragmatic response, again neither 'good' nor 'bad' given that the externalisation of advisory processes invokes both challenges and opportunities by disrupting the role of advising within government. The internal advisor must negotiate advice in more

Table 6.1: Policy advisory system actors classified by policy types

	Short-term/reactive	Long-term/anticipatory
Procedural	***'Pure' political and policy process advice*** Political parties, parliaments and legislative committees; regulatory agencies. Internal as well as external political advisers, interest groups; lobbyists; mid-level public service policy analysts and policy managers; pollsters.	***Medium- to long-term policy steering advice*** Deputy ministers, agency heads and executives; *expert advisory councils*; royal commissions; judicial bodies. Agencies, boards and commissions; crown corporations; international organisations (for example, OECD, ILO, UN).
Substantive	***Short-term crisis and fire-fighting advice*** Political peers (for example, cabinet); executive office political staffs. Expanded ministerial and congressional political staffs; cabinet and cabinet committees; external crisis managers/consultants; political strategists; pollsters; NGOs and community organisations; lobbyists; media.	***Evidence-based policymaking*** Statistical agencies and units; senior departmental policy advisors; strategic policy units; royal commissions; expert advisory councils. Think tanks; scientific and academic advisors; open data citizen engagement-driven policy initiatives/web 2.0; blue ribbon (eminent persons) panels.

Source: Craft and Howlett, 2012: 91 (with expert advisory councils added)

challenging, exposed, politicised circumstances, where advice giving is contested, competitive and at times mediatised. Substantive knowledge must be supplemented by astute, shrewd and subtle advisory skills (Prince, 2007) as well as by active policy brokerage, boundary spanning and robust management of advisory processes.

A focus on the state in PAS research necessarily leads to a focus on the policy work internal to government as critical to the sourcing, mediating and uptake of policy-relevant information that is critical to complex problem-solving. The circumstances of this work have changed markedly. However, as a practitioner, Smith (2018) embraces the disruption. She advocates innovation, boundary jumping by talking with stakeholders rather than for them, and forming compacts on problem-solving with citizens. Internal processes must be improved to develop new capabilities (Scott and Baehler, 2010). Heinrichs (2005) embraces the disruption too, but more systematically, with his typology for assessing and optimising advisory structures, with design options for improved management processes. Advisory structures, internal advisory actors, as well as the state itself, must adapt to the complexities of PASs within pluralistic knowledge societies. Heinrichs is not a PAS theorist, however, his advisory typology offers promising scope for future PAS research.

From first to second wave analysis

The PAS literature has usefully identified and explained policy advising in changing circumstances. It acknowledges the forces of globalisation and neo-liberalism and the impacts that are emphasised in this book, such as the constrained capacity of government. It tended towards descriptive analysis early on, but is evolving beyond that. Initially, Halligan (1995) depicted advisory sources in terms of their proximity to government and the control that government had over their information. Prasser then distinguished between 'cold' *rational* and 'hot' *political* advice, the former being impartial, evidence-based, strategic and anticipatory, and the latter opinionated, partisan, reactive and short term. 'Cold' advice is public-oriented, proposing optimal solutions, while 'hot' advice seeks consensus for electoral gain (Prasser, 2006: 13). Craft and Howlett (2013: 187) later explored externalisation and politicisation in terms of the 'interactive or synergistic effects of parts of the policy advice system of actors'. Beyond this 'first wave' analysis, Craft and Wilder (2017) discern 'second wave' analysis, that is, less focused upon internal-external advisory boundaries, and more on the space between the two.

This approach draws on governance theory, seeing the state as not central to, but a collaborator in, policy advisory processes in domain-specific circumstances, reflecting more porous public-private borders (Chapter 5) and enhanced policy networking. It is less about the location and character of country-specific systems, institutions and interlocking practices (Halligan, 1995), and more about the connective dynamics of policy analysis by a range of actors within policy domains. The unit of analysis is not the public service, but advisory systems or domains themselves; the location of interest is the subsystem level; and the focus is on 'why advisory systems combine in particular policy instances and with what effect' (Craft and Wilder, 2017: 215). This approach draws on networks, subsystems, advocacy coalitions and collaborative governance literature in its acknowledgement, for example, of ideational disposition, subsystem coherence, openness and stability, and the efficacy of working relationships. This analysis moves from descriptive to more theoretical accounts of advisory processes, with an interest in expert and non-expert advisory dynamics but at the domain-specific, subsystem level with little, if any, emphasis upon the state.

Second wave analysis emphasises much that is already familiar in the PAS and policy literature, and depicts advisory subsystems as networks and communities. The PAS approach already states that 'analysing single actors yields an incomplete picture of the realities of policy advice' and advocates a more complex, differentiated, systems approach (Veit et al, 2017: 87). It already explains the dynamics of diminished bureaucracies, contestation over facts and values, enhanced politicisation, changing advisory roles and evidence-based policy challenges. Nevertheless, in terms of problem-solving, the subsystems highlighted by second wave analysis could generate domain-specific policy-relevant information to help shape decision-making. These policy results would invariably range from political to procedural, but may include the generation of advice that informs policy-based learning, for example, or instrumental problem-solving (Craft and Wilder, 2017). Second wave analysis therefore draws attention to the nature of domain-specific settings, at the policy problem-solving level, and it is to this level that we next turn by employing the combined insights of governance and systems theory.

Governance, systems and policy advice

By focusing on the nature and workings of PASs and by advocating the study of subsystems, the second wave approach returns to the network and policy community focus that inspired governance theory. We see this as cognate with systems theory, which captures relations, linkages and networks, albeit within structured contexts that map policy systems, and acknowledge political contexts and therefore authority and accountability. The combined insights of governance and systems theory – with their dual emphasis upon cross-relational dynamics and settings – thus have utility in reconsidering advisory subsystems. Governance theory, in Bell and Hindmoor's (2009: 191) state-centric relational account, emphasises that 'governments have *enhanced* their capacity to achieve their goals by developing closer governance relationships with non-state actors'. The state has changed and its capacity may or may not have diminished, but its authority remains, including its agenda-setting powers and the manner in which it seeks or receives advice from external sources (Chapter 4). This broader 'policy-generating systems' (Scott and Baehler, 2010: 166–7) context and emphasis upon the changing state is missing from the PAS literature but is highlighted by the governance and systems approaches. We reconsider advisory subsystems within this context.

Advisory subsystems reconsidered

Halligan (1995) had already described PASs in terms of the work of policy advisors within distinctive ideational and institutional settings, but also within policy domain, sectoral and network circumstances. Craft and Wilder focus on the subsystem logic in this scholarship. They observe that systems and subsystems approaches focus on interest mediation, resource and power dependencies, state-non-state exchanges and structural and ideational traditions. Policymaking is 'the product of forms of public-private actor relations accruing in bounded policy areas' by 'semi-autonomous decision-making networks'. While subsystems scholarship is overly descriptive and neglectful of causal mechanisms, some studies have 'linked subsystem configuration and operation to distinct patterns and propensities for policy change'. Ideational coherence and disposition, and openness to new ideas, are distinguishing features of advisory subsystems. Advisory subsystems will also vary widely, in terms of coherence and openness for example, between loosely defined discourse communities, and attentive publics, and regularised networks (Craft and Wilder, 2017: 221–3).

We suggest that governance theory enriches this account because it is more explicit about the role of the state in subsystems. Bell and Hindmoor (2009: 189), for instance, don't see any policy networks as semi-autonomous, but influenced by government as it directs governance partnerships and relationships. This makes sense, although there is likely scope for exploring the extent to which advisory subsystems operate closer to, and further from, government. We do not assume that advisory subsystems are necessarily all coherent entities, coalitions or communities, nor that they are necessarily entirely removed from the orbit of government. They are representative instead of a variety of formal and informal advisory sources internal and external to government at times in distinctive policy domains. In a systems-based sense, they may cohere simply by drawing attention to causal factors in terms of policy problems, and of the various interventions that may be required to address them (Scott and Baehler, 2010: 181). Advisory subsystems do not, however, offer any structured or guaranteed means of achieving policy outcomes, nor do they have any guaranteed connection to the state or its policy-making apparatus. 'At the most', just as with advisory systems, as Halligan (1995: 152) argues, they 'might exercise indirect influence'.

Governance theory and problem-solving contexts

More broadly, we have seen that governance theory provides a narrative of the changes that have occurred in 'the practice of governing human societies to solve problems' (Bouckaert, 2017), with implications for policy capacity that explain trends in PASs. Critical policy challenges, international and domestic, and the emergence of wicked problems (Crowley and Head, 2017a; Head, 2018), global warming for example, coupled with unprecedented opportunities as a result of innovation, liberalisation and globalisation, have impacted governing practices. 'This is all happening in the context of the retrenchment of the state, austerity for our welfare systems, decreasing legitimacy and trust in institutions, and changing power balances', Bouckaert observes. Whether the public sector is part of the solution or not, and the extent to which PASs are included, will vary in terms of ideological, geographical and political setting. However, the governance response has been to formalise informal networks, in varying fashion – depending on jurisdiction, domain and the issue at hand – in terms of networked coordination and implementation (Bouckaert, 2017: 45).

Some argue that the solving of complex problems requires complex advisory mechanisms (Scott and Baehler, 2010). Governance discourse suits the notion of complexity in general, and of complex problems and complex means of addressing them, particularly within liberal democracies. However, the more open PASs and subsystem networks are in the governance era, the more likely they are to generate conflict over, and contested advice about, complex problems, and the more likely the state is to want to maintain some control. Steven Ney (2009) argues that this control is not necessarily rule- and compliance-based, but the consequence instead of the state's collaboration in cooperative relationships with advisory actors and institutions. He sees the once monolithic state as now part of a networked polity scattered across a range of discrete networks that focuses on the resolution of problems. The literature sees PASs as more open today, while recognising that, despite the trend to more connected governance, some policy systems and subsystems in some jurisdictions and policy domains will likely remain exclusive. This raises issues about the dynamics of advisory systems.

Broad systems-based analysis

How might systems theory itself throw light on the nature of PASs? Systems theory acknowledges interactivity, as one might find in an advisory system or policy community, and maps a policy problem against its context (Chapter 2). Lasswell, who was not a systems theorist, rationally approached problem-solving analysis as a series of steps by mapping: i) decision processes; ii) values and institutions; iii) social processes; and iv) intellectual tasks. Rittel and Webber (1973) rejected this as *first generation* systems rationality, such as we still see today in the policy process literature, in their path-breaking investigation of wicked problems. They turned to *second generation* systems theory in order to define 'interacting open systems' and to ask not simply 'what are they made of', but 'what do these systems do', and furthermore 'what should they do' to assist problem-solving? If we look at PASs and advisory subsystems this way, by focusing on dynamics and behaviour, we would ask 'by what processes and interactions do they transmit advice in a usable form to decision makers?'(Cobb and Elder, 1972: 85; Craft and Wilder, 2017: 217).

The role of advice is implicit rather than explicit in this analysis, other than as an intellectual task, but systems theory is useful because, as Bevir (2009: 202) observes, it acknowledges the set of parts that form a whole, or macro-structures in relation to their units. He suggests bringing together systems and governance theory, and sees governance theorists as system theorists because governance is considered to be 'the product of a complex network of interdependent systems' (p 203). He evokes policy networks, communities and subsystems descriptively and operationally, with systems 'a set of subsystems or processes that are coordinated to accomplish defined goals' ... 'within an environment that is defined by fixed factors that constrain the system' (p 203). Systems and subsystems are explicitly decision-making or goal-seeking, rather than advisory, however, Bevir's depiction aligns with second wave analysis and its emphasis upon subsystemic advisory units and contexts. Indeed these authors distinguish their second wave approach by its application of 'policy subsystem theory to advisory system dynamics' in order to show how 'context may shape advisory system component configuration, operation and influence' (p 221).

The PAS literature has thus reconnected with subsystems that were the early focus of governance scholars. This literature is expanding in terms, for instance, of concern with the systemic character of advice, and the nature and operation of distinct domains. There is scope for deeper analysis (see Table 6.2). The blurred boundaries, collaboration and goal-seeking or intent that the governance literature assumes could be investigated in terms of advisory systems, as could the contexts and dynamics that systems theory acknowledges. Varying types of advisory systems could be conceived, for example: political, administrative, hybrid, domain-specific, subsystems and advocacy-based systems, as could the variance of systems that are institutions-, operations-, network- and/or advocacy-based. The nature, location, character, focus and activity of differing advisory systems may vary in ways that could be investigated (see, for example, Craft and Wilder, 2017; Weible, 2008). As could assumptions that advisory systems are interlocking, which may not be true in more complex and/or contingent subsystems that may be without typical systemic dynamics or goal-seeking behaviour. The need for effective advice from within and beyond the state, and for charting its generation, delivery and efficacy, will see this scholarship continue to flourish.

Table 6.2: Exploring advisory subsystems – scope for future research

Depiction	Traditional	Systems-based	Governance-based	Advocacy-based
Nature	Internal/hybrid	Hybrid	Hybrid	External/hybrid
Location	Government/ largely	Inside-outside	Inside-outside	Communities/ largely
Character	Individuals/ teams	System members	Collaborators	Network members
Focus	Truth to power	Operation	Multiple voices	Persuasion
Activity	Advisory	Problem-solving	Goal-seeking	Advocacy
Knowledge	Expert, political	Expert, operational	Expert, partnering	Expert, community

Expert advice and systems-based problem-solving

The degree of difficulty involved in the translation of expert advice into a process of problem-solving that addresses wicked problems is illustrated on a number of fronts, in particular with longstanding social and environmental issues (Crowley and Head, 2017b; Head, 2018). This draws attention to the role of experts, expertise and policy advisory bodies within contemporary advisory systems. Not only have advisory systems externalised from within to increasingly beyond government, but also advisory bodies themselves, which are more externalised and interactively engaged as a result. Our reconsideration of policy advice and advisory systems in the context of complex problems would not be complete without linking the changing dynamics of advice, and the current focus on policy systems, with a consideration of the role of expert advice. While there has never been a direct or causal link between professional, impartial advice and government decision-making (Head, 2016), the emergence of a complex, and at times a highly contested, advisory landscape in an era of changing state capacity has been challenging for the uptake of expert advice.

Advisory bodies, knowledge brokering and uptake

The challenge is well illustrated by recent literature (Van Damme et al, 2011; Reinecke et al, 2013; Schultz et al, 2015;) and *International Library of Policy Analysis* studies on the changing role of expert advisory bodies (Wang and Chiou, 2015; Yamaya, 2015). In Craft and Howlett's (2012; Table 6.1) schema for advisory system actors, expert advisory bodies provide medium- to long-term, anticipatory policy steering advice, which is procedural more than evidence-based, although they may commission or generate evidence in order to inform their advice. They are established by government, but typically operate with some degree of independence thereby illustrating the 'need for reliable and authoritative advice on matters where technical understanding of complex issues is paramount' (Crowley and Head, 2017a: 182; see also Prince, 2007). However, while there will always be a role for independent advisory bodies within government, such bodies are under pressure to externalise their focus and activities, and to adapt to the changing advisory contexts and expectations. As well as their 'inwardly focused' provision of expert advice, they are therefore increasingly 'outwardly engaged', as expected either by government and/or the community, in order to harness not only expert, but also increasingly lay, knowledge.

In this way such bodies assume the features of 'boundary organisations' (Van Damme et al, 2011) engaging across PASs with a shift in emphasis from their role as entirely knowledge providers to knowledge brokers. The uptake of their advice is impacted notably by the externalisation that the PAS literature has identified, but also by enhanced contestation, and thus politicisation, around notions of expertise in the more open governance era. Competent boundary spanning (Williams, 2002), exercised in inter-organisational, network, system or policy domain-based circumstances, is thus a critical skill for the uptake of policy advice to resolve complex problems in collaborative circumstances. Although knowledge brokering and boundary spanning stretches the role of expert advisory bodies, those that do engage with sectoral interests and value-based groups are, however, likely to be better placed to leverage and support policy traction on difficult issues (Crowley and Head, 2017a: 181; also Chapter 9). Related to the increased complexity and openness of the advisory landscape is a more open, deliberative process of knowledge generation across traditional boundaries (see Cash et al, 2002; also Chapter 5) with policy diffusion and learning new facilitative mechanisms for the uptake of ideas. Advisory bodies now drive this uptake where they engage in domain-specific circumstances.

There has been a trend therefore, away from independent advisory bodies solely acting to provide expert advice, towards a new dynamic where such bodies interact and communicate with PAS stakeholders inside and outside government. This contrast is depicted in Table 6.3 and parallels the transformation of policy advising from an internal to an external process. Nevertheless recent cross-national and single-country studies that have documented transformation, diffusion and variability issues in terms of expert advisory councils (Wang and Chiou, 2015; Yamaya, 2015 and Merklova and Ptackova, 2016) reveal no uniform response to the pressures to adapt to changing advisory contexts and expectations. Not all advisory bodies have made efforts at brokering advice and working across the community to ensure the uptake of knowledge, with many advisory councils remaining squarely within the traditional space (Table 6.3) or only partially externalised. Institutional context remains responsible for such cross-national variations – with differing socio-political contexts, whether pluralist, neo-corporatist, post-communist or newly democratic, affecting the degree to which advisory bodies are externalised. It follows that this will have a bearing on the levels of politicisation, boundary activity, knowledge brokering and ultimately on policy diffusion and the uptake of policy advice (Crowley and Head, 2017a: 191). This area is under-researched.

Table 6.3: The 'externalisation' of idealised advisory bodies

Traditional, professionalised advisory bodies	Modernised, interactive, responsive advisory bodies
Impetus – Policy needs to move towards greater professionalisation (specialised, expert advice)	*Impetus* – Policy needs greater interactivity (political responsiveness for legitimacy and sustainability)
Policy advice needs to be effective/efficient	Policy advice needs to be open to challenge
Advisory bodies provide advice efficiently/direct to government	Advisory bodies provide advice accountably/in transparent fashion
Advisory bodies as government add-on	Advisory bodies as countervailing force
Short term instrumental advice	Long term strategic advice
Provide advice on demand	Provide pro-active advice
Advisory bodies linked to 'mother' department	Advisory bodies at a critical distance from government
High isolation of policy advisory expert bodies	Expert bodies now boundary riders between interests
Advisory bodies stability derives from isolation	Stability derives from being responsive to stakeholders
Government links constrain network activities	Interactivity strengthens dialogue between actors
Advisory and political realms need clear demarcation	Advisory-political interaction promotes uptake of advice

Source: Adapted from Craft and Howlett, 2013; Crowley and Head, 2017a; Reinecke et al, 2013; Van Damme et al, 2011

Climate policy work at the boundaries

In terms of complex problem-solving in the governance era of externalised advisory systems, climate change represents a 'super-wicked' problem (Levin et al, 2012) with a record of policy failure in spite of a knowledgeable global advisory community keen to forge workable solutions (Ingold, 2011). The climate PAS is itself a complex one (Miller, 2001), with international governance and advisory-based efforts, including the Intergovernmental Panel on Climate Change (IPCC) which was established by the United Nations (UN) and World Meteorological Organisation in 1988 to provide authoritative scientific assessments (www.ipcc.ch). In addition, the UN's Framework Convention on Climate Change, and processes such as the Kyoto Protocol, have established a range of knowledge generation, brokering and learning environments that coalesce around meetings of the signatories (conference of parties, or COPs) to agreed actions (Brunnée and Streck, 2013). Not only are there transnational climate policy networks, including advisory bodies, but also national, regional and local networks, with varying emphases from knowledge generation to brokering to advocacy to simply partnering of state-based efforts, and a combination of these roles. Reinecke et al (2013) have mapped the role of climate policy knowledge brokers (councils, networks, hubs, service providers) in a diverse advisory landscape within the European Union and found their roles carefully balanced between generating legitimate advice and brokering its uptake.

Advisory bodies in climate policy systems must retain their professional credibility but work 'close to the political and societal sphere to ensure their relevance' and therefore to engage in broad consultation and collaborations in order to achieve policy leverage (Reinecke et al, 2013: 91 and 95). The primary focus of such bodies is upon boundary management to ensure knowledge uptake and policy action, but also upon ensuring that the boundaries that protect the legitimacy of professional knowledge production, do not prevent broader communication, collaboration and action (Cash et al, 2002: 1). While the PAS more broadly is only just beginning to consider the implications of empirical mapping of advisory systems and is not as focused on knowledge uptake as it is say upon policy capacity, Hoppe and Wesselink (2014) have conceptualised a framework for boundary work. This maps the policy (advisory) network against the problem of climate change within distinctive and influential political-cultural contexts in order to consider the links between policy expertise, boundary arrangements and the public sphere in terms of implications for advice and action. It may be that such policy domain specific analysis is required to generate this level of more detailed consideration of advice uptake, because the climate policy advisory literature is extremely focused on problem-solving, as we saw with Heinrichs's (2005) typology for optimising advice.

The problem of climate change is illustrative, therefore, of the utility of the problem-solving approach to policy analysis in the governance era, which we adopt in this book (Chapter 1). It illustrates, by way of the actions and inaction of nation states on mitigating emissions, for example, that the role of the state is paramount, but that, while internal advisory systems remain prominent, external expertise, brokering, advice and advocacy are significant influences. PAS analysis that neglects the state, for example by simply mapping the external advisory landscape, would not suffice as an explanation of policy generation. Hustedt and Veit (2017), for instance, emphasises the relevance of institutional *and* policy-level factors in analysing climate advice, explaining that an advisory system comprises internal, advisory influences and influential external actors. In these terms, a policy network, domain or system emphasises knowledge provision (see also Castells and Cardoso, 2006). An advisory system therefore refers to a set of components that all deal with providing knowledge for policymaking in a given policy domain (Hustedt and Veit, 2017). Hustedt also reminds us that the structuring of solutions to complex problems like climate change is challenging given diverging values and beliefs, and opinions on what constitutes climate policy knowledge.

Conclusions

Policy advice and advisory systems tend to be underplayed or neglected in much of the policy-making literature despite robust policy advisory research efforts, and recent concerns with the character and dynamics of domain-specific advisory systems within and beyond the state. We have argued that the state nevertheless remains a significant policymaker in varying contexts despite policy advisory trends and practices, including trends towards greater externalisation, polycentrism and politically competing sources of advice (Crowley and Head, 2017a: 184; Halligan, 2010). We therefore do not see the state as necessarily diminished by its reliance upon more diverse advisory sources, but caught up instead in a complex web of advisory relations that are contingent, in terms of their character and dynamics, upon the problem at hand. However, we have emphasised the challenging circumstances of garnering advice that is fit for messy or wicked problem-solving, in particular because such advice is increasingly deliberatively derived in contested circumstances.

It is not necessarily a failing of government that it relies on external advice, but there are downsides. While advice has always been open to interpretation, contestation is notable in open advisory systems. Information is challenged and expertise less prominent, as inclusivity, ideology, power, resources and politics assume greater emphasis (Chapter 7). Furthermore, enhanced citizen engagement (Delli Carpini et al, 2004) complicates decision-making and policy change (Chapter 9). Science can be negated, for example in the literal burning in the streets of a plan to return environmental flows to Australia's parched Murray-Darling River basin (Australian Broadcasting Commission (ABC), 2010). Neither is it ideal where neo-liberal downsizing reduces advisory capacity with the effect that more open processes generate politicised advice and reduce the role of expertise. We have argued that advisory systems are generally viewed less critically, with less emphasis upon displaced expertise or diminished capacity, although with some concern for politicisation and system-like dynamics.

The study of policy advice and advisory systems tends to be descriptive, but our focus has been on the dynamics of problem-solving, and hence the relevance of both governance and systems theory for the analysis of advisory activity and the uptake of evidence-based advice. We have canvassed various policy challenges including the problem of climate change and found that advisory skills such as knowledge brokering are evolving as essential to knowledge generation and uptake in more connected, complex circumstances. Given the scope and longevity of pressing social and environmental problems, greater research attention should be paid to the transmission of problem-solving, evidence-based advice in contemporary governance and systems-based domains. From our perspective, policy advice and advisory systems research should address issues around the politics, process and efficacy of advice giving in dynamic, changing circumstances in terms of the solving of complex problems, many of which are currently defying resolution.

7

Reconsidering *information*

Introduction

Information (observations on and about the world) is the basic material of all public policies, and appears in many guises across a wide range of policy-related literatures. These literatures include analyses of how policies are made, as well as inquiries into the content of policy in the form of ideas and knowledge. In this chapter, we suggest that information, broadly understood, warrants a prominent place in the general analysis of public policy. It is not as if information is ignored in contemporary analysis, but rather, that its presence is taken for granted. Information needs to be problematised if the implications of the growing complexity and difficulty of 'doing' policy are to be understood and addressed. In this chapter, 'reconsidering' means using information as a lens with which to clarify both the content and conduct of policy.

Two streams of reconsideration are explored: information within public policy, and information as an object of public policy. The first stream brings together key concepts in policy analysis, and enables us to scope the importance of informational processes within policy systems. Reconsidering in the second sense enables us to identify shifts in the relationship between information and public policy as a field of action. Both perspectives help us to draw conclusions about the relationship between public policy and the state.

Information matters because governing is impossible without information on the governed. At a very basic level, states cannot survive without taxation, which requires information on citizens – who they are, where they live and what they own. Tax policies shape and refine relationships with the state based on this information. Similarly, health and pensions policies exist in and through the information that is held on citizens and the way it is deployed.

In addition, information has an intimate relationship both to governance (Peters, 2016) and to public policy. At the policy level, the neo-liberal ascendancy in Western democracies has privileged market-oriented governance in the form of national and international deregulation (and re-regulation), and a dispersal of decision-power away from the nation-state and towards corporate interests and other (more strategic) states.

At the same time, the effects of cross-boundary problems such as climate change have become more intense. In the face of these challenges, states seem mired in bureaucracy when more agile responses are needed. In an age where more data is collected and processed worldwide than ever before, it is disappointing that policy-making capacity (ironically, at least in part as a result of policy-related decisions) has developed insufficiently to take full advantage of these resources. Part of the problem is that more data does not necessarily mean more information. Information communicates: data (of itself) does not.

Policy scholarship has a role to play in teasing out this multi-stranded story and assessing its implications. Throughout, we link this discussion with the general framework of the systems thinking we developed in Chapter 2. This broad schema gives three main sections to the chapter, covering:

- policymaking as an informational process;
- information and governance; and
- information, accountability and the state.

We begin by defining information.

What is 'information'?

There can be no hard and fast definition of information: information is coloured by the context in which the term is employed. However, we believe it is important to trace a link to information theory, which stresses the uses to which information is put. From this perspective, information is knowledge that is relevant to a particular situation. Information reduces uncertainty. It is not the same as data or even 'big data': data may provide the raw material, but not (without further analysis) the relevance. Thus, information lies somewhere 'in between' data and knowledge (Marschak, 1996).

An important result for the study of public policy flows from this definition, which we will return to throughout the chapter. In Chapter 2, we argued for a systemic conception of public policy based on its role as a key means of communication between the political system and its environment. Our definition of information suggests that public policy plays its communicative role by reducing the uncertainty in which the political system operates. Policies do this by interpreting and responding to needs for action emanating from the environment. To the extent that these responses are adaptive, policies may be seen as successful in their effects.

We emphasise that we are not putting forward an alternative way of judging the success of specific policies, which will necessarily rest on a number of dimensions (McConnell, 2010b). Rather, we suggest that there is a relationship between the health of political systems and the effects of the ensemble of public policies that have built up over time. The informational aspects of the underlying processes – their appropriateness and accuracy – become a useful tool of policy critique. For example, policymakers may make emotional or intuitive judgements about the impact of events (Maor, 2012). Valuable insights can also be obtained in this way into the impact of knowledge use in different parts of the political system (Radaelli, 1995).

Conceptualisations of information in the policy literature

Information has appeared in the policy literature in a number of ways, and in different guises. Scholars such as Christopher Hood identified information as one of the tools of government (Hood, 1983). Thus information (as, for example, when governments promote preferred behaviours) was seen as an instrument of policy. Hood's 'nodality' (government as a point of convergence across many spheres) is also an informational concept, in that it depicts the drawing together of different knowledge in the act of governing. From a systems perspective, Geoffrey Vickers related informational needs to the problems of 'steering' the state (Vickers, 1965: 107–9). Subsequent research into the role of knowledge and expertise in policy has highlighted the intricacies of these relationships (Newman et al, 2016). In an era where knowledge may increasingly be counterfeited or faked, the policy sciences highlight the impact of such activities on the legitimacy of the policy process (Perl et al, 2018).

The 'network' revolution in governance analysis implicitly included information as a vital factor in network function (Keast et al, 2004). The 'how' of public policy shows policymakers operating in communities defined by particular informational backgrounds and forms of knowledge (Hale 2011: 1; Dunlop, 2016). The concept of policy 'diffusing' across boundaries implies an informational transmission mechanism of some kind (Chapter 5). In a 2016 study, Esmark explored the political logics associated with different types of informational use and control, focusing on the 'nudge' factor implied by network governance (Esmark, 2016).

If information is conceptualised as 'flowing', policy-making structures can be seen as shaping or channelling these flows in various ways. Beginning in the 1990s, Baumgartner and Jones began to develop a theory of agenda setting that interpreted the key institutions of the American state from an information-processing perspective (Baumgartner and Jones, 1993). The key resource of 'attention' shaped the ways in which Congress and the bureaucratic executive dealt with unceasing and often undifferentiated inputs of information.

Another stream explored information as an object of policy. For economists, information displayed unique properties, requiring the protection of intellectual property, and to some degree, public support for early stage innovation. From the 1970s onwards, policy scholars focused on the issues involved in governing the new technologies and the corporations that, increasingly, produced them (see, for example, Lamberton, 1986).

More recent scholarly interest in 'e-government' reflected, not only the ubiquity of information and communication technologies, but their power to transform administration – for better and for worse (Bovens and Zouridis, 2002; Dunleavy et al, 2006a). The power of the state to know more than ever about citizens, down to the smallest details of their lives, sharpened the values conflict between privacy and security. In authoritarian China, clear signs are emerging of 'digital dictatorship' (Carney, 2018).

From the early 2000s, the research agenda began to include the potential impacts of surveillance-related information on state power, as states struggled to assure the security of their citizens, in times of (to many) inexplicable terrorism and violence. Twenty years on, the research agenda has expanded to include the implications of new social media, the rise of 'fake' news and the fragmentation of the public sphere.

This brief overview has suggested the ubiquity of information in policy analysis. In a highly fragmented field, we rely on our systemic understanding of public policy to focus our approach. In reconsidering information, we seek to use an informational 'lens' to focus more clearly on the character, limitations and potential of public policy.

Policymaking as an informational process

Information is functionally important in policy settings (we would argue, much more so than conventional policy theory allows). Drawing on our discussion in Chapters 2 and 4, we claim that a state will be adaptive to the extent that its policies and policymaking reflect the demands of the environment in which it operates. The transmission of appropriate information will help to shape this adaptiveness. However, in making this claim, we must also give due weight to the political nature of information. In policy settings (as in politics) information is not neutral, but reflects the interests, values and perspectives of those wanting to influence outcomes. Evidence is often contested and its use ('evidence-based policy') subject to changing and changeable policy processes. Information technology does not, of itself, augment objectivity. Data collection and processing are deeply structured by context and purpose (Dourish and Bell, 2011).

In highlighting the adaptive and interpretative roles of information in policymaking three activities stand out: agenda setting; sense-making; and using knowledge (that is, evidence).

Information in agenda setting

Agenda theory tells us how political systems sort and select those policy ideas that will receive serious attention through the deliberative processes of government. While the agenda literature is not 'informational' in itself, agenda-setting processes enable political systems to focus resources, by discarding or overlooking some ideas, and prioritising others. Agendas create and select information in a way that enables governments to use it (see, for example, Burstein and Bricher, 1997).

The notion of an 'agenda' conveys the idea that not everything can be simultaneously important – that priorities are partly set (by agents) and partly assigned (by circumstances). The 'weight' of the agenda is expressed through informational sources, which can be used to measure both agenda content (in terms of priorities at any point of time) and agenda setting (in terms of the selectivity of processes). These processes filter the vast number of potential policy signals down to those with which governments are prepared to deal.

The empirical basis for these claims originates largely from work done in the US. This reflects, not only the numerical weight of American scholarship, but also the need to observe the necessary links between ideas and agency, which is difficult in most political systems. In those with Westminster institutional structures, key debates are hidden within the shield of executive power. The more open US system enables much more of the work of problem definition to be observed. Kingdon's policy 'streams' flow more visibly in this context.

Baumgartner and Jones use a systems model that relates input signals, information-processing costs and outputs to hypothesise that politics, by mobilising attention to certain issues, could cause disproportionate (essentially nonlinear) responses to input signals by reducing processing costs (Baumgartner and Jones, 2005). Punctuated equilibrium surmised that change itself is predicated on the emergence of supreme moments of focus and attention; in other words, agenda setting is not a continuous process. Work on political decision-making took this perspective wider. In *The Politics of Information* (2015) Baumgartner and Jones argued that the attention span and processing capacities of governments structured the content of policy agendas.

This approach has been extended by Workman et al (2010) who analyse the relationship between power, structure and responsiveness by using an information-processing approach. They argue that all decision makers (whether elected or appointed) are short of time; their attention spans are limited.

Bureaucracies develop routines for prioritisation. But importantly, they can organise themselves around their informational needs. Therefore, the role of bureaucracy in governance is best understood as a process of simplifying, ordering and 'parsing' (placing) problems in specified 'solution spaces (that is, units and subunits in agency bureaus, program offices and divisions in the bureaucracy)' (Workman et al, 2010: 624).

While Workman's account seems plausible, little empirical work has been done on the ways in which bureaucracies help to set agendas through the informational roles they play. The prevalence of systemic, or underlying agendas, suggests that an enculturation or paradigm-setting process may be involved as well as a structural one. Certainly, the parts of policymaking visible to 'outsiders' remain the tip of a very large iceberg.

Overall, agenda in the policy literature is a process-related rather than a content-related concept. The policy agenda allows for information to be filtered down into usable forms. Using the informational lens helps us to focus on how (and where) this filtering occurs. Following on from this, we suggest that agenda is itself a form of information, and reflects both institutional capacities and the tasks of political management. We suggest that work on agenda, which explicitly makes these links, might provide a useful focus on the travails of much modern policymaking, as democratic leaders struggle to assert their authority in increasingly fractious environments.

Information in policy construction (sense-making)

Information is transferred in ways that are not neutral, reflecting interests and power differentials. Information is selected, not only by the demands of time and space, but those of power (Blom and Vanhoonacker, 2014). Individual political actors select information in ways that are significant in relation to their power in the political system (Walgrave and Dejaeghere, 2016).

Issues are propelled into prominence through a variety of different processes – economic, media, opinion polls, legal shifts, international relations (treaty changes), technology, demographic shifts (Althaus et al, 2007). The information that emerges in these ways is pruned and shaped politically. Information that is deemed 'policy-relevant' captures attention, serves interests; information is generated/sifted/ interpreted by policy communities, and also at the individual level.

Beyond this, consideration of the content of the policy agenda becomes ontological, or related to the generation and understanding of meaning. We know that policy-relevant information is socially constructed, or framed according to values, interests and beliefs. Some targets of policy are constructed as worthy, others less so (Schneider and Ingram, 1993). Policy 'numbers' (quantitative data) are not neutral (Stone, 1997).

If what is important (that is, the heart of agenda formation) is 'constructed', the role of information becomes, logically, subordinate to that of interpretation and argumentation in policymaking. Here, we bump up against one of the oldest debates in public policy – the extent to which we can see the project of policymaking as a 'rational' process. If information is to have independent significance in the policy-making process, we are reliant on an account of policy that draws on the use of evidence (see Chapter 9). Just as policy analysis (in the sense of seeking causal explanations for outcomes) has become increasingly data dominated (Blume et al, 2014) so analysis of policy process must follow the track of information.

Evidence-informed policymaking

For practical policymakers, information, data, evidence are essential for policy argumentation. Indeed the evidence-based/evidence-informed policy literature reflects this priority (while finding that in practice, 'evidence' is an ambivalent and contested concept, and that its use is highly context-based – see Head et al, 2014).

We know that evidence is shaped and pruned by politics; we know, too, that evidence is not randomly ignored. Those who find it does not align with their interests will ignore it. This is the calculation of knowledge and power. Institutions 'mobilise bias' through the values they embody, and the rules and procedures they enact (Bachrach and Baratz, 1962).

Under conditions of complexity, however, a simplifying 'politics as usual' approach will not be adequate. As Baumgartner and Jones note there is, or should be, a correlation between the information that is needed, and the complexity of the decision under consideration. Searching for information will always entail costs. 'Decision-making with less information may be easier but it is not necessarily better' (Baumgartner and Jones 2015: 142). On the other hand, there is limited time and attention to absorb complex arguments, in which case reputational information becomes critical.

Another approach to complexity is to move our attention beyond policy-as-decision to policy as reflection or learning (see Chapter 8). Using the systems approach from Chapter 2, we see that evaluation constitutes the authentication of the 'signal' from policy outputs. When evidence from evaluation is not used, policy will be sub-optimal. Research suggests that formal evaluations rarely find their way into policy practice. This is true whether the evaluations are undertaken by academics, or by practitioners (Sandison, 2005).

Why does policy ignore the 'information of evaluation' to the extent that it does? Many reasons have been adduced: from the purely technical, to the prevalence of short-term, adversarial politics and the over-arching role of values (and value conflicts) in policy settings. Emotions are also involved, as when modestly successful policies are over-hyped and others receive insufficient attention (Maor, 2012). Empirical work suggests that high-conflict policy arenas may be particularly resistant to the use of evidence from evaluation (Stewart and Jarvie, 2015; Chapter 9) Poor incentives for participation may also be a factor. Local knowledge and lay understandings of issues are often discounted in favour of expertise that is engaged and validated 'from the top' (Radaelli, 2008).

Combining systems thinking with information does not resolve these issues, but it does emphasise their importance. Without input from evaluation, the systems engaged by policies will still produce effects, but they may be far from those intended. To the extent that policies ignore evidence, it is likely that 'old mistakes' will simply be repeated. Where policy capacity is reduced, one of the main casualties will be evidence and the ability to use it. Our stance, as policy analysts, should be directed by the need to find better ways to include evidence, rather than finding more 'evidence' that evidence has minimal impacts.

Part of the problem may be that evidence is too narrowly defined. Head (2008) describes three knowledge types that help us to understand the potential for evidence use. There is politically oriented knowledge; scientific information and analysis; and professional experience and expertise. Each of these knowledge types resides in a variety of organisations and is used in particular ways.

Where policies have a high political salience, evidence will be selectively acquired and used. Scientific and social science information and analysis have the advantage of rigorous production but often inter-mesh unsatisfactorily with the policy process. Professional experience lodges in a variety of organisations (see Chapter 7), but its use is subject to the workings of relationships in policy networks and communities.

An information-based perspective suggests further insights. For highly political policies, whatever balance is produced is (by implication) that of the political process itself: the result of many contingent and often-unpredictable factors. But institutional structures, which are more durable, will also play a role (Chapter 3) In theory, where governments are produced by negotiation and consensus, as is often the case in multi-party polities, there is a possibility that conflicting policies may be reconciled in this way. For Westminster-style democracies, where there is a strong dialectic of government and opposition, policy positions may 'see-saw', rather than merge.

Studies of the research-policy interface have revealed generally uneasy or unsatisfactory relationships (see Davies et al, 2000; Edwards, 2004). An informational perspective suggests that improvement might result from a better understanding of systemic interconnections and incentives. In a professional perspective on the problem of managing water-use, Hatton and Young point out the importance of high-level commissioning of research in translating results into the policy sphere (Hatton and Young, 2011). In further work, Head found that 'organisational cultures and practices that value expertise and rigorous evidence' were of high importance in determining the extent to which public servants used research and information in their work (Head et al, 2014: 98).

The 'how to' knowledge of those working in public or other involved agencies, such as not-for-profits, is not usually codified and relies on person-to-person contacts or on the rituals of policy communities for transmission. Yet these forms of knowledge, which relate to implementation more than policy design, are arguably the most important of all (Chapter 8). The informational perspective advanced here suggests that organisations should do more to support the dissemination of these implementation-related insights.

Information and governance

The very centrality of information means that the nexus between public policy and information is multi-faceted. Trying to make public policy *about* how information is used is to attempt the impossible, because of the power of the technologies involved and, when allied with flexible business models, their almost infinite capacity to change the way people relate to each other. At the same time, standard economic theory authorises policy action, because forms of information have significant public good characteristics (Lamberton, 2001). Once created, they can be consumed by one person while remaining available to another (implying that unless some form of ownership of the product can be established, there will be little incentive to create it). According to economic theory, the role of public policy in intellectual property issues is underpinned by this need.

The information society has added a technological twist to this characteristic. As computers have been linked via the Internet, and the cost of computing power has fallen, the cost of distributing information has been reduced to the point where communication of any given piece of information (for example, via Twitter) has become virtually costless both to the producer of the Tweet and to the user. In this environment of ubiquitous social media, information is arguably over-produced, with associated difficulties in separating 'the good, the bad and the ugly' (Dwivedi et al, 2018). At the same time, the effects on public debate of the demise of common information spaces (such as conventional newspapers) have been noted by a number of critics (see, for example, Starr, 2009).

Policy concerns have mirrored understandings of the technology. In the 1980s, the policy task was seen as coming to terms with the information economy, understanding it, measuring it, perhaps controlling aspects of it (Jones, 1982). Access to information was a problem – perhaps governments could help? As access to home computers developed, there was concern about the 'information rich' and the 'information poor'. In most developed countries, the provision of an adequate Internet connection is regarded as a fundamental service, in the same way as power and water and (in past years) a landline. But to a degree technology itself, in the form of mobile phones, obviated the basis for these concerns. Even in otherwise poor countries, the average citizen is not necessarily data poor.

Since the 2000s in particular, the technologies themselves have expanded to the point where the idea of 'regulation' becomes increasingly meaningless. It is difficult to regulate what you cannot anticipate. While the provision of informational infrastructures has significant public goods characteristics, the extent to which states have become involved varies widely, reflecting the importance placed on values such as user privacy (see Solon, 2018).

Old agendas have been superseded. The merging of information and communication technologies, and the continuing rapidity of technological change, has made the regulation (by governments) of the purveyors of information increasingly problematic. The demise of printed newspapers, difficulties in monetising digital versions and the proliferation of net-based media and streaming services have created an incredibly dynamic marketplace.

While the remaining old-style media barons remain powerful, new forms of market dominance and manipulative power have also emerged. Google has been fined for anti-competitive behaviour, and for violating copyright; Facebook has been called out for repeated violations of the privacy of users; elections themselves are increasingly open to manipulation through targeted political marketing. In all this, governments are playing catch-up, rather than a controlling, or even shaping, role.

Information and governance structures

Information defines governance structures. From basic cybernetic theory, we know that it is through flows of information (signals) that the state adapts (or not) to change, so information is critical to adaptation. Bureaucracy, networks and markets have different informational characteristics based on their permeability to these information flows. We can think of these major kinds of structures as types of information-processing array, differing one from the other in the ways in which they use information to achieve coordination (Stewart, 2013).

The 'classic' hierarchical bureaucracy, which prioritises control over adaptation, is often seen as too rigid and unchanging to satisfy policy demands in a fast-changing world. But the reality of structural effects on behaviour is difficult to determine (Olsen, 2006). The traditional bureaucratic paradigm, so notably challenged by new public management, itself remains contested (Lynn, 2001). Bureaucracies remain useful because they continue to be repositories of knowledge and professional expertise (Goodsell, 2005). On the other hand, the political contexts in which public bureaucracies work may constrain the use of knowledge and research (Weiss, 1978; Davies et al, 2000: 31).

We gain key insights into administration by understanding how agencies collect and process information. Work from different traditions has enriched this stream. Scholars working in the field of public management have demonstrated the ways in which hierarchical organisations structure information and how this, in turn, affects decision-making (see Hammond, 1993; Egeberg, 1999).

The bigger picture, relating to the informational nodality of the state, remains clouded. Classic globalisation scholars such as Castells seem to write off the state in a networked world (Castells, 2004). Nevertheless, the state has risen to the challenge to some degree in the form of integration strategies, working across boundaries (both institutional and geographic) through the rise of relational forms of governance (Bell and Hindmoor, 2009). In these arrangements, persuasion (in our sense, a form of information) acts as a complement to hierarchy in sustaining the policy 'reach' of the state (Bell et al, 2010; see also Chapter 4).

Administrative capacity and IT

In the day-to-day sense, information is much more vital to administration (that is, implementation) than it is to policymaking. Policies are instantiated in the form of information technologies. These technologies are aptly termed the 'info'structure of government: the underlying foundation of information resources and associated people, technologies and facilities (Levitan, 1987).

However, the extent to which information technologies may be shaping the policies they implement is not well understood. IT systems automate processes and reduce labour costs. At a practical level, system constraints may inhibit some forms of policy change. (For example, a radically new policy approach may require expensive new information systems and software). Existing policies require safeguards to ensure their continued viability: the need to protect systems from hackers and saboteurs has given birth to a suite of public sector encryption technologies.

Paradoxically, however, the importance of computerisation in public management has not been paralleled by a corresponding consciousness of this reality, either within the senior reaches of public services, or among scholars of public management (Dunleavy et al, 2006a: 9). At the practical level, IT skills are usually contracted-in to agencies, and the work that is accomplished through them is usually seen in a technocratic way. The more routine the task, the more likely it is to be framed in this way.

For the scholar of public management, it is the organisational consequences of information that are of more interest. Information flow may be impeded by old-style hierarchy; but looser governance structures derived from outsourcing may lead to losses where key variables are not (or cannot be) covered by performance reporting. IT systems may have related, or independent effects. Arguably, a deeper understanding of the importance of information flow may lead to a clearer conception of the applicability of implementation choices in particular policy situations. A greater appreciation (within the public management literature) of the implications of IT would appear to be essential here.

Information, accountability and the state

The extent to which government decisions reflect the preferences of citizens (the elusive social welfare function) represents the 'gold standard' of democracy. Democratic systems are held, at least potentially, to come closest to this standard. Yet the policy-making apparatus of the democratic state has been under fire, most fundamentally because it has become too removed from citizens (Fung, 2006). To some extent, this issue of democratic responsiveness is a revival of debates about representative versus direct democracy. But the role of information and information technologies takes us further, to questions of governance and accountability – to the very nature of the state itself. Does an informational state inevitably use information for purposes of dominance?

The policy analysis literature has followed many streams in pursuing versions of the 'direct' democracy argument – the need for a more 'deliberative' democracy; the need for policy consultation; and most recently, the problems and opportunities posed by e-democracy (the relationship between democratic values and the technologies of social media and the Internet). In this section we consider the implications for the public sphere of the rise of social media; and the policy values of Internet development and regulation.

Social media – a transforming force?

The power of media, particularly social media, to shape political behaviour (and hence policy) is highlighted by the informational perspective. If new media are revolutionising the way politics happens, what does this mean for the policy-making process? Is 'the state', as the most powerful, concretised form of information, pulling in one direction, while more fluid forms of communication are bypassing the realm of public policy altogether? The politics of information and the working of public policy through information may draw in different directions, with significant implications for the legitimacy and adaptiveness of the state.

The empirical verdict is mixed. 'Mediatisation' (the priorities of a teeming media environment) tends to produce fragmentation and over-simplification of policy ideas (Peters, 2016). The need to provide constant material for media consumption burns out political leaders, makes them vulnerable to journalistic fishing expeditions and leads to a crassness of public debate that undermines deliberative policy.

The key question, however, may not be how can we re-imagine democracy in the era of the information revolution but rather, in what ways can information technology enhance the capacity of political systems to understand and adapt to change? Can the vast amounts of data that are available both within and outside the state be harnessed to this purpose?

Participatory democracy

Information and communication technologies have altered the shape of political communication (and of political organising). The technical preconditions for the emergence of a fully participatory democracy would appear to be closer than ever; opportunities are abundant for discursive engagement with other citizens in a proliferant public realm. Experience suggests, however, that attitudes are more likely to be reinforced than transformed by these processes.

Discursive will-formation, as originally envisaged by Habermas, involves citizens resolving differences through discourse, developing their capacities for doing so through democratic participation (Warren, 1993). The most ubiquitous social media platform (Facebook), notwithstanding the connectivity and communication it inspires, is seen by some critics as essentially a vehicle for selling users to advertisers (Roberts, 2014: 106; Heyman and Pierson, 2015).

Political parties everywhere have struggled to maintain membership and trust. At the same time, they have become adept at political marketing, using techniques derived from the private sector to tap into public sentiment. Information technologies have turbo-charged these capacities. Parties (and candidates) are able to collect information about voters on a massive scale, using this information to tailor customised advertising and appeals for support: the higher the stakes, the more valuable the information becomes. US Presidential candidates rely increasingly on data analytics to shape campaigning.

Despite the salience of these 'privatised' forms of information use, some progress has been made in understanding the ways in which public information systems can assist democratic processes, particularly at the local level. Public administrators will always have at least some information which is generated by their own purposes. Information (in the form of open data) expands possibilities for engagement according to the extent to which open data platforms bring together the 'activity systems' of administrators and citizens (van den Hoven, 2005; Ruijer et al, 2017).

In the context of participatory governance, experts and citizens are mutually enriched by bi-directional flows of information. Citizens often know, or can learn, as much as many experts about particular policy domains of interest to them. Technically savvy citizens 'on the spot' can instantly communicate both data and opinion. For their part, experts bring broader context and an understanding of complexity to deliberative debates (Fischer, 2009; Chapter 3).

The utility of data held by the state is not necessarily known in advance to users. As the Australian Productivity Commission puts it: '[T]he substantive argument in favour of making data more available is that opportunities to use it are largely unknown until the data sources themselves are better known, and until data users have been able to undertake discovery of data' (Productivity Commission [Australia], 2017). In an era of rapidly advancing machine intelligence, these opportunities may prove significant in generating new outlooks on policy-relevant questions.

Some caveats seem necessary, however. For citizens, the forms of this information may not necessarily be helpful. In particular, the comprehensibility and accessibility of information, and citizens' ability to manipulate the information in meaningful ways, will shape the level of use (Kellogg and Mathur, 2003).

Information flow in itself is not enough. Moving forward in policy terms requires the skills of the boundary-rider, the knowledge broker, the person who can help reconcile multiple conflicting perspectives, or at least help to define the key points of difference (see Chapter 6). Scientific knowledge needs translation into value-informed terms the layperson can understand and relate to (Stewart and Jones, 2003: 134–8; Fischer, 2009: 164).

Tensions have been observed through these processes. Achieving the advantages of open data requires a stance towards openness. States vary considerably in their attitudes towards freedom of information. On the other hand, states are expected to protect their citizens. In order to achieve this goal, information is tightly held, not only on citizens who are deemed to be a risk, but also on all citizens. CCTV cameras on every corner in many cities and widespread use of facial recognition databases are now considered the norm. Privacy may be a thing of the past. In upholding the values it is supposed to protect (that of the safety of citizens and their society), the state risks undermining its own legitimacy (that is, it becomes an autocracy).

Secrecy and the state

Because information confers tactical and strategic advantages, power differentials and power structures determine who gets what in the information field. Thus, powerful forces operating within the state (and between the state and corporations) counterbalance moves to e-democracy. While globalisation stresses the dissolving of informational borders, states use cyber-techniques to infiltrate the critical control systems of other states, and to spy on citizens. In 2013, whistle-blower Edward Snowden disclosed the extent of cyber-surveillance of citizens by (in particular) the US National Security Agency (Greenwald, 2014). State-sponsored Russian interference in the 2016 US Presidential election has been well documented (Intelligence Community Assessment (ICA), 2017).

The so-called 'deep state' draws its power and continuity from control over these processes, which are constructed as 'secret'. Citizens want the state to protect them. Mediated through politics, these demands produce enhanced institutions of control. The creation of these reservoirs of information reflects technological capabilities and organisational practices.

In general, we see that the less democratic the state, the more secretive it is, both about its decision-making processes, and in its informational relationship with citizens. Generally speaking, the nastier the government, the more it will try to keep its activities hidden. Information remains the lifeblood of accountability.

Public policy itself aims to strike a balance between the rights of individuals and the need for collective security. Most governments have strict rules about the information that is collected, how long it may be kept and to what purposes. Privacy legislation is intended to govern the activities of firms in the private sector, as well. But such is the power of technologies, and so grave do the threats appear to be, that individual privacy and civil liberties are steadily eroded. As the state penetrates deeper and deeper there is a need for policies (values) to control these processes (Bannister, 2005).

Applying the informational perspective

We have argued that the project of policy analysis should revisit the problem of producing better policy, by taking a broader perspective on what policy does. The informational perspective developed in this chapter suggests that it is the extent to which public policies both gather and transmit information that will shape the adaptability of political systems.

This approach implies, in turn, a research agenda that revisits existing policy concepts, in a critical way. Such a research agenda might include: a renewed and expanded emphasis on approaches to public policy that are implicitly informational, for example, policy learning and evaluation and evidence-based policy; as well as using the informational 'lens' to discern new themes and new approaches to old problems. The following applications put forward some methodologies through which these potential advances might be achieved.

Application 1: improving policy through information: the case for meta-analysis

As we have seen, there is a continuing theme in the literature: policy should be evidence-based, but rarely is. The key question is not: how much information goes in or out, but what can be done to improve its application? Which kinds of information tend to have an impact, and which don't?

This is difficult terrain to research. But we may know more than we think we do. For policy-oriented researchers, the problem is not a lack of empirical data, but rather finding ways of synthesising and learning from widely scattered research, much of it constructed around particular policy fields, such as health. Relevant 'generic' material crops up in a wide range of journals, from public administration through to those with 'public policy' in the title.

Even within the one journal, such as *Science and Public Policy*, the shape-shifting nature of public policy means that work relevant to knowledge-into-policy appears in many guises. Papers here often focus on many instances and themes relating to the incorporation of scientific knowledge into policy, and it is the nature of the theme that shapes the analysis. For example, the intensely difficult work of regulating science and its applications tends to be seen through a 'risk and regulation' lens. Managing (or encouraging) the progress of science tends to be seen through an 'innovation' lens. An informationally informed program of research could constitute a meta-analytic way of making more use of this wide variety of material.

Application 2: improving the informational 'reach' of public policy

There has been extensive research on the use of adaptive forms of governance for the clarification and resolution of a wide variety of policy problems, from urban planning, to ecological management, to regulatory improvement. Are there ways of 'designing-in', perhaps at the institutional level, optimal informational characteristics for forming particular kinds of policies?

Reconsideration of the policy instruments literature reminds us of the informational content of concepts such as Hood's nodality (Hood, 1983), and Schneider and Ingram's hortatory policy instruments (Schneider and Ingram, 1990). Wherever policy works through behavioural means (whether via exhortation, punishment or education), there is a strong informational or communicative content. Information may provide a unifying thread for the discussion of policy instruments in different institutional settings (see Le Gales and King, 2017).

Systems thinking gives additional purchase on the role of the state. At the macro-level, a comparative institutionalist approach could prove fruitful. Is it true, for example, that coalition-based states with proportionally based electoral systems make better use of information (in the sense of linking the political system with its environment) than those that are majoritarian? New Zealand (which changed its electoral system in 1996 to restrict majoritarian dominance) could be a suitable case study to test this out (Chapter 3).

At the meso-level, the large literature on engagement and public administration suggests a research agenda that explores, not only the forms and patterns of governance, but also the types of practice, that relate most easily to engagement. Public managers may need to think and act differently, 'outside the square' of public management norms and values to create better forms of engagement (see, for example, Boxelaar et al, 2006; APSC, 2007). Interestingly, this conclusion has also been reached by those investigating problematic issues from a policy learning perspective (Jarvie and Stewart, 2011). Information-as-control may frustrate information-as-enabler.

Application 3: analysing accountability systems

Not surprisingly, the huge changes wrought by new technologies, and new and emerging media platforms and markets, have engendered a plethora of research approaches and interests. There is no simple way to navigate these literatures. However, if we align 'information' and 'system' we come very close to a core concept, that of accountability. Accountability is built around relationships: in public life, officials and political executives are accountable to someone for something. Without information flowing through these channels, there is no content to the process: information is the lifeblood of both formal and informal accountability.

We know that governments everywhere seek to restrict, control and mould what those 'outside' know of their activities. Yet key questions remain unanswered. While the processes and implications of accountability systems have been extensively studied, the role of information in underpinning these systems is usually seen, in policy studies, through the lens of freedom of information legislation. The role of the media in sustaining information flow is acknowledged, but not well developed.

The advent of the Internet has further complicated the analysis. Two opposing views have emerged in the literature. Some scholars point to the part played by the Internet in the loss of a genuinely collective public 'space'. In this view, the loss of advertising revenue (which had largely supported this space) has undermined the capacity of the press to play its traditional accountability role. The decline of investigative journalism gives citizens fewer avenues to understand and to react to government actions (or inactions) in ways that might produce policy change.

From a traditional accountability perspective, therefore, societies appear to be losing critical information at a rapid rate. On the other hand, there is evidence that social media can enhance the agility of protest movements, and that citizen journalists with mobile phones and cameras can provide news services with immediate and graphic images from anywhere in the world. New forms of civic engagement may bypass the state, or prove unsustainable in the face of traditional forms of power. The perspective advanced here suggests that the yardstick will be the extent to which power is held to account through these changes.

Application 4: balancing flexibility and control in governance

The exploration/exploitation dichotomy has been explored in administrative contexts (Duit and Galaz, 2008). Governance scholars have addressed the pros and cons of collaborative governance in supporting policy outcomes, particularly in the environmental field (Newig et al, 2018). Translating these concerns into informational terms, we might discern an interesting link between the structures through which policy is made and implemented, and the extent to which information flow is inhibited or promoted.

Many questions relating to the working of bureaucratic organisations, in particular, remain unanswered. Hierarchy impedes and stylises information flow (briefs are extensively re-written, for example, as they move from one approver to the next). Information is carefully controlled in this way. But when the policy agenda determines a clear need, information is at a premium. The bureaucracy becomes a sponge, soaking up ideas from everywhere, before reverting to more crystalline forms.

The flow of ideas within the 'black box' of government and between government and organisations outside it remains poorly understood. The rules governing who public servants may talk to, and to what effect, protect ministerial control at the expense of adaptive understanding. The way in which these values are balanced within public organisations, particularly in Westminster systems, is critical for both accountability and response in an era of adaptive governance. Empirical work which attempts to penetrate these opaque areas, while generally thought of as belonging to mainstream 'public administration' could (if well contextualised) be given much more prominence in the scholarly journals of policy and governance studies.

Conclusions

The informational reconsideration of public policy presented in this chapter brings together both the content and function of public policy in new ways. By aligning the broad idea of 'information' with systems thinking, political and other processes can be conceptualised as linking the collective apparatus of the state with the external environment.

Policy analysis has much to gain from this informational perspective. Information channelling or processing enables policy-making structures to be illuminated in new ways. Reconsideration leads to a stronger emphasis on key activities such as agenda setting. The role of evidence and its relationship to politics and the role of social media becomes an issue of the first importance.

Information offers a fresh perspective on the role of the state, opening up the possibility that the long-term responsiveness and viability of states can be understood and evaluated via the adaptation/legitimacy lens. States need information to adapt through policy. At the same time, states use information to spy on their own citizens, threatening both their adaptiveness and their legitimacy.

Information and information technology are often used interchangeably; yet they are analytically distinct concepts. The technologies that advance uses of information are subject to the same, context-based, calculations of cost and benefit as affect other technologies. While the pace of technological change is stunning, politics remains surprisingly durable. It is easy to talk via social media, and to orchestrate petitions, but old-fashioned movements and organisation are still necessary to attract serious political attention. Technology gives political parties added opportunities for rationalisation and manipulation of voting. But voting continues to occur within institutionally prescribed informational frameworks.

There are technical issues about which too little is known. From a policy-process point of view, policy analysts should pay much more attention to the routines of e-government (particularly in relation to implementation), the use of information technologies in cyber-warfare and surveillance, as well as the challenges and opportunities for administration posed by the information age more generally.

Technological determinism, based on a perception of an unholy alliance between IT and capital, does not take us very far. Reconsideration suggests that the way to understand IT and the state is through the information, rather than the technology. This perception leads to a more nuanced view of the state's role. The state's informational capacity is extensive, but so is that of civil society, particularly business. The state's reach beyond its borders, which in peacetime draws on international diplomacy, negotiation and agreement, is far less direct than that of business. Private citizens, too, can communicate beyond their own immediate situation. We see a strange contest of wills between citizens, business and government that is played out in the sense of who controls what information.

Despite the possibilities of e-governance, there can be no clear-cut path of influence from technologies to governance (Dunleavy et al, 2006a: Chapter 9; Afterword). There is little evidence that bureaucracies have been changed by the new technologies to operate in more holistic ways, although they have altered at the margins (Reed, 2005). Two decades into the 21st century, the familiar worlds of management and politics continue to dominate hopes of a more open communicative order. While the informational dimensions of *realpolitik* may be exposed by the same technologies (as for example, via Wikileaks), states have no problems in hunting down human whistle-blowers.

Fundamentally, the capacity of states rests upon their ability both to use and to control information, in particular the information that is generated through governing. Use and control may run counter to each other. If we can see a conflict, it occurs when the politics of information gets in the way of the policy (that is, information as adaptation) – the more expansive the scope of governmentality, the more the balance between citizen and state tips towards the state.

Overall, the issue we draw from the literature, is that of a disjunct between what we might call older or more traditional approaches to the analysis of public policy and the state, and approaches highlighting the effects of the information revolution itself (Meijer and Bannister, 2009). Some have seen at least the potential for profound change, while others have remained sceptical.

Within the smaller world of day-to-day public policy, information can still make a positive difference – within each policy 'construction', there is a core space that can be utilised to good effect. For policy analysis, the challenge is, armed with this knowledge, to determine good (or at least less bad) ways of incorporating information in the policy process.

8

Reconsidering *implementation*

Introduction

Public policy in a democracy is ideally about the successful pursuit of collectively agreed goals and desired outcomes. The democratic policy-making process needs to generate a reasonable level of agreement and clarity about these goals and outcomes. 'Implementation' consists of the organisational processes through which policy goals are pursued and realised. In practice, these goals become further refined through the managerial and negotiation processes of implementation, especially in complex programs involving many stakeholders.

The realities of policy implementation in modern governance are far from being neat and predictable. Firstly, policy needs to be understood in a holistic sense as including the program management, monitoring and evaluation processes. Policy is not just the initial 'idea' of what needs to be done, but includes the practices that constitute the policy delivery and consequent impacts. Secondly, the mechanisms of implementation are seldom simple, often requiring multi-organisational partnerships or contractual oversight relationships. Thirdly, the interpretive and persuasive dimensions of policy remain very active during 'implementation', with service-delivery staff having to deal with emerging uncertainties and managers having to make professionally informed choices during program implementation (Laws and Hajer, 2008). And fourthly, while attempting to address and manage complex or wicked issues, the underlying problems may continue to evolve, and various stakeholders might engage in disputes or reinterpretations of the required actions.

We argue that closer attention should be given to understanding and improving policy implementation, but we also need to identify and absorb the lessons already known. In seeking out these lessons, much can be harvested from studies that do not always bear the label 'implementation'. For example, there is much value in exploring the relationships between traditional managerial 'implementation' literature and the large reservoirs of knowledge encompassed by governance studies and complexity studies. The former emphasise the relational networks underpinning policy design and policy management, while the latter emphasise the evolutionary and unpredictable nature of emerging issues and organisational responses. Implementation processes often encounter governance challenges that were unforeseen, arising from difficulties in the coordination of partnerships or from rapid changes in external events.

Implementation research has been the 'poor cousin' within public policy scholarship, where much of the excitement has centred on policy change and innovation. This contrast in valuation has been mirrored within public service organisations themselves. In both instances, implementation has generally been accorded a lower status than the analysis and practice of policy design and policy reform. This division was exacerbated by the new NPM-style public service culture from the 1980s, such as the UK 'Next Steps' agenda, which required clear separation between the roles of priority setting, policy design, regulatory oversight and service delivery. Ambitious executives often perceived a more attractive career path in policy rather than delivery. This deliberate and artificial separation of roles has been unfortunate, because lack of integration between 'policy' development and 'implementation' practice undermines the quality of policy systems. Central policy units, with their responsibility for steering the priorities of government, cannot be fully effective as strategic policymakers without a deep appreciation of the administrative and coordination challenges of program delivery on complex issues. Failures to achieve program goals in cost-effective ways are detrimental not only for financial efficiency and accountability, but for their negative effects on public trust, legitimacy and governance capacity.

This chapter recognises that the previous literature on policy implementation has grappled with many important questions in public policy and management – policy design, effective management, hierarchies of control, network coordination, evaluation and learning. However, both the research literature and the managerial practices of government need to be continually updated – owing to the rapidly changing global contexts canvassed in this book, and the changing fashions in public management itself. Accordingly, this chapter outlines the contributions of the main schools of analysis in implementation studies, together with the emerging challenges confronting researchers and practitioners. In particular, we argue that, in the context of increased complexity and increased demand for collaborative capacity, scholars need to explore the capabilities required for program delivery that rely on multiple actors (O'Toole, 1986), and utilise a wide range of instruments, from traditional top-down legislative and regulatory mechanisms through to negotiated codes of conduct with non-state actors. There is a substantial risk that public management arrangements lack an appropriate balance between reliability and flexibility, thus hindering effective and adaptive responses to complexity and crisis.

These challenges are even more evident at the international level, where norms, principles and standards are negotiated on various emerging issues – security, economy, environment and human rights. The diffusion of norms through treaties and agreements (Betts and Orchard, 2014) has been patchy and contested. Even the well-established system of European Union Directives has come under severe strain owing to national differences and exogenous shocks (as noted in Chapter 5). Ambitious attempts to develop global policy approaches for the big issues like 'environmental sustainability' are confronted by implementation dilemmas that are quite different from those highlighted in the older literature which contrasts 'top-down' and 'bottom-up' approaches to decision-making and stakeholder engagement. Sustainable development agendas are inherently fluid and contentious, given the scientific uncertainties, the evolving nature of the issues and the diverse range of knowledge and interests among actors. Examples of joined-up approaches for sustainable development include the UN Millennium Development Goals in 2001 and the UN Sustainable Development Goals in 2015 (Clegg, 2015); the Kyoto Protocol on Climate Change in 1998, and the Paris Accord on Climate Change in 2015 (Howes et al, 2017). The political search for joined-up solutions at regional and global levels has required new thinking about how to build multi-lateral support. Governments have an important role in seeking innovative and collaborative approaches for complex issues, but these strategies require stakeholder support and incentives for action at all levels.

Implementation matters

We argue that policy scholars need to give enhanced attention to implementation processes because of the insights available about policy success and failure, monitoring and evaluation, and policy capacity and learning. A better understanding of implementation is necessary for improving policy design and for enhancing policy outcomes. Understanding how policy decisions transition into successful program management is central for understanding state capacity and system capacity, especially in more complex problem areas. Implementation entails structural and process challenges which test governmental and partner capacities, and which shape the boundaries of policy success or failure (Peters, 2014; 2015a). Moreover, the increased reliance on outsourced, contractual and networked service-delivery models has challenged and stretched the policy and administrative capacity of governmental systems.

For policy researchers, a closer understanding of implementation provides insights into some of the key concerns and puzzles of contemporary policy studies – including how complex policy fields become sites of ongoing struggle, and how complex implementation practices ultimately define and shape policy evolution. As noted in Chapter 7, research in the managerial and administrative domains of public policy also provides important insights into the information and analysis needs of government (for example, for program management, monitoring and review), and greater understanding of how organisational cultures impinge on government agencies' capacities for evaluation and policy learning.

Implementation is sometimes seen as the routine or even boring part of public governance. However, good administration is critical for the achievement of outcomes for citizens and for the credibility of government itself. Narratives about the success (or otherwise) of policy implementation are central in many debates – for example, about accountability for the use of public resources, or about the distributional impacts of programs. Implementation can be managed well or badly. Scholars have long discussed the reasons for poor or patchy results (Gunn 1978; Hogwood and Gunn 1984: 198–206). In the case of large infrastructure projects, which often have delays and cost over-runs, Ministers are attracted by the political allure of announcing public investment in mega-projects; but research has continually shown that the cost/benefit statements provided by powerful corporate investors tend to exaggerate benefits and understate costs (Flyvbjerg, 2014). With the ongoing litany of failures and fiascos in the public sector (Bovens et al, 2001; King and Crewe, 2013), increased attention of both practitioners and scholars has focused on the conditions necessary for 'good' implementation. For example, it has often been found that political imperatives for rapid action lead to rushed planning and implementation (Shergold, 2015), with the result that some new programs are badly managed and the intended benefits fail to materialise.

The longstanding literature on the theory and practice of implementation has assumed that governmental leaders or ministers have the politico-legal responsibility to decide on policy goals and directions, whereas public servants have the operational responsibility for managing the administrative arrangements and delivery mechanisms. In this traditional model, the theory and practice of implementation rests upon two rationalist assumptions: firstly, that *what* is to be implemented (policy design, program strategies, performance indicators) can be clearly specified by political leaders and senior executives; and secondly, that the subsequent implementation activities undertaken by service providers can and should be faithful to this enunciated policy design (program 'fidelity').

Both of these assumptions have been seriously undercut by several decades of analysis and experience. The division of functions envisaged by the traditional approach rests on the notion that 'policy' can be clearly separated from the sphere of implementation. However, as Susan Barrett argued many years ago:

> many so-called implementation problems arise precisely because there is a tension between the normative assumptions of government – what ought to be done and how it should happen – and the struggle and conflict between interests – the need to bargain and compromise – that represent the reality of the process. (Barrett and Fudge, 1981: 145)

Moreover, the blurring of policy and implementation within an ongoing interactive process occurs at every level of governmental systems – from the macro level, where high-level policy bargaining occurs, and the meso levels of inter-organisational adjustment and coordination, through to the micro level of front-line services where the professional judgement and discretion of staff can modify or extend policy intent. However, popular notions of accountability seem to demand that specific managers or delivery agencies will be held responsible for efficient and effective activities to achieve the desired results. The assessment of policy 'success' (or alternatively, of policy failure) is generally understood in terms of whether the stated policy goals have been translated into well-designed programs, which in turn have been 'implemented' in a competent way to meet those stated goals (McConnell, 2010a; 2010b).

Finally, the challenges faced by modern governments have arguably become more complex and urgent in recent decades. Three brief examples indicate the scale of these challenges. Firstly, responses to unpredictable security and policing crises have required significant coordination, restructuring and up-skilling of agencies, as well as the need for implementing new policy instruments. Secondly, in social services and health care, complex new arrangements for service delivery, whether through competitive outsourcing or through network collaboration, have stretched the capacity of government agencies to monitor performance and understand the factors driving success or failure. Thirdly, in climate change and environmental protection, designing and implementing even mild reforms has been difficult, owing to widespread resistance by vested interests and limited funding to leverage change programs.

In complex or rapidly changing areas of policy, the precise steps required for success are very difficult to map or specify in advance. This inherent feature of complex programs adds to the difficulties of undertaking evaluation in complex service-delivery arrangements with multiple goals and many diverse stakeholders. Outsourcing and contracting of service delivery, and privatisation of key utilities, also brought many non-state actors into the complex web of program implementation. In moving beyond the top-down and contractual models of New Public Management, new forms of integrated service delivery are being developed. There are significant challenges in attempting to shift from top-down or principal-agent models towards decentralised 'place-based' collaborative models which value interaction, adaptation and mutual learning. These 'place-based' experiments focus on localities, and involve deep engagement with local stakeholders (Sabel and Simon, 2011; Marsh et al, 2017). As a recent comparative study concludes:

> Established architectures, built in the era of New Public Management (NPM), emphasised central determination of outcomes, accountability based on these goals, and service delivery based on arms-length contracts. But place-based action implies variability of outcomes across sites, their progressive development, discretion for on-the-ground staff to tailor approaches to local circumstances, and individual/ community engagement in decisions that affect them. (Marsh et al, 2017: 445)

The evolving history of implementation studies

Over time there have been ebbs and flows of scholarly attention to implementation studies within the wider domain of policy studies. Implementation research, including both conceptual frameworks and the empirical investigation of case studies, has evolved over several decades. Areas of focus reflect the variety of policy interests among scholars and their range of preferred research methods. The fundamental starting point was always the framework of laws and regulations, as determined by legislatures and executive government, which authorise administrative actions. Public servants require these authorisations in order to undertake regulatory and service functions.

The classical accounts of implementation in the 1960s and 1970s broadly adopted a 'top-down' model of implementation, understood as executing the instructions and directions of legislatures and executive government. Implementation was regarded as a set of administrative challenges for competent professional managers, given that policy decisions had already been taken and instruments selected after taking account of political and financial circumstances. For example, Bardach (1977) provided an influential account of the process by which a policy proposal in the US achieves a legislative or regulatory mandate; he also emphasised the importance of providing dedicated resources for implementation and enforcement, and the clear allocation of responsibilities to a designated agency. This 'top-down' notion of implementation as following instructions was expanded in the 1980s and 1990s in the light of further experience with new service models. Bardach later noted that additional elements were needed for success:

> Mandates defining regulatory programs will often require compliance resources from businesses or ordinary citizens. Service-delivery programs will often need participation from citizens who perceive the availability of the program, are willing to make the effort to establish eligibility, and can manage to sustain continued participation. The responsible agency may also wish to involve relevant non-profit agencies. Other program agencies with overlapping jurisdictions or responsibilities must sometimes be asked to cooperate. (Bardach, 2001: 7235)

A similar pattern of shifts in thinking is evident in the most famous US study of implementation by Pressman and Wildavsky (1973). Their chosen case was a complex federal government program to fund job creation projects. The intended beneficiaries were unemployed people willing to work on public works projects at municipal levels. Pressman and Wildavsky outlined the many policy implementation failures in the federal program ('dashed expectations', 'ruined hopes'), and they sought to explain why resources approved by the federal government in Washington were not producing the intended outcomes in disadvantaged local areas (such as Oakland). They focused on institutional and structural complexities and 'veto points'. The federal program relied on diverse other agencies or actors, whose interests were not necessarily aligned with the intentions of the central decision makers. Hence, the initial 'lesson' for rational planners in Washington was that they should devise strong structures to minimise the discretion and bargaining available to other actors. However, Pressman and Wildavsky were sceptical about whether such top-down structural controls could work (given that they required intensive coordination and vast flows of timely information).

Pressman and Wildavsky produced two later editions (1979; 1984) which illustrate how policy scholars were beginning to modify their learning about how means and ends are intertwined in complex programs. The key insight was that the problems were as much behavioural and attitudinal as structural. The authors now suggested that a degree of dissonance and flexibility was inherent in managing decentralised federal programs. Implementation would require negotiations with relevant stakeholders, and some minor revisions in the detailed objectives might be expected. Moreover, policies might continue to evolve in response to the various forces and the local contexts in which they were located. In short, they argued that simple tasks depend on complex chains of interaction, each part of which needs to be constructed with a view to strengthening these relationships among actors.

In recent decades, the major debates in implementation studies are between those who continue to take a 'top-down' approach to implementation (rational planning and accountability, as specified in performance indicators and audits: see Barber, 2008), and those who are more concerned about understanding the actual behaviour of local leaders and 'street-level bureaucrats' who try to adapt large programs to local needs. The latter 'bottom-up' approach highlights the organisational behaviours and motivations that explain variations in program outcomes. One of the classics in the latter camp is Michael Lipsky's study *Street-level Bureaucracy* (1980). This and many later works have focused on the relationships between local officials, various client or 'target groups', and the impact of wider socio-economic contexts (Riccucci, 2005; Behn, 2017). Local flexibilities have been championed as necessary for responding to the complexity of programs, and for seeking innovative solutions to achieve outcomes (for example, Durose, 2011). The conflict between top-down concerns for efficiency and predictability, and bottom-up perspectives highlighting relational practices for problem-solving and service enhancement, has sometimes become unproductive. Other forms of synthesis have emerged from the engagement of policy studies with major issues of complexity, the mix of policy instruments, and collaborative learning.

Changing contexts and challenges for implementation

From the late 1980s, scholarly interest in implementation theory was reshaped by research agendas focused on the system-level changes transforming the public sector. Firstly, as noted in Chapter 7, information technology (IT) rapidly became a vital strand in policy design and service planning. IT has transformed the capacity of service systems to produce extensive data, not only for monitoring program performance within government but also for communicating with citizens and service clients (Dunleavy et al, 2006a; 2006b). Digitisation has fostered service innovation, ranging from intermodal transport ticketing through to online client services (payments, service information, and so on). The massive expansion of stored information has also led to major concerns about cyber-security and privacy of these databases.

Secondly, as noted in Chapter 4, there was widespread debate about the legitimacy and capacity of state agencies to take the lead role in directly providing services where alternative non-state providers were available or where a service market could be created. The delivery of public services solely by governmental bodies became somewhat less common in many countries since the 1980s, with privatisation of government-owned business enterprises (Colley and Head, 2013). However, as Peters notes, this trend has been variable:

> While accepting the general premise that implementation has become more multi-organisational, some important public functions remain peculiarly governmental and may be managed by a single public organisation. At the national level, public pensions fit that more *étatiste* model in many countries. At the local level, functions such as sanitation, water, and the like remain in the public sector and may be implemented through relatively simple structures. (Peters, 2014: 132)

In the UK during the Thatcher era, the NPM advocacy of efficiency was underpinned by ideological debates about privatisation and small government, refocusing on the 'core' roles of government, and opposing the incremental growth of 'big government' (Dunleavy and Hood, 1993). As state agencies moved towards 'steering' roles (setting priorities and measuring performance), policy implementation increasingly focused on new models of service delivery – especially service contracting or 'commissioning', and the coordination of joined-up service arrangements. NPM generated extensive restructuring of agencies and redefinition of public sector roles, in a search for efficient and effective business models for service delivery. Parallel developments in the US included the pro-market stance of the Reagan era and the 'Reinventing Government' movement of the Clinton era (Frederickson, 1996). The rhetoric of this period emphasised not only commitments to results-based management and cost-effective programs, but also encouragement for local innovation to improve outcomes for clients (Osborne and Gaebler, 1992).

Despite the flurry of reform efforts to encourage both efficiency and improved outcomes, policy failures continued to occur and governments received the blame. Policy success (or otherwise) is often measured on three dimensions: the managerial or administrative competence of the organisations (managing the programs in a timely and efficient manner); the delivery of the intended services or outcomes for clients; and ultimately the political-electoral rewards for the government (McConnell, 2010a; 2010b). According to Hogwood and Gunn (1984: 197–8), 'perfect' implementation is an unattainable fantasy, owing to a wide range of political and organisational factors; and failures arise from 'bad execution, bad policy or bad luck'. There are many reasons why program outcomes are weakened along the road from policy design to detailed implementation practices (Edwards, 2001). These reasons include 'incomplete specification; inappropriate agency; conflicting objectives; incentive failures; conflicting directives; limited competence; inadequate administrative resources; and communication failures' (Althaus et al, 2007: 168–74).

In responding to evidence of poor or incomplete implementation, two types of response are evident. The first approach has been to tighten the requirements. According to this view, funding agencies should closely specify the accountabilities for particular tasks and ensure disciplined coordination where necessary. Articulating the classical view of implementation as competently following clear instructions for resource management, management consultancy firms have propagated the art and science of service delivery. In this approach, skills in project management, contract management and risk management have been identified as requiring significant enhancement. This top-down NPM managerialism reached a high point with the 'Delivery' mantra of former UK mandarin Michael Barber (2008; 2015). This orthodoxy involves several steps in clarification, assignment of roles, scheduling and monitoring. After a minister or department has been assigned leadership responsibility for a policy or service reform, a detailed plan is required for integrating and sequencing the implementation activities; together with processes to support and monitor progress. Ongoing concerns about the effectiveness of implementation led to the establishment of 'Implementation Units' in several jurisdictions, including the UK and Australia (Lindquist, 2007). Key functions of these central units included keeping track of promises and milestones, putting pressure on those accountable for delivery and signalling cases requiring central intervention. The attraction of this approach may be linked to the distinctive rhetoric of centralised executive power in Westminster systems; it has been less attractive in other nations. Importantly, it is also at odds with the 'governance' trends towards networks and multi-stakeholder collaboration, as noted in the work of R.A.W. Rhodes (1997; 2007):

> Governments fail because they are locked into power-dependent relations and because they must work with and through complex networks of actors and organisations. To adopt a command operating code builds failure into the design of the policy. Such centralisation will be confounded by fragmentation and interdependence which, in turn, will prompt further bouts of centralisation. (R.A.W. Rhodes, 2007: 1258)

Thus, the efficacy of the top-down performance management approach has been queried from several sides. Empirical studies have consistently shown that various actors in a complex multilevel program exhibit a range of knowledge, values and dispositions. They contribute various resources, skills and capacities. In working *with* this diversity rather than suppressing it, the implementation challenges are seen as relational, behavioural and motivational as much as contractual. In complex programs where partners need to cooperate to achieve collective purposes, the need for flexibility and judgement is more pronounced, along with the need for increased collaboration across organisations and sectors (O'Flynn et al, 2014). Research concerning 'new public governance' (Osborne, 2010) has highlighted the importance of network coordination and cross-sector collaboration, and the role of third-sector partners in the delivery of public services. As noted in Chapter 2, complex implementation practices may have 'system' features that need to be identified and managed. The shift towards studying governance arrangements for devolved service networks has placed more emphasis on the perspectives of network actors and the importance of continuous negotiation and interpretation (Klijn and Koppenjan, 2015). Indeed, the communication flows that underpin service planning and delivery are vital aspects of implementation success. This accords with recent research trends towards interpretive accounts of policy and management, and studying implementation practices rather than rational plans (Hill and Hupe, 2003; 2014; Carey et al, 2015).

Factors influencing implementation

There is a considerable body of experience showing that certain types of programs or interventions are very likely to have major problems. Examples include:

- designing and installing new IT systems for complex organisations – typically involves major problems with timeliness, cost, and functionality;
- rapid expansion of front-line services – typically constrained by insufficient supplies of skilled labour, communication systems and other resources;
- constructing a large number of physical facilities (offices, clinics, schools, roads, and so on) – typically requires long-term planning and scheduling;
- foreign interventions and armed conflict – the 'fog of war' entails high uncertainty and unpredictable costs; and
- the 'war on drugs' – the disparate nature of the wicked problems and the networked character of the actors mean that success is deeply problematic.

In addition, some policy areas are subject to complex structural arrangements, such as those found in the multilevel governance systems of the European Union. There are inherent tensions between national preferences and European integrative tendencies, requiring negotiated trade-offs between conformance to European directives, national diversity and policy performance (Heidbreder, 2017; Thomann and Sager, 2017). Similar challenges occur within the complex policy settings of federal systems (such as the US, Canada and Australia) where the central and provincial governments may be seeking inconsistent goals in the same policy field and therefore struggle to provide seamless and effective services (Kettl, 2014). In some areas of service delivery, from infrastructure to social care, the use of coordinated public/private partnerships has become widespread; but these have proved difficult to manage without constant stakeholder communication and negotiation (Williams and Sullivan, 2011; Hodge et al, 2012).

A key part of implementation success is making wise choices in relation to the available 'policy instruments'. This deliberative choice process is described by Howlett as 'policy design'. Much of this literature is about 'matching' the task or public purpose to the most suitable tools and instruments (Howlett, 2011). Poor choice of instruments undermines the achievement of desired outcomes. For example, sole reliance on a voluntary code of conduct by industry to prevent hazardous chemical pollution of the environment has been shown to be ineffective internationally; regulatory standards with credible enforcement are crucial for programs aiming to reduce environmental harms. More generally, there are important relationships between the types of policy problems and the choice of remedies, and some choices are more appropriate than others. Specific instruments are often vital for crafting an effective solution. For example, risk analysis, resource coordination and community mobilisation are crucial for responding to disasters and emergencies; and in preparing for future shocks and challenges.

The factors influencing implementation have been much discussed in the literature (Hogwood and Gunn, 1984; Hill and Hupe, 2014). According to Van Meter and Van Horn (1975), different areas of policy decision will display specific processes, structures and relationships that influence implementation of public policy. Two generic dimensions often identified by scholars are (a) the amount of change involved (small changes are easier), and (b) the extent to which there is goal consensus among the participants in the implementation process (disagreement leads to inconsistent or negative results). Some factors are largely under the control of implementing agencies and others are given by the political context and socio-economic environment (Van Meter and Van Horn, 1975: 483). Other important aspects concern the complexity of the challenges, such as the range of stakeholders, their level of conflict, and the degree of ambiguity in the policy proposals. These dimensions led Matland (1995) to suggest a matrix of four types: low conflict-low ambiguity (administrative implementation), high conflict-low ambiguity (political implementation), high conflict-high ambiguity (symbolic implementation), and low conflict-high ambiguity (experimental implementation). From an organisational standpoint, capacity issues are crucial, such as the informational and managerial resources available, the cultures of implementing agencies, and arrangements for inter-organisational cooperation where joint action is required.

Such attempts to theorise the diversity and complexity of implementation draw attention to the need to overcome the simple dichotomy between 'top-down' and 'bottom-up' approaches. Indeed, it has proved to be a false debate, as the conditions for either perfect 'top-down' or for perfect devolution are never met. Several scholars (for example, Winter, 2012; Hill and Hupe, 2014) have attempted to develop a more integrated analytical framework. One point of agreement is that policy arenas are different; and that there are many actor perspectives at work – such as those of politicians, managers and front-line service workers (May and Winter, 2009). Stakeholders have different perspectives on the nature of issues and solutions. Recent frameworks, such as the 'policy regime' perspective, focus on the relationship between the political context and organisational capacities. May (2012; 2015) argues that this highly political relationship determines whether a specific policy reform, such as the US Affordable Care program, can develop an enduring sense of legitimacy, policy coherence and policy durability. The survival of reforms has strong political dimensions, and does not depend simply on administrative competence.

Moving beyond domestic policy issues, divergent perspectives on goals and policy success are widespread. In relation to overseas development aid programs, for example, there are strongly held political claims by donor countries that foreign aid provides benefits for both the donors and the aid recipients (Radelet, 2017); however, the political drivers for program delivery often outweigh the evaluation evidence (Kennedy and Crowley, 2018). From a critical perspective reflecting practitioner experience, Mosse (2004) suggests that keeping a coalition of interests together is essential in development aid programs, and requires ongoing effort. Hence for Mosse, a primary function of development aid policy is to mobilise and maintain multilevel political support, or in his terms, to legitimise practice rather than to provide a rational roadmap for project implementation (2004: 640). Implementation, in his view, is driven not just by design objectives but also by inter-organisational concerns to preserve administrative order and the agreed delivery paradigms (2004: 664).

The prevalence of top-down design approaches in development aid prompted a range of more participatory approaches. In these alternative frameworks, local issues are given top priority, local skills are developed and adaptive learning capacities are encouraged (Andrews et al, 2017). Brinkerhoff (2005; 2014) shows that in fragile states and post-conflict societies, major links need to be built between the legitimacy, effectiveness and security dimensions of governance. In most cases, such governance systems have to be constructed and continuously modified over time, taking account of the interplay between local and national levels, and the importance of informal governance and cultural practices. Even in a large and rapidly developing country such as India (Gupta, 2012), state implementation capacities are limited by insufficient resources, corrupt networks, fragmentation of agencies and lack of experience with successful reforms.

Improving capacities for successful implementation

Policy design and implementation depend on a range of factors concerned with capability, context and support. In the Organisation for Economic Cooperation and Development (OECD) countries, analytical capacity and financial resources are only two of many factors important for excellence in policy design, implementation and evaluation. Thus 'policy capacity' includes the capacity to undertake strategic relationships with ministers, other public agencies and with external stakeholders (Wu et al, 2015; Head, 2015). Importantly, 'policy capacity' to deal with big issues requires strategic foresight and a focus on longer-term considerations, going well beyond the competent management of immediate programs (for example, OECD 2010; Chapter 4). Policy management has also become much more difficult in complex service contracting environments. In turn, the skills and competences of senior officials have expanded to meet the practical and professional challenges of navigating this complex relational environment (Hartley et al, 2015).

Policymakers consistently face external shocks and international instability. The global context has been marked by major conflicts linked to economic resource security, together with other large-scale threats such as financial crises, pandemics, natural disasters, terrorism and cyber-crime (OECD, 2011). These major shocks have generated increased needs for national preparedness and international cooperation, both of which necessitate strengthening policy coordination and regulatory capacity. At a national and regional level, the risks and threats arising from disasters and crises have occupied an increasing part of government policy attention and program coordination effort (Christensen et al, 2016b) The complexities and uncertainties of wicked problems require the policy and implementation systems to transcend their 'normal' operational range – which is essentially that of bureaucratic monitoring and fine-tuning. The need to manage high levels of uncertainty places major stresses on actors throughout the system. Political and administrative leaders are being challenged to find avenues for problem management that go well beyond the skills of conventional project management. One requirement is the building of relational or collaborative capital across sectors and organisations (APSC, 2007; Head and Alford, 2015). This co-production paradigm in turn requires enhanced trust and appropriate levels of devolved authority. Bureaucratic cultures, however, are generally built on the premise of maintaining central control to ensure the efficient attainment of specific results, and genuine devolution and collaboration therefore tend to be resisted (Stewart and Jarvie, 2015).

Improving the capacity for successful implementation thus depends on the type of policy proposal and the actors who need to be involved. As outlined previously, the assumptions underlying rational models of policy planning – and their assumed transitions from policy intentions into organisational practices for implementation – have been widely criticised. The process of implementation is often not predictable and thus not controllable in detail. The actual experience of the implementation process may disclose defects in the policy design. In that sense the most viable solution (if it exists) can only be known retrospectively – a normative challenge for those concerned with accountable government, and a practical problem for officials who need to provide reliable information to ministers.

Auditors-General have an important role in scrutinising program implementation and suggesting improvements. But they tend to assume that program goals and managerial systems are capable of precision and that the failure to produce desired or predicted outcomes can be attributed to specific failures by managers and political decision makers. The argument is that clear specification of goals and targets, combined with good project management, will deliver the required results (for example, Australian National Audit Office (ANAO), 2014; National Audit Office (NAO), 2015). These assumptions about professional knowledge and foresight, and capacity to control the actions of third parties, have been widely abandoned in the public policy literature, which has recently been coming to terms with limited or 'bounded' rationality, incomplete knowledge, political contestation of strategy and unreliable cooperation among actors. The alternative approaches tend to favour 'adaptive' management (Brunner 2010; Chaffin et al, 2014), which are consistent with our theme of highlighting policy capacities to address crises and complexity.

The assessment of success or failure in policy implementation can be undertaken from different perspectives. As noted above, policy success can be measured on three dimensions: the managerial or administrative competence of the organisations (managing the programs in a timely and efficient manner); the delivery of the intended benefits for clients; and the political-electoral rewards for the government

(McConnell, 2010a; 2010b). The criteria for determining policy failure are inherently contentious. For example, one program might have been well crafted, but poorly implemented; whereas another program may have been poorly targeted but efficiently implemented. Another program might have achieved its own stated goal, but also had additional unintended effects; while another program might have been competently managed but has now become politically unpopular (Bovens et al, 2001). The scale and complexity of some wicked problems require much more than competent management. Nevertheless, better thinking about implementation requirements during the 'design' stage of policy development will help to avoid many pitfalls.

Performing, evaluating and learning

Implementation studies have become re-oriented toward contemporary concerns about policy effectiveness and performance evaluation. We have noted that senior policy practitioners and consultants (for example, Barber, 2008; 2015) and audit bodies (for example, ANAO, 2014; NAO, 2015) have expressed strong views about the elusive art of effective implementation. The dominant approach – enunciating a set of rules, procedures and schedules – is clearly in the top-down tradition of following clear instructions in a principal-agent model of authority. Here, learning can occur through fine-tuning (optimising the dominant model through minor incremental adjustment). The top-down and polarised aspects of Westminster styles of government are not always conducive to policy learning. Another approach to learning about policy effectiveness is collaborative leadership for problem-solving and service improvement (O'Leary and Bingham, 2008; Williams and Sullivan, 2011; Crosby et al, 2017). Here, learning occurs through the sharing of knowledge and experience among stakeholders, specific attention to learning about successful cross-boundary implementation and iterative approaches to problem-solving.

There have been longstanding debates over whether to assess implementation through conformance criteria (doing what was envisaged) or through performance-outcomes criteria (where the desired results may be pursued through a variety of appropriate methods). This dichotomy mirrors the entrenched tension in evaluation studies between audit-focused perspectives and innovation-focused perspectives. As Behn (2003) reminds us, evaluations and reviews can be conducted for many purposes, from providing the basis for judgemental sanctions and budget controls, through to instilling positive motivation, and promoting collective learning for improvement. In recent decades, there has been increased attention to more experimental approaches (Sabel and Simon, 2011; Marsh et al, 2017), in which the desired results and the appropriate methods are both open to adjustment and mutual learning.

Program evaluation activities have been the backbone of evidence-informed policy design and professional implementation in OECD countries (Head, 2016). However, there has been a major contention surrounding research methods for securing reliable knowledge. As the CEO of the Campbell Collaboration notes (White, 2016), there has recently been much greater use of randomised controlled trials and impact evaluations to assess program effectiveness. But the implementation and design failures that underlie weak performance need to be tied more closely to rigorous evidence about program impacts (White, 2016). The argument for strengthening the scientific character of program evaluations has been forcibly made by many professional evaluators. The essential challenge for scientific approaches to evaluation is to clarify and stabilise that which is to be tested. Thus, for Durlak and DuPre (2008: 329), the key point is to emphasise the need for 'fidelity' and consistency of application, rather than a tolerance of local interpretations.

This concern with positivist scientific certainty is inconsistent with the realist view of policy implementation that began to emerge in the 1980s (Dickinson, 2011). Policy implementation was seen as strongly influenced by negotiations and trade-offs by the actors involved. Policy thus becomes seen as 'what is done' rather than as 'what was rationally imagined'. This dilemma is fundamental to policy studies: how can policy implementation be sensibly evaluated if the stated objectives seem to be modified and adapted through a complex interactive process, and how does the measurement of outputs and performance outcomes help us to assess policy success? Hence, the recent discussion of policy success and failure has taken a broader political and institutional approach, by taking account of administrative competence, the delivery of the intended benefits or services, and the impacts on governmental reputation (McConnell, 2015). But if policy success is to be sustained over a lengthy time period, other factors become important. Patashnik argues, in relation to the US, that successful reforms 'realign public authority' and generate 'positive feedback effects'. 'Reforms endure not because they are "frozen in place" or because their background conditions do not change. Rather, they endure because they reconfigure the political dynamic' (Patashnik, 2008: 155).

One of the standard methods for policy learning and for reflection on implementation issues is the establishment of a public inquiry into a policy issue or crisis that has raised public disquiet. Such inquiries would normally be expected to produce deeper understanding of policy implementation – both its strengths and weaknesses – together with extensive suggestions about ways to improve implementation in specific contexts. And yet there are numerous examples of where the findings and recommendations of public inquiries have failed to generate necessary reform. For example, in the UK, Susan Benbow (2008) examined the history of abuse of older people with mental health problems in NHS facilities. She drew attention to continuing cultures of neglect and indifference that amount to persistent systemic failures. She concluded that despite improved protocols for service delivery, there have been large blockages to learning from inquiries on topics of socio-cultural sensitivity. In a related example concerning institutional sexual abuse, an Australian research report considered why so many recommendations from previous public inquiries into child sexual abuse had not been implemented (Parenting Research Centre, 2014). Some of the reasons included insufficient resources, staff training, cross-agency coordination and the complexity of undertaking law reform on matters affecting many organisations; but some recommendations also foundered because they had not been drafted with an eye to practical feasibility and clarity of purpose. In complex policy areas, cross-organisational issues and associated communication are fundamental to the achievement of program outcomes and implementation success.

In the literature on policy and managerial learning, the 'capacity to learn' is demonstrated in implementation actions that reflect substantive changes in organisational culture, procedures and practices. When proposed new policies require agencies to undertake new tasks or to build new relationships, many concerns arise about the capacity of agencies to innovate. Risk aversion is seen as a 'normal' protective mechanism for large organisations. Nevertheless, there is also evidence that with good leadership and sufficient time, public agencies can learn from their own experience through confronting the behavioural, cognitive or technical demands arising in the implementation of policy change. In a study of a UK NHS program, Schofield (2004) proposed that public managers have to 'learn a range of often new and detailed techniques in order to implement what are often ambiguous policy directives'. Schofield develops a model of 'learned implementation', which shows how learning can occur across several organisational dimensions, and how this experiential knowledge assists in practical problem-solving and new operating procedures.

The policy literature concerning public inquiries and policy reviews underlines the multiple functions they may perform. On the one hand, governments might genuinely be searching for answers to difficult policy puzzles, or may be seeking reassurance that their preferred policy direction will be feasible and defensible. Formal public inquiries – for example, about disasters and emergency situations – may be partly aimed at settling community debates about the causes of the crisis, and partly aimed at finding an appropriate balance between detailed emergency planning and the need for rapid adaptation in response to fast-evolving crises. Stark points out that such inquiries are about 'making sense' of complex and troubling issues (Stark, 2014). In discussing the public inquiry into an industrial disaster on a North Sea oil platform, Brown (2004) suggests that inquiries have not only forensic and informational purposes but also ritualistic and symbolic functions. Establishing a credible narrative is essential for inquiry reports in order to depoliticise disaster events, legitimate institutions, and reduce social anxieties by affirming future capacity to control events (Brown, 2004). As Hood (2010) reminds us, public inquiries are sometimes established by government as blame-avoidance devices.

One strategy for improved learning is through case studies. The case for building and refining policy theory through comparative case analysis is well known. As Elinor Ostrom argued: 'Without the capacity to undertake systematic, comparative institutional assessments, recommendations of reform may be based on naive ideas about which kinds of institutions are "good" or "bad", and not on an analysis of performance' (Ostrom, 2011: 9). Understanding a range of cases, with detailed regard for the contexts and consequences of action, is a necessary complement to theory building. In particular, a full understanding of implementation cannot be derived simply from examining the key performance indicator (KPI) metrics of program performance, which provide only a 'dashboard display' for how program activities are being managed. A deep understanding of how and why a program succeeds (or otherwise) requires detailed fieldwork over a period of time (Beyer, 1997: 20). Such an analysis would necessarily reflect the wide range of perspectives of the various players – those directly involved such as public officials, service-delivery contractors and program clients, as well as political leaders, auditors and media commentators. A well-rounded understanding would also take account of multiple academic knowledge disciplines, their various research methods and the various levels of institutional analysis. In other words, we need more empirically grounded theory, and better ways of drawing lessons from the various case studies.

Learning from implementation is perhaps even more challenging for the practitioners themselves. Public sector contexts may undermine the capacities and incentives needed for effective review and reflection. In examining a range of cases, we might also distinguish between implementation arrangements that are internal to the public sector, arrangements that rely on market mechanisms and arrangements that use network governance and cross-sector collaboration. Thus it might be possible to develop a detailed typology of political and institutional forms and challenges affecting implementation.

Conclusions

Policy implementation has been a relatively neglected theme in policy studies since the 1990s, both in theory and in practice, except for a continuous stream of cases demonstrating the many failures of implementation after the legislative framework and budgets have been approved. But fortunately, the field is much richer than this. Much of the recent work on governance, complexity and crisis management is really about complex implementation under conditions of uncertainty. Additional complexities in implementation arise from multilevel governance (including vertical coordination and role allocation issues) and from the multi-layered nature of service planning and delivery (Carey et al, 2015; Stewart and Jarvie, 2015; Marsh et al, 2017).

We have argued that complex implementation practices ultimately define and shape policy evolution. Recent calls for developing fresh approaches to implementation theory and practice recognise the need for more effective approaches to complex policy problems in the 'era of governance'. Complex problems cannot be resolved primarily through greater technical expertise and specialisation; instead, they require closer connections between policy designers, program managers, key stakeholders and citizens. Policymakers need to acknowledge these contextual and relational aspects more clearly in their design thinking, and take a more nuanced approach to accountability.

The public policy literature on implementation has not resolved the normative issue about whether the exercise of local-level discretion in the application of policies should be applauded for its responsiveness or criticised for its un-authorised character. This dilemma is not easily resolved, but needs to be managed afresh in response to changing social and physical contexts. Insistence on prediction and control will not produce optimal outcomes in many cases. Some of the difficulties arise from budget pressures or from the need to implement poorly crafted political promises. A better understanding of the limits of 'planned' implementation, as revealed by systems thinking (Chapter 2), would improve our capacity to forge more creative and effective solutions.

But achieving a consensus on such matters is unlikely. Hajer (2009) claims that the conditions which shaped the 'classical–modernist' framework of the democratic nation-state have been undermined, not only by globalisation but also by the cultural fragmentation facilitated by new media channels. These new pressures tend to generate deficits in legitimacy, in implementation capacity and in policy learning. These deficits, according to Hajer, can only be remedied through the cooperative modalities of network governance (Hajer, 2009: 24–33). Thus, we come back to the importance of relational and collaborative approaches. Implementation requires deeper understanding and judgement about contexts, resources, stakeholders and values. These insights will only emerge from deeper consideration of implementation case studies, where practitioners and researchers jointly develop grounded understandings and lessons for practice.

9

Reconsidering *policy change*

Introduction

Policy change occurs when the goals, methods or effects of a policy are modified. Policy change can occur at many levels and scales, ranging from small adjustments to existing regulations (for example, minor reductions in corporate income tax), through to introducing new social security programs or new environmental protection policies. For many leaders, managers and citizens, the arguments about policy change are the centrepiece of public policy debates. To understand the dynamics of these debates and understand how policy change occurs, we must focus on the interplay between actors, ideas, interests, institutions and political contexts. These dynamics occur under conditions of complexity and uncertainty, and operate at various levels – local, national and global.

This chapter focuses on the theories and frameworks developed by scholars for explaining how policy change actually occurs, and how proposals are modified through conflict and compromise, in the real world of public policymaking. The absence of change in the face of large challenges – such as climate change – deserves close attention and explanation, because the failure of policy systems to learn from knowledge and experience and to develop more effective policies is a major indicator of their capacity for good governance.

Policy debates and negotiations, whether in favour of policy reform or policy continuity, are always conducted within structured contexts. Firstly, policy decisions are embodied in programs and practices that, by their very nature, are institutionalised in rules that operate at several levels (see Chapter 3). Thus, explanations of policy change and stability need to take into account the rules and practices of organisations, which themselves are shaped by the interplay between complex systems – socio-economic, technological, organisational and environmental (see Chapter 2). Secondly, in democratic regimes, explanations of policy change also need to address issues of leadership in mobilising organisational and network support for various options, conservative or radical. Key policy actors – whether government leaders, public sector managers and diverse stakeholders – will typically exhibit a spectrum of views about the feasibility and desirability of modifying existing practices. Thirdly, explanations need to address the capabilities of public decision makers to select appropriate policy instruments and to undertake the 'steering' required to orchestrate the cross-organisational arrangements necessary to achieve agreed public purposes.

While many issues are handled through incremental fine-tuning (Lindblom, 1979), some of the big policy problems facing modern societies require concerted efforts and new thinking. Reformers argue for development of robust and enduring responses rather than cosmetic adjustments. Major crises and new challenges may spark the opportunity for innovation in policy goals, methods and partnerships. The Great Depression of the 1930s provided the seedbed for the emergence of Keynesian macro-economic policies with an expansionary role for the state, a paradigm that gradually achieved substantial dominance for several decades. The economic recessions of the 1970s provided opportunities for a shift towards neo-liberal approaches, marked by a more constrained view of the state's role, privatisation of public assets, and the adoption of corporate business models in public management and service delivery (see Chapter 4).

The scholarly study of public policy and governance has always taken a strong interest in explaining both policy shifts and policy stability, or the dialectic of continuity and change. Much of the policy literature has focused on either the political persuasion aspects of policy debate and decision-making ('why' specific policy agendas changed or otherwise); or on the institutional aspects of how the policy system operates under various conditions ('how' specific proposals for policy change were handled and managed in a complex system). These two aspects have been integrated in the conception of a 'policy regime' that comprises the components of a policy arena at any given point in time (May and Jochim, 2013). Key themes include: (a) how specific tools and instruments of public policy and service delivery have been developed, modified, or endured over time; and (b) how the processes for undertaking policy deliberation and governance have been adapted over time.

The study of policy change has been dominated by two complementary approaches. Firstly, many studies have focused on the policy dynamics and processes of particular nation-states[1] (for example, UK, USA, France, Germany, Brazil, and so on), together with the various international organisations and networks in which they participate such as the European Union or the Organisation for Economic Cooperation and Development (OECD). Secondly, other studies have focused on particular policy domains (for example, environment, social welfare, agriculture, technology, economic development, and so on) and their associated policy-process arenas (for example, Brans et al, 2017; Dodds, 2018).

Debates about policy change, and the success factors for achieving policy change, are central to understanding the policy process and deeply affect the outcomes for citizens (Weible et al, 2012). This chapter focuses on the explanatory frameworks that can help account for patterns of policy change and policy continuity. We identify approaches that assist in understanding the impact of diverse contexts and processes in public policymaking. Explanatory frameworks are important for helping us understand how concrete proposals for policy change are either facilitated or constrained, and how policy ideas gain support (or otherwise) from decision makers, policy managers, service providers and stakeholders. We are not seeking an integrated or universal theory of policy change (see Howlett et al, 2016; John, 2018), but rather seeking to examine how policy frameworks help us understand a range of policy scenarios, from business-as-usual through to managing crises and tackling wicked problems.

Explaining policy change in recent scholarship

Policy change has many dimensions, which need to be recognised in considering the nature of policy challenges in the modern era of complex governance. We distinguish here between a focus on: (a) analysis of policy ideas, arguments and persuasion, linked to advocacy, support and leadership; (b) analysis of the intended and actual effects of policy changes; and (c) analysis of the factors that account for change and sustainable outcomes. Policy studies generally focus on explaining policy change in the context of the *interaction* between actors, ideas, interests, institutions and political circumstances. Diverse policy actors seek to influence and persuade others, or exercise power and authority over others, under conditions shaped by previous debates and settlements (Bachrach and Baratz, 1970; Lukes, 2005).

The institutional and ideational contexts have changed significantly in liberal democracies in recent decades. Increasing reliance on outsourced, contractual and networked models of service delivery has stretched the 'internal' policy capacity of national government systems. The rise of New Public Management helped to encourage the creation of a 'policy market', extending beyond the policy platforms of mainstream political parties. Diverse 'external' (non-state) sources of advice have emerged (Craft and Howlett, 2013; Howlett and Migone,

2013), facilitated by the massive growth in digital communications utilised by lobby groups, consultants, think tanks and advocacy organisations (see Chapters 6 and 7).

Scholarly debates on how to explain policy change also reflect a broader debate, underlying all the social sciences, between structural-institutionalist approaches to understanding social and political action, on the one hand, and constructivist-agency focused approaches on the other hand (see Chapter 3). Thus, some policy analysis frameworks tend to emphasise continuity and 'path dependency' (Mahoney, 2000), showing how institutional arrangements and policy settings tend to persist over time, supported by organisational cultures and vested interests. In the 'punctuated equilibrium' variant of this approach (Baumgartner and Jones, 1993), patterns of continuity and change are linked to how political attention is 'disproportionately' focused on certain policy topics and how information is processed in political and policy systems (see Chapter 7). Policies tend to be relatively stable, but punctuated by occasional sharp changes. These changes in policy are typically foreshadowed by changes in policy agendas, priorities and issue framing, such as the new directions arising from a change of government (Baumgartner and Jones, 2005). For example, the Trump administration in the US in 2017 disrupted and overturned established approaches in many areas of social policy and international relations, including such initiatives as reducing the rights of immigrants and introducing high tariffs as an instrument for pressuring trade partners in international treaty renegotiations.

Many academic approaches to policy change emphasise the role of political activists and organisational actors in reinterpreting existing mandates or in mobilising support for change (for example, the 'advocacy coalition framework': Sabatier, 1998). A central feature of the policy process is the building of momentum for policy reforms through issue-based alliances of stakeholders – or conversely, building conservative coalitions to resist change (Sabatier, 2007). Kingdon (1995) claims there are always several policy solutions (or preferred actions) circulating in public debate and that political leaders necessarily focus on just a few issues at a time. Opportunities for policy change may develop when the political and media systems draw attention to issues that are seen to require a high-priority response, and policy brokers and entrepreneurs increase their efforts to join up possible solutions to these salient problems.

Depending on the timescale of the analysis, shifts in policy might be mapped as a series of incremental changes over an extended period, or might be seen as more abrupt changes in direction (for example, urgent responses to perceived crises and challenges). Hence, explanations of change often turn on how key actors interpret and respond to challenges and opportunities in political or socio-economic developments (Hall, 1989; Thelen, 1999). The scope for actors to leverage policy change depends partly on existing bureaucratic practices and organisational cultures, and partly on the capacities of leaders to build coalitions for reform. In all circumstances, ideas and persuasion are central in policy debates and in deliberative decision-making. This requires attention to both the 'structure' and 'agency' perspectives, as outlined previously. In addition, we have argued that systems thinking (Chapter 2) invites us to consider more broadly the nature of the causal processes, emergent situations, and feedback or learning opportunities that shape the way actors interpret and attempt to influence the policy process.

For understanding policy change, we argue for a pragmatic approach that focuses on several factors: the importance of ideas and interests, the role of advocacy and mobilisation, the skills and resources of key actors, and the significance of institutional structures and political contexts – which provide pathways and constraints for various policy debates and outcomes. These debates and associated power struggles occur under conditions of complexity and uncertainty. In this chapter, we consider these factors by examining five themes in the governance and policy-making literature. These themes are selected as being helpful for understanding and addressing the challenges of complexity and uncertainty – the role of policy crises, policy ideas, policy problem 'frames', reasons for success and failure, and the prospects for strengthening policy learning.

Crises and responses to policy challenges

In 2008 the collapse of several prominent banks precipitated an international recession, leading to a decade of fiscal austerity in many countries. A series of cumulative impacts generated negative expectations and accelerated the recession. Recriminations emerged about why regulatory standards and risk management had become so lax in the core financial markets of the US and UK, and why early warning signs had been ignored. Short-term responses included selective bailouts and guarantees for major corporations, while longer-term measures included credit restrictions and tighter prudential standards (Nelson and Katzenstein, 2014; Bell and Hindmoor, 2015). There was a massive debate about the causes of the crisis and the adequacy of proposed solutions. The slow recovery was overshadowed by the politics of austerity, and populist political parties were able to attract increased electoral support. These serious policy challenges were exacerbated in many countries by a large influx of refugees, who were either escaping areas of economic stagnation or fleeing from terrorism and civil wars. As Galston notes (2018: 8): 'concerns about immigration largely drove the Brexit referendum, the 2016 US presidential election, and the gains of far-right parties across Europe'.

Crises and wicked policy challenges tend to undermine established arrangements; as institutions come under stress and demands for action intensify, risks and opportunities emerge for leaders to steer new directions and initiate substantial policy changes (Drennan et al, 2015). Crises are sometimes followed by public inquiries that examine the factors that precipitated the disaster and evaluate the adequacy of crisis responses. Such inquiries can produce evidence and testimony that leads to policy learning and improved crisis readiness. The term 'crisis' denotes a disruptive situation characterised by urgency of decision, large harmful impacts, and raising a discussion of system restructuring (Shrivastava, 1993: 25). There are many policy fields in which crises occur – including financial, ecological, health systems, natural disasters and terrorist violence. And there are many aspects of effective crisis management: coordination, communication, governance, protecting organisational reputation, and so on. Some perceived crises lead to widespread disruption, re-prioritisation of policy attention and the restructuring of state agencies (May et al, 2009). Regardless of whether the issues arise from natural disasters, civil conflict, or poor decision-making by political leaders, a widespread perception of crisis may trigger intense conflict about the nature and causes of the predicament, who is to be blamed for the situation, and debate about appropriate response measures (Boin et al, 2009; Howlett, 2012). The 'blame game' is often a battle between the advocates of contending solutions.

Leaders can sometimes achieve major reforms in a short time frame, more rapidly than could accrue through a series of minor incremental adjustments. The institutionalist approach in policy literature generally emphasises the conditions favouring continuity rather than policy disruption. To the extent that major policy change is truly 'exceptional', rather than a normal everyday occurrence, policy theories need to identify those special circumstances that might facilitate 'switching' or transformative change. The relevant literature highlights how leaders interpret and respond to 'critical junctures' in political or socio-economic developments (Thelen, 1999). In many cases, this may simply mean that changes in government arising from electoral competition will allow new political elites to gain opportunities to implement their different agendas.

Thus, two main styles of explanation for major policy change are evident – one ideational and the other situational. The first explanation (centred on political values and ideologies) takes seriously the value differences embedded in the policy platforms of alternative coalitions within a democratic political system. Changes in policy direction are here seen as the outcome of electoral contestation, especially where there are sharp divergences between the policy promises made by the major political coalitions. The second explanation (situational) depends on the notion of a dramatic trigger event, or 'focusing event' (Birkland, 1998), which calls into question the adequacy of existing policy and planning arrangements. The novel situation provides an opportunity for leaders to shift the policy agenda – for example, by claiming an urgent need for new policy directions to deal with the emerging crisis.

The quality or appropriateness of the policy response depends on many factors, including policy capacity. This capacity includes both individual and organisational skills, resources and commitment to testing alternative options. According to Wu et al, (2015), policy capacity refers to 'the competencies and capabilities important to policymaking' including the deployment of 'analytical, operational and political' skills, and the capabilities for policy work at the 'individual, organisational and system resource levels' (2015: 165). Public managers and advisors also require a clear understanding of government priorities and institutional contexts. Without such understandings, policy workers cannot develop fit-for-purpose policy options. Ideally, robust policy development will serve not only the current needs of government but also provide stewardship of public governance and integrity processes.

Technical skills may be sufficient to examine the causes of failure in a business system or engineering system. But other skills and capacities are essential for managing complex issues in the era of multi-stakeholder partnerships and collaboration to ensure concerted action. New forms of leadership may be needed for policy issues demanding urgent action under conditions of uncertainty. A crisis may provide a trigger for policy change, but effective leadership is necessary to generate new directions and to persuade key partners to work together. Crises linked to volatile and urgent policy issues (such as a sudden influx of refugees) are characterised by fears, emotions and value conflicts that can make resolution very difficult. By their nature, policy responses to these 'wicked' crises are seldom driven by evidence and rigorous analysis. The appraisal of risk and future scenarios is 'not based on strict probability logic and evidence, but on clues, heuristics, and rules of thumb' (Coletti and Radaelli, 2013: 1064), and this is exacerbated by crisis conditions.

While crises might provide conditions under which policy change is facilitated, crises do not necessarily produce effective policy changes, since leaders can make mistakes and ideological approaches may generate unforeseen negative impacts. Moreover, major shifts in policy are not triggered solely by an exogenous shock. Thelen argues that the pace and nature of policy change can be variable, and does not necessarily require external 'shocks' to trigger the possibility of change (Thelen 2004; 2009). She argues that substantial policy change can occur through a variety of channels including through continuous incremental processes. In her model, therefore, 'strategy, conflict, and agency' are always important and 'not just in those rare moments when structures break down entirely' (Thelen, 2009: 493). This perspective is echoed by Taylor (2009), who argues that a preoccupation with policy transformation arising from 'critical junctures' leads us to overlook the significance of incremental adjustments arising through responses to the everyday challenges of governance.

Significant changes in policy paradigms certainly arise from time to time, as shown in the rise of Keynesianism in the 1940s, the rise of feminism, environmentalism and human rights in the 1970s and the rise of neo-liberalism in the 1980s. In some cases, the new paradigms, ideas and practices can substantially displace the previous orthodoxies, but in other cases the new and the old co-exist in ongoing competitions for influence. Successful new policy paradigms involve reframing of goals and methods, and building coalitions of political support. Béland (2007) examined three major episodes in US social security policy reform. Contrary to the 'path dependence' assumptions of scholars who focus on factors that reinforce institutional continuity, Béland argues that systematic attention to ideational processes can shed important light on the nature of policy and institutional changes. For example, in some cases, policy change may be 'layered' onto existing arrangements, whereas in other cases the existing programs and organisations are redirected ('converted') toward new goals over a period of time (Béland, 2007).

Hogwood and Peters (1982) argue that policy reform generally involves policy 'termination', succession or replacement. In some cases, political leaders are determined to terminate an existing policy inherited from a previous government, and they attach symbolic significance to this transition. Deregulation of the economy, and restructuring of welfare programs, have been key areas of conspicuous termination and succession since the 1980s. But in some other cases, policy and organisational arrangements persist over time even where a government has introduced new directions (Jordan et al, 2013). This continuity might be partly explained by the influence of political coalitions attached to these older arrangements (Geva-May, 2004). These dynamics operate differently across time and place. The public sector in most western countries was substantially restructured in the 1980s and 1990s (New Public Management, market-based policy instruments, outsourcing of service delivery, and so on), especially when incoming governments had clear control over budgetary and legislative programs. Other policy areas are subjected to ideological and political reversals – for example, President Trump has followed a policy 'dismantling' agenda – especially on environment protection (Dennis, 2018).

The role of policy ideas

Policy ideas fuse together the issues, goals and solutions in public policy discussion. Policy ideas shape and motivate policy debates and political advocacy. In liberal democracies with relatively open communication and debate, there is a robust marketplace in policy ideas. Policy ideas are already embedded in existing programs, and filter how actors assess the feasibility of new alternatives. Policy ideas that are not currently being advocated can remain potentially influential; many such ideas are stored in a virtual policy warehouse,[2] readily available to be revived, refreshed, extended and re-circulated. The persuasive capabilities required for policy advocacy, brokering and entrepreneurship are widely distributed across modern policy systems. Think tanks, business lobbies, community non-government organisations (NGOs), consultancies, research centres, media channels and government policy units are all actors in the policy market. Taking policy ideas seriously can illuminate the likely outcomes of policy change and the challenges faced by leaders and managers.

How do ideas gain traction and shape policy change? The contexts of policy debate and decision-making in open democratic countries are dynamic. Because policy debates have increasingly been focused on 'selling' ideas, the role of 'policy entrepreneurs' and brokers has been more widely examined in policy analysis, especially in the US and several other OECD countries (Kingdon, 1995; Mintrom and Norman, 2009; Mintrom and Luetjens, 2017). Policy activists and entrepreneurs exhibit a range of roles and strategies for influencing policy debate. In water policy, for example, these roles have included developing new ideas, selling and advocating these ideas, building advocacy coalitions, identifying windows of opportunity, selecting appropriate policy venues for maximising influence and managing support networks (Huitema and Meijerink, 2010). There are many factors determining the relative success or failure of the policy ideas promoted by entrepreneurial individuals and organisations, and their success is situationally contingent. Clearly there are factors related to the skills of the actors, the timing of available opportunities, the resources available and the formation of coalitions supporting various viewpoints. Prominent individuals (for example, policy 'celebrities' of high standing) can sometimes be successful in specific circumstances but they can also fail badly in other cases (Beeson and Stone, 2013).

Policy ideas range from entrenched defence of the status quo to various arguments for change. Conservatives generally accept the need for micro-adjustments to maintain social stability, whereas reformers generally seek bold new goals and directions. New policies are always shaped through new formulations of policy ideas. Given the centrality of policy competition and contestation within the democratic policy-making process, the role of policy ideas has attracted considerable attention in recent scholarship. Relevant ideas or beliefs include broad values (for example, appeals to equity and fairness, or appeals to religious and cultural identity), as well as more specific preferences for certain policy instruments (for example, redistributive taxation, market-based mechanisms and voluntary codes of practice).

A rich 'interpretivist' school of analysis has highlighted the role of ideas, values, mentalities and meanings that are constructed by diverse policy actors – whether individuals or organised groups (see Fischer, 2003; Hajer and Wagenaar, 2003; Colebatch, 2006b; Schmidt, 2008; Zittoun, 2009; Colebatch et al, 2010; Fischer and Gottweis, 2012). The interpretivist approach highlights the importance of narratives, persuasion and agenda setting as essential features of policy debate, whether directed toward preserving the status quo or challenging it. The beliefs, motivations and values of individuals and groups are seen as embedded in everyday practices within networks and organisations. But these beliefs and practices are not fixed; they are subject to ongoing modification and development by actors in the course of interpreting and managing emergent situations, threats and opportunities (Weick, 1995; Yanow, 1996; Kay, 2009; Bell, 2011; Boswell, 2013). In cases of value disagreements and intractable disputes, group processes to mediate discussion can lead to imaginative new thinking (Schön and Rein, 1994).

The binary tension in policy studies between structural and ideational explanations needs to be resolved in order to achieve well-grounded explanations of policy change and policy continuity. Some writers have argued that these binary oppositions are artificial and that ideas are the essential medium through which actors interpret situational contexts, construct views about their interests and formulate their preferred courses of action (Stewart, 2009; Béland and Cox, 2011; Mehta, 2011; Smith, 2013; 2014). Other writers have made pragmatic attempts to deal with these complexities by distinguishing between the political, administrative and ideational dimensions of policy change. From this perspective, policy reform ideas (for example, Keynesianism in the 1940s or neo-liberalism in the 1980s) can be seen to have gained traction under three conditions: when the policy ideas themselves were coherent and compelling, when key political parties and leaders provided strong support and when the administrative agencies have had the capacity to implement the new strategies (Hall, 1989; Lieberman, 2002). Yet others have argued for a two-way-influence conception of policy systems, in which contexts always 'matter', but the relevant situations and institutions are themselves always in flux because of the value-driven actions and struggles among the actors (Schmidt, 2009; Taylor, 2009; Bell, 2011; Pollitt, 2013).

The importance of policy ideas also arises in another context. There has been much research in recent decades on the use of 'evidence-based' policy ideas. In many countries there has been increased public investment in data collection and program evaluation, and improved processes for accessing reliable evidence in policymaking. The 'evidence-based policy' movement seeks to optimise the use of research evidence to improve the quality of policy decisions and improve the effectiveness of program implementation (Cairney, 2016; Head, 2016). Many ideas for policy reform are pitched at an operational design level (is there evidence that a proposed instrument will produce the desired result?); whereas other ideas for policy reform are pitched at a macro cultural-ideological level (is this proposal consistent with core social values?). The rationalist notion that scientific evidence can or should displace political interests and democratic priorities is naïve (Majone, 1989). We argue that policy arguments and policy ideas, not data and evidence more narrowly, are the currency of policy debate and serve to structure the decisions about government programs. The central challenge is not so much to enlarge the 'scientific' basis of decision-making processes, but rather to seek better governance of decision-making. As Sheila Jasanoff puts it, the central focus needs to be on: 'how to exercise power with reason, how to make good decisions in the face of epistemic as well as normative uncertainty, and how to strike an accountable balance between the sometimes conflicting pressures of knowledge and norms' (Jasanoff, 2015: 1724).

The co-existence or even fusion of science and values in policy debate is evident in all dimensions of the policy process, from scoping the problem, debating the options, through to evaluating current programs and reviewing experience elsewhere. Much of the disagreement about policy problems and solutions is anchored in value differences. In this regard, the policy literature has provided important insights into how the debates on problem 'framing' are not only widespread but are also essential to achieving high-quality and feasible policy solutions.

Conflicts in framing policy problems

Modern policy debates seem to be marked by both complexity and polarisation. The mass influx of refugees from the Middle East and Africa into Europe in the last decade, and the politically exaggerated concerns of the Trump administration about Mexicans entering the US, have drawn attention to the polarisation of views about the nature of complex social problems and appropriate ways to resolve such problems. Mass migration movements can be interpreted either as security threats to host countries or as humanitarian crises for the victims of civil war or persecution. In the same way, people enmeshed in long-term unemployment can be seen either as unwilling to adapt to new opportunities and develop relevant skills, or seen as the unfortunate byproduct of system failures and structural change.

In seeking to understand policy change (and efforts to resist change), the scholarly literature has convincingly shown that the framing of problems is fundamental. In other words, a better understanding of how 'policy problems' are conceptualised, prioritised and contested can provide a solid platform for understanding the dynamics of policy debate, policy decision-making and policy change. This insight applies at all levels, from the micro and local levels through to the macro and international levels. The way in which policy problems are defined and scoped is central to political and ideological debates (Dery, 1984; Gusfield, 1989; Peters, 2005).

The definition of a policy problem is not self-evident; indeed, the scholarship of 'problem framing' has become an exercise in de-mystification. It is essentially about problematising how policy problems are defined, debated and acted upon (Schön and Rein, 1994; Bacchi, 2009; 2012; van Hulst and Yanow, 2016). The analysis of how policy actors frame problems allows scholars to gain a closer understanding of the effects produced by different ways of framing policy issues, and understanding whose interests underlie particular framings. By interrogating or questioning the common-sense meanings and values that are embedded in claims about policy problems and solutions, it is possible to clarify and reveal the underlying interests, ideological positions and cultural assumptions. Thus, the way issues are framed is often controversial. Modern processes for the media framing of complex issues are strongly influenced by governmental and economic power, but also subject to debate and counter-vailing pressures.

Peters (2005) focuses on how 'problems' emerge in a particular context, and how they are interpreted by various actors in the light of issue history, the balance of key participants, and the dominant ideologies and interests. The way a problem is framed has a large bearing on the way that solutions (including tools and instruments) are selected by key actors, including the preferences of organisational actors such as government agencies, business and community stakeholders. The way a problem is defined is closely tied to the type of solution that is proposed (Peters, 2005; Bacchi, 2009). For example, if poverty is seen as an individual-centred problem, generated largely by deficits in personal skills and motivation, the solutions proposed will be oriented toward encouraging individuals to develop their skills and work-orientation. By contrast, if poverty is primarily seen as an enduring structural feature of society, generated by economic systems and market forces, the solutions proposed are likely to be oriented toward social security, employment programs and income safety-nets.

The contest over problem definitions and priorities generates the public policy agenda. This agenda-setting process is crucial, because it shapes the selection of issues deemed worthy of attention, the ways in which they are considered and the nature of solutions regarded as feasible and supportable. Agenda setting involves the exercise of power and influence, understood as a contest of ideas and priorities. There are key phases in policy debate where the nature and scope of problems are intensely debated (Dery, 1984), but the subsequent decisions seldom resolve the issues permanently. Agenda-setting and framing contests are continuous and iterative, providing a background to the policy decision-making process in which choices are made from among contending policy ideas.

In filtering out some proposed courses of action and favouring others, framing contests have significant consequences. In environmental policy, for example, the debate over how to construe 'sustainable development' has been bitterly polarised between pro-growth advocates and those seeking to protect environmental and social values and to minimise threats of irreversible harm (Adger and Jordan, 2009; Dovers and Hussey, 2013; Schandl and Walker, 2017). In this context, there has been heated debate about the policy triggers for invoking the 'precautionary principle' – which essentially requires that high-risk projects (for example, industrial projects or medical technology innovations) should not be authorised to proceed in the absence of scientific research demonstrating there are no long-term adverse impacts (Ravetz, 2004; Van Asselt and Vos, 2006; Stirling, 2008; Metz and Ingold, 2017).

The dynamics of each policy field are different, including how open or closed is the inner circle of stakeholders and decision makers, and what forms of evidence are used in policy arguments. The central role of policy framing and reframing is widely understood by the actors in each policy field, along with their tactics in providing supportive evidence to buttress their preferred policy stance. Numerous cases have shown how this proceeds in policy areas marked by emotion and controversy. In foreign policy and defence policy, for example, the restricted and secretive processes and the need for urgent decisions can lead to rapid shifts. The analyses of the US and UK engagement with Iraq (and the role of advisers and intelligence services in filtering information about key issues such as the existence of weapons of mass destruction) suggest that the objectives of public policy changed over time as the strategic and operational context changed (Jamieson, 2007; Houghton, 2008; Thomas, 2017).

Similar adjustments to changing external realities have been evident in the shifting policy frames for 'processing' displaced people who are seeking asylum or refugee status. At various times, such people have been positively welcomed as tragic victims of oppressive regimes, while at other times demonised as illegal immigrants who should be separated from civil society in remote locations (Boswell, 2009). In relation to climate policy frames, there are deeply contrasting perspectives including denial that problems exist. Dewulf (2013) found there were serious differences in policy framing across three key dimensions: (1) the tension between adaptation and mitigation perspectives; (2) the contrast between framing climate challenges as tame technical problems, as against wicked policy governance problems; and (3) the framing of climate policy as a state security issue, rather than centred on human well-being and security.

In examining the nature of policy frames and policy issues, it is evident that many of the big issues are marked by complexity, uncertainty and diversity of viewpoints – these are 'wicked' policy problems (Rittel and Webber, 1973; Head and Alford, 2015). Some issues are more complex and contested than others – they seem to be chronic, persistent and intractable. Policy framings of 'wicked' and intractable problems – such as refugee immigration, illicit drugs, or sustainable development – are closely linked to the ideological worldviews and value preferences of policy actors. This means that such issues are less amenable to resolution through data analysis and appeals to scientific evidence. However, such issues can dominate the policy agenda owing to public controversy and media pressures.

Policy changes addressing wicked issues are usually partial, tackling only a small piece of the problem. Changes are often driven through new political leaders who make electoral commitments to specific solutions, for example, 'tough on drugs', 'control our borders', and so on. The prominence of ideological doctrines in relation to wicked policy problems suggests that policy outcomes on such matters are primarily generated by political conflict around polarised electoral commitments. Dryzek (1983) cautioned some decades ago that the politics of complexity and uncertainty sometimes seem to 'crowd out' professional policy analysis. Instead, he argues, *more* analysis and more discussion are required to deal with the politics of complexity and uncertainty. These deeper forms of analysis must extend well beyond choosing between 'pre-specified' technical instruments (1983: 345) that can only address one aspect of these complex problems. We agree with Dryzek that evidence-informed debate is crucial for addressing issues with higher levels of complexity and uncertainty.

Success and failure in policy design and change

According to Howlett (2011), policy design is about creating and implementing effective policies that produce desired results. In other words, decision makers should formulate and implement policies that 'work'. In the real world of policymaking, however, the choices made by decision makers are often not informed by best-available evidence – rather, the policy decisions are formulated on the basis of emotional fears, cultural identities, economic interests and personal or ideological preferences. A classic example of policy failure is the UK 'poll tax' introduced by the Thatcher government in 1990 as a local government financing measure, following several years of high-level political manoeuvring to replace local rates; the measure was poorly conceived and highly unpopular, and was withdrawn in 1991 (John, 1999; King and Crewe, 2013, Chapter 4). In this example, Ministers clearly set the policy agenda, determined the preferred option and suffered the electoral backlash. In other cases, policy bureaucracy is likely to play a larger role in researching options, analysing risks and preparing advice on feasibility and likely outcomes.

The literature on policy success and failure has centred on three sets of criteria: managerial effectiveness, the policy outcomes for clients and the electoral implications for political elites (McConnell, 2010a; 2010b). In other words, policy success requires the administrative competence of responsible agencies (managing the programs in a timely and efficient manner); the delivery of the intended services or outcomes for citizens; and ultimately the political-electoral rewards for the government (McConnell, 2015). In a similar fashion, policy effectiveness or success is claimed to be assessable on three dimensions: technical, operational and political (Wu et al, 2015). Firstly, a good policy design must demonstrate that it is technically equipped to achieve the desired objectives. Secondly, the policy design should pay attention to operational feasibility in specified contexts, and be mindful of how costs and benefits fall on various groups. Finally, it should be recognised that a single policy instrument will seldom operate alone, but will co-exist with competing and potentially inconsistent goals and instruments (Wu et al, 2015). Careful attention should be paid to be sequencing and interaction effects of the instruments. The composition of 'policy mixes' (Howlett, 2014; Rogge et al, 2017) also raises concerns about the coherence and consistency of public policy within a specific country and its fitness for purpose. For example, a study of crisis management institutions in six European countries found a significant diversity in policy responses, with different mixes of coercive, coordinative and cooperative arrangements (Christensen et al, 2016a).

Policies are more likely to 'work' when there is clarity among stakeholders and decision makers about the nature of the problems and about the likely impact of various options. But this is less likely with complex and controversial policy issues. The policy literature has increasingly focused on the design and communication challenges of turbulent policy issues, where responsibilities are ambiguous and entangled. Ackoff and others have examined policy fields that are 'messy' in this sense (Ackoff, 1974; Ney, 2009; Roe, 2013). Generally, the recommended approaches are collaborative and procedural in the first instance, aiming to bring the disputants together; rather than urging a cognitive-driven approach that calls for 'more science', and gathering a vast store of information. In some policy fields, collaborative networks (Chapter 3) may play a useful support role in brokering policy improvement on difficult topics (Klijn and Koppenjan, 2015).

The various scales of problem complexity are important for policy analysis and decision. At a specific or micro level, one narrow component of a broad issue can be carved out for close consideration. For example, in relation to traffic congestion, it is possible to use CCTV to monitor traffic flows and link these data to algorithms governing traffic signal systems, thereby optimising traffic flow within the existing road network. Here, the scope of the problem is well defined within agreed technical parameters, derived from experimental results from engineering studies under various scenarios. A workable consensus can be achieved about technical knowledge and problem-solving, but only if the overall problem ('congestion') is defined narrowly in terms of technical considerations about the role of information technology.

At a more complex level – the design of policy programs – it is evident that relevant knowledge needs to be much deeper and more nuanced than experimental research can provide. Program evaluations are highly prized as a systematic and focused type of appraisal and assessment (Head, 2016), but the knowledge required to understand the dynamics of program management and civic outcomes may be complex (Stewart and Jarvie, 2015). Depending on the multiple behavioural relationships within each program, a mix of research knowledge, practitioner knowledge and citizen experience will be needed. In public health, for example, policies to reduce obesity have drawn on a range of measures (information, incentives, regulation), and have sought to influence a wide diversity of stakeholders – children, parents, teachers, health practitioners, food retailers and food producers (Clarke et al, 2016). The perspectives of key stakeholders are essential elements of the knowledge required both for mapping the dimensions of the problem and for implementing cooperative measures to tackle the causes and impacts of obesity.

Some discussions of policy change fall within the realm of managing 'normal' problems – those with known levels of risk and known outcomes, as identified by trusted experts. On the other hand, addressing larger complex problems must engage with diverse perspectives about risks, causality and policy effects. Complex problems require expanding our conception of how to generate useful knowledge, drawing upon the collaboration of an 'extended peer community' (Funtowicz and Ravetz, 1999). Inclusive or participatory methods are recommended for producing and constantly reviewing the provisional knowledge that is produced (Ravetz, 2004). Where policy innovation is required but the traditional tools of program development seem insufficient, there has been increasing support for collaborative design methods (Bason, 2014; Torfing, 2019) as a method for exploring creative solutions. The intent is to seek effective policy innovation through collaborative approaches (Hartley et al, 2013; Crosby et al, 2017). While the feasibility and effectiveness of collaboration under various conditions has been keenly debated in the policy literature, there is agreement on the need for reliable and relevant stakeholder knowledge for effective policy design.

Policy learning and policy change

In principle, policy decisions and program outcomes should improve over time as a result of better evidence and learning from experience. However, few scholars and practitioners believe that this optimistic narrative is widely applicable in practice. In some cases, necessary policy changes are blocked by vested interests or resisted by political elites concerned to protect their ideological worldview. In other cases, effective policy options are well known (for example, to address homelessness) but are not pursued because the government has other priorities for investment. In other cases the policy settings to address a challenge are manifestly inadequate, such as the regulatory response to the global financial crisis that emerged in 2008 (Nelson and Katzenstein, 2014; Bell and Hindmoor, 2015). In other complex cases, such as policies intended to benefit and protect Indigenous minority peoples in Canada, the US and Australia (Stewart and Jarvie, 2015; Maddison, 2016), the most effective policy options are implicitly ruled out because they would entail high levels of self-determination by the stakeholders.

Learning in professional contexts can be understood as increasing one's capacity to take effective action (Kim, 1993). However, 'learning' can occur at many levels (individual, organisational, institutional system). Different actors are likely to 'learn' multiple lessons, in different ways, and with diverse consequences. Accounts of policy-relevant learning need to clarify 'who learns, what they learn, and the effects of learning on subsequent policies' (Bennett and Howlett, 1992). Important connections between policy learning and policy reform have been widely asserted in the policy studies literature (Dunlop and Radaelli, 2013; 2017; Heikkila and Gerlak, 2013). And yet there has been little emphasis on 'learning' in most accounts of policy change.

An optimistic perspective is that individuals, organisations and systems can learn from experience, including learning about effective methods for building support as well as cognitive learning from engagement with evidence and reasoned argumentation. Differences nevertheless arise on what counts as sound 'evidence' and how trusted knowledge can be used in generating policy ideas and policy recommendations. A pessimistic perspective, on the other hand, is that 'learning' is so tainted by partisan interests, emotions and ideologies that any improvements in policy settings would seldom be the result of 'learning'. This perspective is reinforced by the widespread rejection of rationalist evidence-based models of how policymaking actually occurs. Thus if 'politics rules', and if emotional slogans generally prevail over reasoned arguments, then the prospects of policy learning are diminished. A realist perspective might conclude that learning is uneven and subject to competing forces, including entrenched power structures; but that progress in policy learning is possible when strategic alliances can be formed among groups committed to improving and embedding reliable knowledge about policy effectiveness.

Three arenas of policy learning might be suggested. Firstly, in the political sphere, leaders and activists might learn from experience about which political tactics and political communications are more effective or more popular (this is not our focus here). Secondly, program evaluations commissioned by public agencies (sometimes using external experts) gather relevant evidence, examine past performance and provide suggestions for improvements. Here, there are clear examples of policy learning over time. For example, improved road safety has arguably resulted from stronger standards and enforcement; governments note these improvements, learn from each other, and a new paradigm is consolidated. Thirdly, public inquiries (independent policy reviews, including investigations of policy disasters) typically engage with stakeholders, experts and the public concerning the causes and consequences of the crisis, examine similar cases, and make recommendations to prevent a recurrence of the failures (Stark, 2018).

Organisations have variable capacities to identify and work with best-available evidence. Even in instances where policy learning has been formally distilled through a process of inquiry and synthesis (for example, a Commission of Inquiry investigating a crisis – see Chapter 8), the lessons may be only partly implemented and codified in new practices, and covert resistance may continue. Moreover, the rationale underlying policy reforms may become dissipated over time. Lessons learned by one cohort of managers and leaders may weaken through the rapid turnover of personnel. Leaders may not have the skills and commitment to inculcate the lessons through mentoring and induction programs. Thus, policy learning is incomplete and dispersed, and lessons are often forgotten over time or deliberately suppressed for partisan reasons (Stark and Head, 2019).

Policy learning is often identified with the evaluation phase of the policy process, and review activities can also be provoked by legislative requirements for regulatory impact statements and by sunset clauses in legislation. But the importance attached to evidence-based review and program evaluation is highly variable across policy systems (Head, 2016). In most countries, the quantum of policy evaluation reporting is quite low. Importantly, even when agencies are committed to the use of rigorous evidence in everyday policymaking, decision-making is heavily constrained by the dominant policy paradigms that guide the direction of government or agency activities (Stevens, 2011; Wilkinson, 2011; Maybin, 2015).

Alternatively, one of the most common short cuts for policy learning is 'borrowing' policy ideas from elsewhere. It is common for states to copy and adapt programs already implemented by similar or neighbouring states. Empirical studies of how policy adoption occurs (Evans, 2004; Benson and Jordan, 2011; Shipan and Volden, 2012), indicate that the intuitive attractiveness of the policy ideas to decision makers is often more important than careful assessment of the conditions enhancing a successful transfer from one national context to another. Policy transfer or policy diffusion can operate through many channels (Dolowitz and Marsh, 2000). Examples include transnational networks and international organisations that promote gender equity (True and Mintrom, 2001), or humanitarian peacekeeping principles (Betts and Orchard, 2014), or educational testing regimes (OECD, 2018). Large consultancy firms with advisory roles in privatisation programs have also been influential in policy transfer; and international development banks have been significant actors in imposing financial reforms in developing countries. In the case of international development aid, the delivery of pre-packaged programs may be convenient for the donor country but may ignore the on-ground context of needs and capacities in the receiving country. For example, when detailed projects (for example, in governance reform, infrastructure or health care) are not working, this may be because 'the fundamental approach is (contextually) wrong' (Pritchett and de Weijer, 2010: 42).

Policy learning, or the construction of policy 'lessons', always occurs under conditions of ambiguity and complexity. These conditions are 'normal' in modern public policymaking. Political leaders and their parties can contribute to ambiguity even when they are striving for particular policy changes. As noted by Schneider and Ingram (1997:

82–4), policy goals can be framed broadly or narrowly, they can be variously framed to appeal to different constituencies and they can serve symbolic or hortatory functions. Policy learning therefore operates in inconsistent ways for leaders, organisations and policy systems.

A frequently observed feature of policy debate is the role of advocacy groups favouring particular solutions (Kingdon, 1995). Rather than invest considerable time and effort in data analysis and the comparative evaluation of options, these groups (recently termed 'instrument constituencies') argue strongly for pre-established solutions – such as specific regulations, market incentives, or standards (Voß and Simons, 2014; Béland and Howlett, 2016; Simons and Voß, 2018). The policy design challenge sometimes takes the appearance of a 'battle of solutions' rather than a debate about the nature of the problem and the evidence concerning measurable improvements. In short, the process for undertaking policy development should be calibrated to the nature of the issues under consideration; and approaches that may be suitable for narrow technical problems are not suitable for broader challenges.

Conclusions

This chapter has reconsidered the utility of classic accounts of policy dynamics and policy change in addressing complex policy problems. To understand policy change, we argued for a pragmatic approach that provides insights into understanding and addressing complexity and uncertainty. Such an approach encompasses the importance of ideas and interests, the role of advocacy and mobilisation, the skills and resources of key actors and the opportunities and constraints provided by institutional structures and political contexts. Policy debates and associated power struggles occur under conditions of complexity where knowledge is fragmented and the consequences of action are uncertain. We have considered these challenges by examining five themes in the governance and policy-making literature. These themes were selected as helpful for addressing the challenges of complexity and uncertainty – the role of policy crises, policy ideas, policy problem 'frames', reasons for success and failure and the prospects for strengthening policy learning.

The institutional contexts of these arguments and decisions are central, and policy theories need to be rooted in institutional understandings. As Frederickson noted 20 years ago:

> It is public administration that is responding to structural and contextual dynamics – the problems of jurisdictions

> and systems disorder, unpredictability and instability. It is no surprise therefore, that theories which explain behaviour under such circumstances come from modern public administration. These theories have much less to do with markets, competition, and individual choice, and more to do with theory of institutions and forms of natural and voluntary cooperation. . . . public administration is naturally interjurisdictional, networked, and comfortable in the new world of governance. (Frederickson 1999: 710)

There is a mass of data and evidence available for policy actors to utilise. But many voices contend in the policy debates typical of the modern 'governance' era. Leaders and stakeholders constantly seek to influence the policy agenda and shape the issues by asserting their interests and strongly felt perspectives. Scientific research plays a subdued role in shaping and activating policy debate. But the capacity for collaboration and reasoned debate seems a necessary foundation for effective policy change under modern conditions of complexity and populist partisanship.

Notes

[1] See the series of country studies in the International Library of Policy Analysis: https://policypress.co.uk/international-library-of-policy analysis.
[2] We prefer this notion of a 'policy warehouse' to the standard metaphor of an organisational 'garbage can' as popularised through the writings of James March and colleagues (for example, Cohen et al, 1972).

10

Reconsidering policy – *our agenda revisited*

Introduction

Analysis of public policy is a daunting task. The esteemed Canadian writer Richard Simeon acknowledged this some decades ago when he rejected the emphasis on narrow analytical policy skills (Simeon, 1976), and instead called for a broad analytic approach that is 'holistic and contextually situated' (Skogstad and White, 2017: 666). However, over the last 40 years, policy approaches have fractured and scattered rather than become holistic and integrated, with theorists attempting to make sense of this variety by identifying strands or families of theory, or proposing models for, or thematic approaches to, theoretical synthesis (Ayres and Marsh, 2013). Some are driven into narrow areas of specialisation where they build sub-fields that, in our view, lose efficacy and relevance for complex problem-solving solving insofar as they neglect broader political and systemic contexts. However, not all policy analysis is concerned to assist with problem-solving and improved policy, as we are in this book, nor concerned with our focus on the governance of wicked problems, crisis responses and the building of more resilient, effective policy contexts.

Our book is inspired by the conviction that useful knowledge comes from building on various sources of policy analysis expertise, while also recognising the wider context of policymaking, and the value of policy theories anchored in evaluative, empirical and comparative case studies. We have also argued that policy studies should refocus on state capacity, and on the roles of politics, policy and institutions in building capacity to effect positive change. We are interested in policy change and policy improvement because of the persistence of challenging problems, like climate change, massive inequalities in health and housing, cyber security, urban congestion and the like – and the longstanding failure of states and policy processes to alleviate or resolve them. We are interested in resilience in the face of crises and in new forms of governance, often collaborative, and the reinvention of the state that is inspired by policy evaluation, learning and adaptation.

We believe, as applied theorists, that policy studies should be relevant to problem-solving. We suggest that making policy analysis relevant requires an understanding of theory and practice, but also engagement with political and institutional structures, processes and systems. We have attempted this by interrogating both policy theory and practice, and by taking a conceptual approach to the issues of policy, politics and governance in the context of contemporary problems.

Simeon (1976) noted that the problem with policy analysis in the 1970s was its narrow and somewhat technical focus on improving policy-settings rather than taking a broader focus on understanding the policy system as a whole, with its messy mix of power, conflict and ideology. The common failing of analysis was to either 'focus on the environment of policy making while ignoring the political process, or on the process while neglecting the policy setting' (Simeon, 1976: 556). Our reconsideration of policy offers a corrective to narrow approaches. Each of our chapters reconsiders policy either at the 'deep' level, which is broad and contextual (policy systems, institutions, the state and borders), or at the 'policy-in-action' proximate level (advice, information, implementation and policy change). The theoretical and conceptual discussions in Chapters 2 to 5 are drawn upon when we reflect on policy in more practical, applied circumstances in Chapters 6 to 9. This approach retains strong empirical relevance, while avoiding 'adjectival' or sectoral policy analysis that can subsume the state, and enables us to reflect, realistically, upon the challenges of evaluation and policy change. We link up policy and governance (implemented action) on the one hand and the state (structured authority) on the other in an approach we have called systemic institutionalism. Each chapter depicts earlier iterations of policy thought, and relates them not only to the complexity of current problems, but also to the immense changes that have occurred in the 21st century.

In this chapter we review our findings and offer recommendations for future research.

Complexity, governance and the state

We have observed that, while policy problems and their circumstances have grown in complexity (Cairney and Geyer, 2015), decision makers and analysts have struggled to develop models and frameworks to assist in understanding the policy dynamics and contributing insights for more effective action. The world in which policy actors seek their preferred futures is an increasingly complex one, not only in the immediate contexts of multilevel issues and multiple arenas, but also arguably in the wider sense of institutional and ecological systems. Although 'systems thinking' has a long, somewhat convoluted history in the policy sciences, we suggest in Chapter 2 that it has the ability to move beyond the specifics of policy problems to identify and depict underlying complexity. It is an approach that foregrounds context, politics and institutions, policy actors; and examines the interconnections, not only between actors, but also between different systems and subsystems. It holds, as Rittel and Webber (1973) did nearly 50 years ago, that policy systems are dynamic, and susceptible to disruption by stakeholders or by other systems, and it draws attention to evaluation, learning, adaptive responses and change. We are beginning to see adaptive responses to the complexity agenda in policy practice, for example in the recognised need for collaborative capacity, for appropriate complex policy instrumentation mixes, and for novel local flexibility options in policy implementation and evaluation processes.

Governance theory (for example, R.A.W. Rhodes, 2007) attempts to make sense of complex social and organisational arrangements, emphasising stakeholder networks and deliberative processes that add new dimensions to policy formation while also creating new challenges. While we appreciate that governance theory threw new light on complexity, connectivity, inclusion of a broad range of policy actors, and new ways of managing policy, we also canvass some shortcomings. Governance studies usefully show us some features of the adaptive state's response to more complex policy circumstances, and governance theory could be itself adapted to acknowledge the centrality of state agencies and state capacity. However, it seems to have largely lost its connection with politics, power, interests and ideas, which, we have observed, are the lifeblood of any active polity, and it has also neglected engagement with those issue-specific policy processes and contexts that are fundamental to policy outcomes and success (Howlett and Ramesh, 2016). We have also argued that governance theory has failed to engage substantially with the big political economy questions underlying the state's battles to contain the massive disruptive forces of late capitalism. The rise of populism, for example, is a massive political disruption that offers a credible threat to 'the assumptions of the governance paradigm and its claim to identify new practices of governing fitted to the needs of the twenty-first century' (Stoker, 2019: 4).

Our concern with problem-solving also has us questioning whether governance-inspired deliberation and connectivity can produce workable policy, in a world where relevant knowledge and authority are outflanked by political, ideological and populist partisanship. Governance analysis has preferred to overlook and decontextualise the role of the state, its authority, its boundaries and its capacities. States remain enduring political institutions that enjoy a monopoly of formal, legal authority over political communities marked by clear borders. Public policy can be seen as the endorsed roadmap or guide for the use of state power to improve outcomes, and this quest for effective public policy is therefore directly related to issues of state capacity. Because we are interested in problem-solving in complex environments, we find the governance concept far more useful to assess ongoing adaptations within the liberal democratic state than as a descriptive label for a novel phenomenon counterpointed to government.

Towards better outcomes

Following Lasswell, we have argued that good analysis is a means of improving policy design, process and practice (Dunn, 2018). By good analysis, we mean a conceptualisation of public policy that links policy actions more precisely with their effects, through an enhanced understanding of the interconnecting systems involved. In particular, we have emphasised the value of lesson learning, not only from successful programs but also from the many instances of policy failure (Peters, 2015b). Although our book reconsiders various aspects of policy theory, its approach is pragmatic and realist with a view to informing and encouraging improved practice. We believe that the issues of better policy design and better policy process remain fundamental, in particular in light of the overwhelming burden of unresolved social and environmental policy challenges. Our approach has been to question the adequacy of governance theorising in terms of theoretical and practical responses to complex problems and crises, while drawing attention to the key functions, and changing roles, of the state in policymaking and problem-solving. Our search for better, or improved, policy processes and outcomes has required a review of policy theory, and has suggested that systems-based analysis is an important mode of inquiry for bringing together the insights from policy studies and governance literature.

Chapter 2 explains that the policy world has changed with an upsurge in complexity-related problems (Cairney and Geyer, 2015). The chapter argues that complexity and systems thinking go hand in hand; with both focusing on incremental feedback, learning, adaptation and adjustment. From an overall systems perspective, public policy is the principal avenue for public-sector responsiveness to changing economic, social and political events. Systems-based analysis also acknowledges the reality of the dispersed nature of the governance landscape. In Chapter 3, we view this schema from an institutional perspective, outlining the ways in which institutions both constrain and enable policy action. The challenges facing policymakers in these circumstances are clear. We see from both policy analysts and from practitioners that innovative, collaborative, flexible and adaptive institutions and processes are the key to pursuing better policy, using, where necessary, networked institutional arrangements (Ansell, 2008). The extent to which networks and stakeholder engagement are required will depend on the nature of the problem, the configuration of stakeholders and matters like inclusivity, expertise, security and confidentiality. Some issues – such as setting interest rates by central banks – depend on good information and independent decision-making, rather than on collaborative networks. We also note that as service delivery models evolve, and traditional institutions develop hybridised approaches to improving outcomes, policy scholars have come to recognise a 'hard-soft', 'formal-informal' institutional dynamism. The changing context of the state is significant. In Chapter 4, we argue that reconsidering the state from a policy perspective suggests an ontology that acknowledges both the strength of autonomous institutions and their varied interactions with civil society. We observe that policy challenges and crises are ushering in new, more complex governance arrangements in search of improved policy processes and outcomes that nevertheless enhance, rather than diminish, the power of the state (Bell and Hindmoor, 2009).

In Chapter 5 we acknowledge that domestic policy problems, such as health and environment, spill over into the international arena, and that cooperative, cross-border policy efforts are often required at the regional and multi-lateral level. This casts implementation analysis in a novel light. We have argued that empirically grounded case study analysis is a key to improved policy, and this is true of both cross-border and domestic policy implementation. Given the enforcement obstacles in extra-territorial policymaking, states are required to relate to each other in much the same ways as states must deal with non-state interests in domestic policymaking. The resulting relational dynamics, which may sometimes include the involvement of civil society, are critical to effective implementation. We have observed, however, that there are many policy and regulatory areas where states are able to cooperate routinely and effectively without the need for civil society actors.

In Chapters 6 and 7, we see the impact on policy advice and information of challenging and contested circumstances, with the consequence that expert knowledge has become more of a disputed commodity in the governance era. Policy advising no longer commands the respectful attention it once did, in circumstances where advice is increasingly politically determined and subject to adversarial opinion-formation. There are no simple solutions to these obstacles to improved policy. Chapter 7 argues that understanding the critical role of information (as distinct from data) is crucial, a point which reinforces the role of evaluation and review. Without input from rigorous evaluation, the policy and service systems will produce effects, which might be inadequate or far from those intended. In Chapter 8 we observe that where flexibility, collaboration and innovation are required for good implementation, project management arrangements need to be adapted to reflect these requirements, despite the strictures of traditional audit approaches that emphasise clear specification and predictability (National Audit Office, 2015). Systems thinking certainly points to the limits of simplistic approaches to implementation. Fresh approaches to implementation scholarship, and a renewed emphasis on managing for results in a complex environment, are crucial to achieving improved policy outcomes in the governance era.

The emphasis in the policy literature on policy failures begs the question of how to achieve positive policy change. In Chapter 9 we observe that the failure of policy systems to learn and to develop more effective policies, for example, in response to climate change, is a major indicator of their capacity, or lack of capacity, for good governance. For understanding policy change, we suggest a pragmatic approach that focuses on several factors: the importance of ideas and interests, the role of advocacy and mobilisation, the skills and resources of key actors and the significance of institutional structures and political contexts – which provide pathways and constraints for various policy debates and outcomes.

Future research options

Given that we are reconsidering not recasting policy theory, we have attempted throughout to identify neglected areas of scholarship, and to point to potential areas of future research. Academic careers in policy research may advance in differing directions, with many scholars keen to specialise by way of making their mark. We have attempted to travel in another direction. We have drawn attention to the broad, politicised, messy, contested, value-laden context of policymaking, and argued that investigating the relationship between the state and society is essential. We have also argued for a reconsideration of systems theory as a way of expanding our understanding of the relationships through which policies, particularly in complex circumstances, achieve their effects. Policy scholars often talk of systems descriptively, in terms, for example, of outlining the features of political systems, policy advisory systems, policy domains, networks or subsystems. Empirical studies that employ systems-based complexity thinking to illuminate actual policy events have been rare, and scholars have been more likely to use 'complexity' as a heuristic (exploratory device), rather than for deeper analysis. Does systems thinking add value to policy analysis? We argue in Chapter 2 that systems thinking, when done well, will bring important perspectives for a better understanding of the problem we are dealing with.

In Chapter 3 we identify scope for scholars to empirically test the claims of governance theory, just as the policy community and network scholars had previously tested the claims of traditional institutional accounts of government decision-making. If networks are characteristic of new institutionalist practice (Bevir, 2009: 112), how do they form; how do they operate; how central or peripheral is the state; do they have a policy impact; are they real or theoretical constructs? And crucially, how can interaction between formal and informal networks/institutions be characterised? We have seen that conflict, norms and values can reshape or redefine domestic and international policy and institutions, which suggests that institutional origins, design, failure and change should be the focus of future research. To characterise our approach, we have suggested the term systemic institutionalism. Similarly in Chapter 4 we suggest that accounts of the disaggregated state could be empirically tested, as well as comparatively tested, by comparing domain-specific policymaking across multilevel architectures. We have also proposed that the concept of boundary spanning policy regimes (Jochim and May, 2010), previously applied to domestic policy arrangements, could be employed to investigate cross-border policy in order to obtain greater purchase on intergovernmental fora, as well as the more fluid situations of international governance (Chapter 5) that have been emphasised by much recent scholarship.

Greater attention should also be paid to the formation and communication of problem-solving evidence-based advice in contemporary governance and systems-based domains. Policy advisory scholarship is gaining momentum and undertaking varied empirical investigations. From our perspective, however, it could give more attention to addressing the political, process and the efficacy dimensions of advice-giving in terms of advice uptake and actual problem-solving. Two frameworks are suitable for application: Heinrich's (2005) advisory typology, and Hoppe and Wesselink's (2014) framework for policy advisory boundary work (Chapter 6). In Chapter 7, we emphasise the role of information in the production of better policy. We see scope for research using the novel informational 'lens' to discern new themes and approaches to old problems. Policy learning, evaluation, evidence-based policy and agenda setting could all be re-examined using this approach that is distinct, say, from media studies or freedom of information research. A politically informed, policy-relevant informational approach could examine the understudied role of the media and new social media in sustaining information flows and affecting decisions. Another area ripe for research is the neglected role of information technology in shaping, constraining or facilitating policies where there may be trade-offs between costs, security, policy utility and change.

In Chapter 8 we argue that implementation analysis should mirror the complex implementation landscape and with it the demand for collaborative capacity, while also asking how much collaboration is actually necessary or new. Empirical research could test such claims that have emerged in governance theory. Nevertheless, scholars also need to explore the capabilities required for program delivery in multiple actor environments within and beyond government (O'Toole, 1986). Any relationships between the traditional managerial 'implementation' literature and the large reservoirs of knowledge encompassed by governance studies and complexity studies could be examined. We argue that scholars need to undertake empirical studies on the efficacy of implementation instruments in complex, multi-actor, networked circumstances in order to identify the design failures that underlie weak performance. Complexity is no reason for abandoning aspirations for improved policy design and outcomes. In Chapter 9 we describe the study of policy change as a robust field focused on policy shifts and policy stability. We advocate a pragmatic analytic approach that provides insights into complexity and uncertainty, while again emphasising ideas and interests, advocacy and mobilisation, the skills and resources of key actors, and any political and institutional opportunities and/or constraints.

The challenges of change

Our concerns with complex policy, wicked problems, crises and improved outcomes leads in each of our chapters and more fully in Chapter 9 to a consideration of policy change. We believe there is a strong case for more research to be framed in this way. While there has always been strong policy and governance-based research about policy stability and change, the roles played by systems, politics and institutions in engendering change have been neglected. We have argued for a refocusing upon these roles, and upon state capacity, because these are not secondary features of the policy system or background context, but rather central elements of problem-solving that deserved recognition in analysis. Our systems approach introduces novel considerations of policy change, not least because systems interact constantly with their environment, such that any changes in the environment will likely cause a change in the system under consideration. This raises issues of what is predictable in a policy system or subsystem, what is irregular, what precipitates change, what the differences are between systems, and in each case we should attempt to explain how and why these dynamics occur. We have called policies 'change interventions', some of which will certainly operate broadly across a policy system, but many of which are more targeted, locally led micro-interventions.

Policy analysis has been grappling with institutional change in the policy environment, as we observe in Chapter 3; policy and governance theorists have well depicted the dynamism in the problem-solving, policy-shaping roles of institutions. New institutional literature, in its many iterations, points to the new norm of constant change. We have seen how values, behaviours, narratives and indeed policies, influence and reshape institutions in order to promote flexibility and adaptation and to overcome failure. We have nevertheless argued that the rise of new institutionalism is itself a symptom of growing complexity in problems and policymaking, including the obstacles to policy change. Change remains difficult to achieve in the absence of a crisis or exogenous shock to shake path dependency. Change is then yet another slippery, contested and multi-dimensional concept. Unlike much policy scholarship, we have argued that an important driver of contemporary policy change results from rethinking the nature of the state, its organisational forms, its objectives and its capacities. Chapter 4 argues that because we live in fast-moving, fluid and turbulent political-economic times, the pace of social and technological changes makes any stable parametric assumption for policymaking hazardous. Adaptive governance has emerged in response, as is widely acknowledged, but the resilient state remains the foundation.

Having integrated change as a key focus of our reconsideration of policy at the deeper level of systems, institutions, the state, and policy/territorial borders, we reconsider change more descriptively at the policy-in-action level in our later chapters. For example, we describe change in terms of changing policy environments and practices, especially the roles that expert advice, information, deliberation and lesson learning can play in policymaking. Chapters 6 and 7 describe changes in the policy advisory context, and the rise of socialised, politicised and mediatised policy knowledge at the expense of evidence-based policy and scientific expertise. Not all policy change can be seen as problem-solving when the dismantling of key policy domains and imposing constraints upon future policy action result from such interventions, as future research will no doubt begin to demonstrate. Policy change, or the lack of it, then assumes broader political and ideological dimensions that must increasingly feature in analysis, given the rise of populism. We also discern the systemic effects of broader change on the quality of policymaking and implementation, such as the loss of policy knowledge in public agencies, the turnover of staff positions, and the increase in contract staff.

The study of policy change has particular utility for examining contemporary problems and their contexts. We can interrogate and reflect upon change strategies – for example, incrementalism as a response to uncertainty, adaptive governance as a response to crisis, or lesson learning as a pragmatic approach to harvesting prior experience. We can reflect upon institutional change, the rise of new, informal institutions, the intriguing formal-informal institutional interface, and the extent to which this operates within or beyond the realm of the state. We have also observed, with our emphasis upon complexity, that the forms and dimensions of change itself are constantly changing, not least so as the connection between politics and policy in the Internet age becomes more immediate, less predictable, and commentary on policy issues can become everyone's business. Finally, we have asked throughout this book how it is that policies fail to change in the face of large challenges, such as climate change, and whether policy scholars are paying sufficient attention to be able to discern the lessons learned.

Conclusions

Our reconsideration of policy studies has been inspired by the need for theorists and practitioners to keep pace with a rapidly changing world, and for policy studies to be revitalised through critical engagement with classic core ideas and a reconsideration of traditional themes. We are interested in a richer, more historically informed portrayal of policy studies, not only in terms of revisiting basic concepts, but also in advancing policy studies systematically, with recommendations for improved practice. We argue the need for a strengthened analytical toolbox in order to create better understanding and design to deal with real world problems. Ours is a broad approach. We reconsider policy at the 'deep' contextual level (policy systems, institutions, the state and borders), and at the 'policy-in-action' proximate level (advice, information, implementation and policy change). We revisit traditional, neglected and emergent scholarship, seeking to better explain business-as-usual policy, crisis management, adaptive responses and the tackling of wicked problems in various contexts from domestic to global. Our approach is realist and pragmatic, informed by our own experiences of policymaking and analysis, and will hopefully inspire debate about the role of policy scholars in understanding and helping to address the complexity, uncertainty and contestability of contemporary problems.

References

6, P. (2003) 'Institutional viability: a neo-Durkheimian theory', *Innovation: The European Journal of Social Science Research*, 16(4): 395–415.

6, P. (2015) 'Governance: if governance is everything, maybe it's nothing', in A. Massey and K. Johnston (eds) *The International Handbook of Public Administration and Governance*, Cheltenham: Edward Elgar, pp 56–80.

ABC (Australian Broadcasting Commission) (2010) 'Angry crowd burns copy of Murray-Darling report'. Available at: www.abc.net.au/news/2010-10-13/angry-crowd-burns-copy-of-murray-darling-report/2296638.

Abrams, J.B., Knapp, M., Paveglio, T.B., Ellison, A., Moseley, C., Nielsen-Pincus, M. and Carroll M.C. (2015) 'Re-envisioning community-wildfire relations in the U.S. West as adaptive governance', *Ecology and Society*, 20(3): 34. Available at: www.ecologyandsociety.org/vol20/iss3/art34/.

Ackoff, R. and Emery, F. (1972) 'Structure, function and purpose', in F. Emery (ed) *Systems Thinking: Volume One Selected Readings*, Harmondsworth: Penguin.

Ackoff, R.L. (1974) *Redesigning the Future*, New York: Wiley.

Adger, W.N. and Jordan, A. (eds) (2009) *Governing Sustainability*, Cambridge: Cambridge University Press.

Adger, W.N., Hughes, T.P., Folke, C., Carpenter, S.R. and Rockström, J. (2005) 'Social-ecological resilience to coastal disasters', *Science*, 309(5737): 1036–9.

Allison, H. and Hobbs, R. (2004) 'Resilience, adaptive capacity, and the "lock-in trap" of the Western Australian agricultural region', *Ecology and Society*, 9(1): 3.

Althaus, C., Bridgman, P. and Davis, G. (2007) *The Australian Policy Handbook* (4th edn), Sydney: Allen & Unwin.

Anderson, B. (1983) *Imagined Communities: Reflections on the Origin and Spread of Nationalism*, London: Verso Books.

Andrews, M., Pritchett, L. and Woolcock, M. (2017) *Building State Capability: Evidence, Analysis, Action*, New York: Oxford University Press.

Ansell, C. (2008) 'Network institutionalism', in R.A.W. Rhodes, S.A. Biner, and B.A. Rockman (eds) *Oxford Handbook of Political Institutions*, Oxford: Oxford University Press, pp 75–89.

Ansell, C. and Geyer, R. (2017) '"Pragmatic complexity" a new foundation for moving beyond "evidence-based policymaking?"', *Policy Studies*, 38(2): 149–67.

Antunes, C., Dias, D., Dantas, G., Mathias, J. and Zamboni, L. (2016) 'An application of soft systems methodology in the evaluation of policies and incentive actions to promote technological innovations in the electricity sector', *Energy Procedia*, 106: 258–78.

APSC (Australian Public Service Commission) (2007) *Tackling wicked problems: a public policy perspective*, Canberra: APSC. Available at: www.apsc.gov.au/tackling-wicked-problems-public-policy-perspective.

Armitage, A. (1995) *Comparing the Policy of Aboriginal Assimilation in Australia, Canada and New Zealand*, Vancouver: University of British Colombia Press.

ASQA (Australian Skills Quality Authority) (2016) *Annual Report 2015–16*, Canberra: ASQA.

Atun, R. (2012) 'Health systems, systems thinking and innovation', *Health Policy and Planning*, 27: 4–8.

Australian National Audit Office (ANAO) (2014) *Successful implementation of policy initiatives: better practice guide*, Canberra: ANAO. Available at:www.tannerjames.com/Articles/ANAO-BPG-Policy-Implementation.pdf .

Axelrod, R. and Cohen, M. (2000) *Harnessing Complexity: Organizational Implications of a Scientific Frontier*, New York: Basic Books

Ayres, I. and Braithwaite, J. (1992) *Responsive Regulation: Transcending the Deregulation Debate*, Oxford: Oxford University Press.

Ayres, S. and Marsh, A. (2013) 'Reflections on contemporary debates in policy studies', *Policy and Politics*, 41(4): 643–63.

Bacchi, C. (2009) *Analysing Policy: What's the Problem Represented to Be?*, Sydney: Pearson Education.

Bacchi, C. (2012) 'Why study problematizations? Making politics visible', *Open Journal of Political Science*, 2(1): 1–8.

Bachrach, P. and Baratz, M. (1962) 'The two faces of power', *American Political Science Review*, 56(4): 947–52.

Bachrach, P. and Baratz, M. (1970) *Power and Poverty: Theory and Practice*, Oxford: Oxford University Press.

Bale, T. and Bergman, T. (2006) 'Captives no longer, but servants still? Contract parliamentarism and the new minority governance in Sweden and New Zealand', *Government and Opposition*, 41(3): 422–49.

Banerjee, S.G., Oetzel, J.M. and Ranganathan, R. (2006) 'Private provision of infrastructure in emerging markets: do institutions matter?', *Development Policy Review*, 24(2): 175–202.

Bannister, F. (2005) 'The panoptic state: privacy, surveillance and the balance of risk', *Information Polity*, 10(1,2): 65–78.

Barber, M. (2008) *Instruction to Deliver: Fighting to Transform Britain's Public Services* (revised edn), London: Methuen.

Barber, M. (2015) *How to Run a Government*, London: Allen Lane.

Barbier, E. (2015) 'Policy: Hurricane Katrina's lessons for the world', *Nature*, 524(7565): 285–87.

Bardach, E. (1977) *The Implementation Game*, Cambridge, MA: MIT Press.

Bardach, E. (2001) 'Implementation: political', in N. Smelser and P. Bales (eds) *International Encyclopaedia of the Social and Behavioral Sciences*, New York: Macmillan, XI: 7234–7.

Barrett, S.M. and Fudge, C. (1981) *Policy and Action: Essays on the Implementation of Public Policy*, London: Methuen.

Barzelay, M. and Gallego, R. (2006) 'From "new institutionalism" to "institutional processualism": advancing knowledge about public management policy change', *Governance*, 19(4): 531–57.

Bason, C. (ed) (2014) *Design for Policy*, London: Gower.

Bauer, J. (2004) *Governing the networks of the information society: prospects and limits of policy in a complex technical system*, St Louis: Federal Reserve Bank of St Louis.

Bauman, Z. (2000) *Liquid Modernity*, Cambridge: Polity Press.

Baumgartner, F. and Jones, B. (1993) *Agendas and Instability in American Politics*, Chicago: University of Chicago Press.

Baumgartner, F. and Jones, B. (2005) *The Politics of Attention: How Government Prioritizes Problems*, Chicago: University of Chicago Press.

Baumgartner, F. and Jones, B. (2015) *The Politics of Information: Problem Definition and the Course of Public Policy in America*, Chicago: University of Chicago Press.

Beeson, M. and Stone, D. (2013) 'The changing fortunes of a policy entrepreneur: the case of Ross Garnaut', *Australian Journal of Political Science*, 48(1): 1–14.

Behn, R.D. (2003) 'Why measure performance? Different purposes require different measures', *Public Administration Review*, 63(5): 586–606.

Behn, R.D. (2017) 'How scientific is "the science of delivery"?', *Canadian Public Administration*, 60(1): 89–110.

Béland, D. (2007) 'Ideas and institutional change in social security: conversion, layering, and policy drift', *Social Science Quarterly*, 88(1): 20–38.

Béland, D. (2009) 'Ideas, institutions and policy change', *Journal of European Public Policy*, 16(5): 701–18.

Béland, D. (2017) Identity, Politics, and Public Policy, *Critical Policy Studies*, 11(1): 1–18.

Béland, D. and Cox, R.H. (eds) (2011) *Ideas and Politics in Social Research*, New York: Oxford University Press.

Béland, D. and Howlett, M. (2016) 'How solutions chase problems: instrument constituencies in the policy process', *Governance*, 29(3): 393–409.

Bell, S. (2011) 'Do we really need a new "constructivist institutionalism" to explain institutional change?', *British Journal of Political Science*, 41(4): 883–906.

Bell, S. and Hindmoor, A. (2009) *Rethinking Governance: The Centrality of the State in Modern Society*, Cambridge: Cambridge University Press.

Bell, S. and Hindmoor, A. (2015) *Masters of the Universe, Slaves of the Market*, Cambridge, MA: Harvard University Press.

Bell, S., Hindmoor, A. and Mols, F. (2010) 'Persuasion as governance: a state-centric relational perspective', *Public Administration*, 88(3): 851–70.

Bellamy, J., Head, B.W. and Ross, H. (2017) 'Crises and institutional change: emergence of cross-border water governance in Lake Eyre Basin, Australia', *Society and Natural Resources: An International Journal*, 30(4): 404–20.

Benbow, S.M. (2008) 'Failures in the system: our inability to learn from inquiries', *Journal of Adult Protection*, 10(3): 5–13.

Bennett, C.J. and Howlett, M. (1992) 'The lessons of learning: reconciling theories of policy learning and policy change', *Policy Sciences*, 25(3): 275–94.

Benoit, E. (2003) 'Not just a matter of criminal justice: states, institutions, and North American drug policy', *Sociological Forum*, 18(2): 269–94.

Benson, D. and Jordan, A. (2011) 'What have we learned from policy transfer research?', *Political Studies Review*, 9(3): 366–78.

Bentley, T. and Wilsdon, J. (2003) *The Adaptive State: Strategies for Personalising the Public Realm*, London: Demos Foundation.

Bernanke, B.S. (2004) *The great moderation*, Speech at Eastern Economic Association, Washington DC, 20 February. Available at: www.federalreserve.gov/boarddocs/speeches/2004/20040220/default.htm.

Bernstein, S. (2002) 'International institutions and the framing of domestic policies: the Kyoto Protocol and Canada's response to climate change', *Policy Sciences*, 35(2): 203–36.

Betts, A. and Orchard, P. (eds) (2014) *Implementation and World Politics: How International Norms Change Practice*, Oxford: Oxford University Press.

References

Bevir, M. (2009) *Key Concepts in Governance*, London: Sage.

Beyer, J.M. (1997) 'Research utilization: Bridging a cultural gap between communities', *Journal of Management Inquiry*, 6(1): 17–22.

Birkland, T. (2007) *Lessons of Disaster: Policy Change After Catastrophic Events*, Washington DC: Georgetown University Press.

Birkland, T.A. (1998) 'Focusing events, mobilization, and agenda setting', *Journal of Public Policy*, 18(1): 53–74.

Blom, T. and Vanhoonacker, S. (2014) 'The politics of information: a new research agenda', in T. Blom and S. Vanhoonacker (eds) *The Politics of Information: The Case of the European Union*, Cheltenham: Edward Elgar, pp 1–14.

Blume, G., Scott, T. and Pirog, M. (2014) 'Empirical innovations in policy analysis', *Policy Studies Journal*, 42(1): S33–S50.

Blyth, M. (2002) *Great Transformations: Economic Ideas and Institutional Change in the Twentieth Century*, Cambridge: Cambridge University Press.

Bodin, Ö. and Crona, B.I. (2009) 'The role of social networks in natural resource governance: what relational patterns make a difference?', *Global Environmental Change*, 19(3): 366–74.

Boin, A., 't Hart, P. and McConnell, A. (2009) 'Crisis exploitation: political and policy impacts of framing contests', *Journal of European Public Policy*, 16(1): 81–106.

Boswell, C. (2009) *The Political Uses of Expert Knowledge: Immigration Policy and Social Research*, Cambridge: Cambridge University Press.

Boswell, J. (2013) 'Why and how narrative matters in deliberative systems', *Political Studies*, 61(3): 620–36.

Bouckaert, G. (2017) 'Taking stock of "governance": a predominantly European perspective', *Governance*, 30(1): 45–52.

Bovens, M. and Zouridis, S. (2002) 'From street-level to system-level bureaucracies: how information and communication technology is transforming administrative discretion and constitutional control', *Public Administration Review*, 62(2): 174–84.

Bovens, M., 't Hart, P. and Peters, B.G. (eds) (2001) *Success and Failure in Public Governance: A Comparative Analysis*, Cheltenham, UK: Edward Elgar.

Boxelaar, L., Paine, M. and Beilin, R. (2006) 'Community engagement and public administration: of silos, overlays and technologies of government', *Australian Journal of Public Administration*, 65(1): 113–26.

Braithwaite, J. (1999) 'Accountability and governance under the new regulatory state', *Australian Journal of Public Administration*, 58(1): 90–94.

Braithwaite, J. (2006) 'The regulatory state?', in R.A.W. Rhodes, S.A. Binder, and B.A. Rockman (eds) *The Oxford Handbook of Political Institutions*, Oxford: Oxford University Press, pp 111–30.

Brans, M. and Rossbach, S. (1997) 'The autopoiesis of administrative systems: Niklas Luhmann on public administration and public policy', *Public Administration*, 75 (Autumn): 417–39.

Brans, M., Geva-May, I. and Howlett, M. (eds) (2017) *Routledge Handbook of Comparative Policy Analysis*, London: Routledge.

Brinkerhoff, D.W. (2005) 'Rebuilding governance in failed states and post-conflict societies: core concepts and cross-cutting themes', *Public Administration and Development*, 25(1): 3–14.

Brinkerhoff, D.W. (2014) 'State fragility and failure as wicked problems: beyond naming and taming', *Third World Quarterly*, 35(2): 333–44.

Brown, A. (2004) 'Authoritative sense-making in a public inquiry report', *Organization Studies*, 25(1): 95–112.

Brunnée, J. and Streck, C. (2013) 'The UNFCCC as a negotiation forum: towards common but more differentiated responsibilities', *Climate Policy*, 13(5): 589–607.

Brunner, R.D. (2010) 'Adaptive governance as a reform strategy', *Policy Sciences*, 43(4): 301–41.

Buchanan, J. (1988) *The Political Economy of the Welfare State*, Stockholm: The Industrial Institute for Economic and Social Research.

Burridge, A., Gill, N., Kocher, A. and Martin, L. (2017) 'Polymorphic borders', *Territory, Politics and Governance*, 5(3): 239–51.

Burstein, P. and Bricher, M. (1997) 'Problem definition and public policy: congressional committees confront work, family and gender, 1945-1990', *Social Forces*, 75(4): 135–69.

Busenberg, G. (2004) 'Adaptive policy design for the management of wildlife hazards', *American Behavioral Scientist*, 48(3): 314–26.

Butler, M. and Allen, P. (2008) 'Understanding policy implementation processes as self-organizing systems', *Public Management Review*, 10(3): 421–40.

Cairney, P. (2012a) 'Complexity theory in political science and public policy', *Political Studies Review*, 10(3): 346–58.

Cairney, P. (2012b) *Understanding Public Policy: Theories and Issues*, Basingstoke London: Palgrave Macmillan.

Cairney, P. (2016) *The Politics of Evidence-Based Policymaking*, London: Palgrave.

Cairney, P. and Geyer, R. (eds) (2015) *Handbook on Complexity and Public Policy*, Cheltenham: Edward Elgar.

Cairney, P. and Heikkila, T. (2014) 'A comparison of theories of the policy process', in P. Sabatier and C. Weible (eds) *Theories of the Policy Process*, Boulder: Westview Press, pp 363–89.

Callaghan, H. (2010) 'Beyond methodological nationalism: how multilevel governance affects the clash of capitalisms', *Journal of European Public Policy*, 17(4): 564–80.

Campbell, J.L. (2004) *Institutional Change and Globalization*, Princeton: Princeton University Press.

Campbell, J.L. and Hall, J.A. (2015) *The World of States*, London: Bloomsbury.

Capling, A. (2001) *Australian and the Global Trading System*, Cambridge: Cambridge University Press.

Carey, G., Crammond, B. and Riley, T. (2015) 'Top-down approaches to joined-up government: examining the unintended consequences of weak implementation', *International Journal of Public Administration*, 38(3): 167–78.

Carney, M. (2018) 'Leave no dark corner', *Foreign Correspondent* 18 September. Available at: www.abc.net.au/news/2018-09-18/china-social-credit-a-model-citizen-in-a-digital-dictatorship/10200278.

Cash, D.W., Clark, W.C., Alcock, F., Dickson, N., Eckley, N. and Jäger, J. (2002) *Salience, Credibility, Legitimacy and Boundaries: Linking Research, Assessment and Decision-making*, Cambridge, MA: Kennedy School of Government, Harvard University.

Castells, M. (2004) 'Informationalism, networks and the network society: a theoretical blueprint', in M. Castells (ed) *The Network Society: A Cross-cultural Perspective*, Cheltenham: Edward Elgar, pp 3–48.

Castells, M. and Cardoso, G. (eds) (2006) *The Network Society: From Knowledge to Policy*, Washington, DC: Johns Hopkins Center for Transatlantic Studies.

Castles, F. (ed) (1993) *Families of Nations*, Brookfield Vt: Dartmouth.

Castles, F. (2007) 'Testing the retrenchment hypothesis: an aggregate overview', in F. Castles (ed) *The Disappearing State?*, Cheltenham: Edward Elgar, pp 19–43.

Cerny, P.G. (2010) *Rethinking World Politics: A Theory of Transnational Neo-pluralism*, Oxford: Oxford University Press.

Chaffin, B., Gosnell, H. and Cosens, B. (2014) 'A decade of adaptive governance scholarship: synthesis and future directions', *Ecology and Society*, 19(3): 56.

Chandy, L. (2011) 'Fragile states: problem or promise?', Washington D.C.: Brookings Institution. Available at: www.brookings.edu/articles/fragile-states-problem-or-promise.

Chapman, J. (2004) *System Failure: Why Governments Must Learn to Think Differently*, London: Demos.

Checkland, P. and Haynes, M. (1994) 'Varieties of systems thinking: the case of soft systems methodology', *System Dynamics Review*, 10(2–3): 189–97.

Child, J. (1972) 'Organizational structure, environment and performance: the role of strategic choice', *Sociology*, 6(1): 1–22.

Christensen, T., Danielsen, O., Laegreid, P. and Rykkja, L. (2016a) 'Comparing coordination structures for crisis management in six countries', *Public Administration*, 94(2): 316–32.

Christensen, T., Lægreid, P. and Rykkja, L. (2016b) 'Ambiguities of accountability and attention: analyzing the failure of a preventive security project', *Scandinavian Journal of Public Administration*, 20(1): 21–44.

Clarke, J. (2004) *Changing Welfare, Changing States: New Directions in Social Policy*, London: Sage.

Clarke, J. (2005) 'Welfare states as nation states: some conceptual reflections', *Social Policy and Society*, 4(4): 407–15.

Clarke, B., Swinburn, B. and Sacks, G. (2016) 'The application of theories of the policy process to obesity prevention: a systematic review and meta-synthesis', *BMC Public Health*, 16(1084): 1–19.

Clegg, L. (2015) 'Benchmarking and blame games: exploring the contestation of the Millennium Development Goals', *Review of International Studies*, 41(5): 947–67.

Clemens, E.S. and Cook, J.M. (1999) 'Politics and institutionalism: explaining durability and change', *Annual Review of Sociology*, 25(1): 441–66.

Cobb, R.W. and Elder, C.D. (1972) *Participation in American Politics: The Dynamics of Agenda-building*, Baltimore: Johns Hopkins University Press.

Coen, D. and Pegram, T. (2015) 'Wanted: a third generation of global governance research', *Governance*, 28(4): 417–20.

Cohen, M.D., March, J.G. and Olsen, J.P. (1972) 'A garbage can model of organizational choice', *Administrative Science Quarterly*, 17(1): 1–25.

Colebatch, H.K. (2002) *Policy* (2nd edition), Milton Keynes: Open University Press.

Colebatch, H.K. (2006a) *Beyond the Policy Cycle: The Policy Process in Australia*, Sydney: Allen & Unwin.

Colebatch, H.K. (ed) (2006b) *The Work of Policy: An International Survey*, Lanham MD: Lexington Books.

Colebatch, H.K., Hoppe, R. and Nordegraff, M. (eds) (2010) *Working for Policy*, Amsterdam: University of Amsterdam Press.

Coleman, W.D. (2012) 'Governance and global public policy', in D. Levi-Faur (ed) *The Oxford Handbook of Governance*, Oxford: Oxford University Press, pp 673–87.

Coletti. P. and Radaelli, C.M. (2013) 'Economic rationales, learning, and regulatory policy instruments', *Public Administration*, 91(4): 1056–70.

Colley, L.K. and Head, B.W. (2013) 'Changing patterns of privatization: ideology, economic necessity, or political opportunism', *International Journal of Public Administration*, 36(12): 865–75.

Considine, M., Lewis, J. and Alexander, D. (2009) *Networks, Innovation and Public Policy: Politicians, Bureaucrats and the Pathways to Change Inside Government*, Basingstoke: Palgrave Macmillan.

Corfee-Morlot, J., Cochran, I., Hallegatte, S. and Teasdale, P-J. (2011) 'Multilevel risk governance and urban adaptation policy', *Climatic Change*, 104(1): 169–97.

Craft, J. and Halligan, J. (2017) 'Assessing 30 years of Westminster policy advisory system experience', *Policy Sciences*, 50(1): 47–62.

Craft, J. and Howlett, M. (2012) 'Policy formulation, governance shifts and policy influence: location and content in policy advisory systems', *Journal of Public Policy*, 32(2): 79–98.

Craft, J. and Howlett, M. (2013) 'The dual dynamics of policy advisory systems: the impact of externalization and politicization on policy advice', *Policy and Society*, 32(3): 187–97.

Craft, J. and Wilder, M. (2017) 'Catching a second wave: context and compatibility in advisory system dynamics', *Journal of Public Policy*, 45(1): 215–39.

Crosby, B., 't Hart, P. and Torfing, J. (2017) 'Public value creation through collaborative innovation', *Public Management Review*, 19(5): 655–69.

Crouch, C. (2004) 'The state and innovations in economic governance', *The Political Quarterly*, 75(1): 100–16.

Crough, G. and Wheelwright, E. (1982) *Australia, A Client State*, Ringwood: Penguin Books.

Crowley, K. (2004) 'Joined up governance: pushing the youth policy boundaries', *Public Administration Today*, Issue 2: December–February, pp 46–53.

Crowley, K. and Head, B.W. (2017a) 'Expert advisory councils in the policy system', in M. Brans, I. Geva-May and M. Howlett (eds) *Routledge Handbook of Comparative Policy Analysis*, London: Routledge, pp 181–97.

Crowley, K. and Head, B.W. (2017b) 'The enduring challenge of "wicked problems": revisiting Rittel and Webber', *Policy Sciences*, 50(4): 539–47.

Crowley, K. and Nakamura, A. (2018) 'Defining regional climate leadership: learning from comparative analysis in the Asia Pacific', *Journal of Comparative Policy Analysis*, 20(4): 387–403.

Crozier, M. (2008) 'Listening, learning and steering: new governance, communication and interactive policy formation', *Policy and Politics*, 36(1): 3–19.

Crozier, M. (2010) 'Rethinking systems: configurations of politics and policy in contemporary governance', *Administration and Society*, 42(5): 504–25.

Cutler, C. (2003) *Private Power and Global Authority: Transnational Merchant Law and the Global Political Economy*, Cambridge: Cambridge University Press.

Daniell, K. and Kay, A. (eds) (2017) *Multi-level Governance: Conceptual Challenges and Case Studies from Australia*, Canberra: ANU Press.

Davies, H., Nutley, S. and Smith, P. (ed) (2000) *What Works? Evidence-based Policy and Practice in Public Services*, Bristol: Policy Press.

de Greene, K. (ed) (1993) *A Systems-based Approach to Policymaking*, Dordrecht: Kluwer.

Delli Carpini, M.X., Lomax Cook, F. and Jacobs, L.R. (2004) 'Public deliberation, discursive participation, and citizen engagement: a review of the empirical literature', *Annual Review of Political Science*, 7(1): 315–44.

Dennis, B. (2018) 'With a shrinking EPA, Trump delivers on his promise to cut government', *The Washington Post*, 8 September. Available at: www.washingtonpost.com/national/health-science/with-a-shrinking-epa-trump-delivers-on-his-promise-to-cut-government/2018/09/08/6b058f9e-b143-11e8-a20b-5f4f84429666_story.html.

Dery, D. (1984) *Problem Definition in Policy Analysis*, Lawrence, Kansas: University Press of Kansas.

Dewulf, A. (2013) 'Contrasting frames in policy debates on climate change adaptation', *Wiley Interdisciplinary Reviews Climate Change*, 4: 321–30.

Dickinson, H. (2011) 'Implementing policy', in J. Glasby (ed) *Evidence, Policy and Practice: Critical Perspectives in Health and Social Care*, Bristol: Policy Press, pp 71–84.

Dodd, T. (2016) 'Education revenue soars to become Australia's $20 billion export', *Australian Financial Review*, 3 Feb. Available at: www.afr.com/news/policy/education/education-revenue-soars-to-become-australias-20-billion-export-20160203-gmke3k/.

Dodds, A. (2018) *Comparative Public Policy* (2nd edn), London: Palgrave.

Doh, J. (2011) 'Connecting the plots: the contributions of Stephen J. Kobrin to international management research', in C. Asmussen, T. Pedersen, T. M. Devinney, L. Tihanyi (eds) *Dynamics of Globalization: Location-specific Advantages or Liabilities of Foreignness?* (Advances in International Management, Vol 24) Emerald Group Publishing Limited, pp 25–31.

Dolowitz, D. and Marsh, D. (2000) 'Learning from abroad: the role of policy transfer in contemporary policymaking', *Governance*, 13(1): 5–23.

Douglas, M. (1986) *How Institutions Think? Key Line of Inquiry in Social Institutionalism*, London: Routledge, Kegan Paul.

Douglas, M. and Wildavsky, A. (1982) *Risk and Culture*, Berkeley, CA: University of California Press.

Dourish, P. and Bell, G. (2011) *Divining a Digital Future: Mess and Mythology in Ubiquitous Computing*, Cambridge: MIT Press.

Dovers, S. (2005) *Environment and Sustainability Policy: Creation, Implementation, Evaluation*, Sydney: Federation Press.

Dovers, S. and Hussey, K. (2013) *Environment and Sustainability: A Policy Handbook* (2nd edn), Sydney: Federation Press.

Drennan, L., McConnell, A. and Stark, A. (2015) *Risk and Crisis Management in the Public Sector* (2nd edn), London: Routledge.

Dryzek, J.S. (1983) 'Don't toss coins in garbage cans: a prologue to policy design', *Journal of Public Policy*, 3(4): 345–67.

Duit, A. and Galaz, V. (2008) 'Governance and complexity – emerging issues for governance theory', *Governance*, 21(3): 311–35.

Dunleavy, P. and Hood, C. (1993) 'From old public administration to new public management', *Public Money and Management*, 14(3): 9–16.

Dunleavy, P., Margetts, H., Bastow, S. and Tinkler, J. (2006a) *Digital Era Governance: IT Corporations, the State and e-Government*, Oxford: Oxford University Press.

Dunleavy, P., Margetts, H., Bastow, S. and Tinkler, J. (2006b) 'New public management is dead: long live digital-era governance', *Journal of Public Administration Research and Theory*, 16(3): 467–94.

Dunlop, C.A. (2016) 'Knowledge, epistemic communities and agenda setting', in N. Zahariadis (ed) *Handbook of Public Policy Agenda Setting*, Cheltenham: Edward Elgar, pp 273–96.

Dunlop, C.A. and Radaelli, C.M. (2013) 'Systematising policy learning: from monolith to dimensions', *Political Studies*, 61(3): 599–619.

Dunlop, C.A. and Radaelli, C.M. (2017) 'Learning in the bath-tub: the micro and macro dimensions of the causal relationship between learning and policy change', *Policy and Society*, 36(2): 304–19.

Dunn, W.D. (2018) Harold Lasswell and the study of public policy, *Oxford Research Encyclopedia of Politics*, Oxford: Oxford University Press, [doi: https://dx.doi.org/10.1093/acrefore/9780190228637.013.600].

Durlak, J.A. and DuPre, E.P. (2008) 'Implementation matters: a review of research on the influence of implementation on program outcomes and the factors affecting implementation', *American Journal of Community Psychology*, 41(3–4): 327–50.

Durose, C. (2011) 'Revisiting Lipsky: front-line work in UK local governance', *Political Studies*, 59(4): 978–95.

Dwivedi, Y., Kelly, G., Janssen, M., Rana, N., Slade, E. and Clement, M. (2018) 'Social media: the good, the bad and the ugly', *Information Systems Frontiers*, 20(3): 419–23.

Easton, D. (1957) 'An approach to the analysis of political systems', *World Politics*, 9(3): 383–400.

Easton, D. (1965) *A Systems Analysis of Political Life*, New York: John Wiley.

Edwards, M. (2001) *Social Policy, Public Policy: From Problem to Practice*, Sydney: Allen & Unwin.

Edwards, M. (2004) *Social science research and public policy: narrowing the divide* (Policy paper no 2), Canberra: Academy of Social Sciences in Australia.

Egeberg, M. (1999) 'The impact of bureaucratic structure on policymaking', *Public Administration*, 77(1): 155–70.

Ellis-Petersen, H. (2018) 'How palm oil ban has made the EU a dirty word in Malaysia', *The Guardian*, 25 April. Available at: www.theguardian.com/world/2018/apr/26/how-palm-oil-ban-has-made-the-eu-a-dirty-word-in-malaysia.

Eppel, E., Matheson, A. and Walton, M. (2011) 'Applying complexity theory to New Zealand public policy: principles for practice', *Policy Quarterly*, 7(1): 48–55.

Esmark, A. (2011) 'Systems theory', in M. Bevir (ed) *The Sage Handbook of Governance*, London: Sage, pp 91–105.

Esmark, A. (2016) 'The informational logics of liberal democracy: making sense of the nudging agenda', *Information Polity*, 21(2): 123–37.

Eulau, H. (1963) *The Behavioural Presentation in Politics*, New York: Random House.

Evans, M. (ed) (2004) *Policy Transfer in Global Perspective*, Aldershot: Ashgate.

Everett, S. (2003) 'The policy cycle: democratic process or rational paradigm revisited', *Australian Journal of Public Administration*, 62(2): 65–70.

Farrell, H. and Finnemore, M. (2016) 'Global institutions without a global state', in O. Fioretos, T. Falleti, and A. Sheingate (eds) *The Oxford Handbook of Historical Institutionalism*, Oxford: Oxford University Press, Chapter 34, pp 572–89.

Ferlie, E., Fitzgerald, L., McGivern, G., Dopson, S. and Bennett, C. (2011) 'Public policy networks and "wicked problems": a nascent solution', *Public Administration*, 89(2): 307–24.

Fischer, F. (2003) *Reframing Public Policy*, New York: Oxford University Press.

Fischer, F. (2009) *Democracy and Expertise: Reorienting Policy Inquiry*, Oxford: Oxford University Press.

Fischer, F. and Gottweis, H. (eds) (2012) *The Argumentative Turn Revisited*, Durham NC: Duke University Press.

Flyvbjerg, B. (2014) 'What you should know about megaprojects and why: an overview', *Project Management Journal*, 45(2): 6–19.

Forrester, J. (1970) 'Systems analysis as a tool for urban planning', *IEEE Transactions on Systems Science and Cybernetics, SSC*, 6(4): 258–65.

Forrester, J. (1992) 'Policies, decisions and information sources for modelling', *European Journal of Operations Research*, 59: 42–63.

Frederickson, H.G. (1996) 'Comparing the reinventing government movement with the new public administration', *Public Administration Review*, 56(3): 263–70.

Frederickson, H.G. (1999) 'The repositioning of American public administration', *PS: Political Science & Politics*, 32(4): 701–12.

Freeman, J.L. and Stevens, J.P. (1987) 'A theoretical and conceptual examination of subsystem politics', *Public Policy and Administration*, 2(3): 9–24.

Friedman, T. (1999) *The Lexus and the Olive Tree*, New York: Picador.

Fukuyama, F. (1992) *The End of History and the Last Man*, New York: Free Press.

Fung, A. (2006) 'Democratizing the policy process', in M. Moran, M. Rein and R. Goodin (eds) *Oxford Handbook of Public Policy*, New York: Oxford University Press, pp 669–88.

Funtowicz, S. and Ravetz, J. (1999) 'Post-normal science: an insight now maturing', *Futures*, 31(7): 641–6.

Furness, H. (2015) 'Jamie Oliver admits school dinners campaign failed because eating well is a middle class preserve', *Telegraph (UK)*, 24 August. Available at: www.telegraph.co.uk/news/celebritynews/11821747/Jamie-Oliver-admits-school-dinners-campaign-failed-because-eating-well-is-a-middle-class-preserve.html.

Galston, W.A. (2018) 'The populist challenge to liberal democracy', *Journal of Democracy*, 29(2): 5–19.

Geva-May, I. (2004) 'Riding the wave of opportunity: termination in public policy', *Journal of Public Administration Research & Theory*, 14(3): 309–33.

Goodsell, C. (2005) 'The bureau as unit of governance', in P. du Gay (ed) *The Values of Bureaucracy*, Oxford: Oxford University Press, pp 17–41.

Gray, J. (1993) *Post-liberalism: Studies in Political Thought*, Abingdon: Routledge.

Greenwald, G. (2014) *No Place to Hide: Edward Snowden, the NSA and the Surveillance State*, London: Hamish Hamilton.

Gresov, G. and Drazin, R. (1997) 'Functional equivalence in organization design', *The Academy of Management Review*, 22(2): 403–28.

Grigg, N., Walker, B., Capon, A., Foran, B., Parker, R., Stewart, J., Stirzaker, R. and Young, W. (2012) 'System resilience perspective on sustainability and equity in Australia', in M. Raupach et al (eds) *Negotiating our Future: Living Scenarios for Australia to 2050*, Canberra: Australian Academy of Science pp 54–92.

Gunn, L.A. (1978) 'Why is implementation so difficult?', *Management Services in Government*, 33(4): 169–76.

Gupta, A. (2012) *Red Tape: Bureaucracy, Structural Violence and Poverty in India*, Durham NC: Duke University Press.

Gupta, J., Termeer, C., Klostermann, J., Meijerink, S., van den Brink, M., Jong, P., Nooteboom, S. and Bergsma, E. (2010) 'The adaptive capacity wheel: a method to assess the inherent characteristics of institutions to enable the adaptive capacity of society', *Environmental Science and Policy*, 13(6): 459–71.

Gusfield, J.R. (1989) 'Constructing the ownership of social problems: fun and profit in the welfare state', *Social Problems*, 36(5): 431–41.

Haas, P. (1992) 'Introduction: epistemic communities and international policy coordination', *International Organization*, 46(1): 1–35.

Habermas, J. (1975) *Legitimation Crisis*, Boston: Beacon Press.

Hajer, M.A. (2009) *Authoritative Governance: Policymaking in the Age of Mediatization*, Oxford: Oxford University Press.

Hajer, M.A. and Wagenaar, H. (eds) (2003) *Deliberative Policy Analysis*, Cambridge: Cambridge University Press.

Hale, K. (2011) *How Information Matters: Networks and Public Policy Innovation*, Georgetown: Georgetown University Press.

Hall, P.A. (1986) *Governing the Economy: The Politics of State Interventions in Britain and France*, Cambridge: Polity Press.

Hall, P.A. (ed) (1989) *The Political Power of Economic Ideas: Keynesianism Across Nations*, Princeton NJ: Princeton University Press.

Hall, P.A. (1993) 'Policy paradigms, social learning, and the state: the case of economic policymaking in Britain', *Comparative Politics*, 25(3): 275–96.

Hall, P.A. and Taylor, R. (1996) 'Political science and the three new institutionalisms', *Political Studies*, 44(4): 936–57.

Halligan, J. (1995) 'Policy advice and the public sector', in B.G. Peters and D.T. Savoie (eds) *Governance in a Changing Environment*, Montreal: McGill-Queen's University Press, pp 138–74.

Halligan, J. (2010) 'The fate of administrative tradition in Anglophone countries during the reform era', in M. Painter and B.G. Peters (eds) *Tradition and Public Administration*, London: Palgrave Macmillan, pp 129–42.

Hammond, T. (1993) 'Toward a general theory of hierarchy: books, bureaucrats, basketball tournaments, and the administrative structure of the nation-state', *Journal of Public Administration Research and Theory*, 3(1): 120–45.

Hartley, J., Sørensen, E. and Torfing, J. (2013) 'Collaborative innovation: a viable alternative to market competition and organizational entrepreneurship', *Public Administration Review*, 73(6): 821–30.

Hartley, J., Alford, J., Hughes, O. and Yates, S. (2015) 'Public value and political astuteness in the work of public managers: the art of the possible', *Public Administration*, 93(1): 195–211.

Hatton, T. and Young, W. (2011) 'Delivering science into public policy: an analysis of Murray-Darling Basin sustainable needs assessment as a model for impact', *Australian Journal of Public Administration*, 70(3): 298–308.

Hay, C. (2005) 'Making hay … or clutching at ontological straws? Notes on realism, "as-if-realism" and actualism', *Politics*, 25(1): 39–45.

Hay, C. (2006) 'Constructivist institutionalism', in R.A.W. Rhodes, S.A. Biner, and B.A. Rockman (eds) *Oxford Handbook of Political Institutions*, Oxford: Oxford University Press, pp 56–74.

Hay, C. (2014) 'Neither real nor fictitious but "as if real": a political ontology of the state', *British Journal of Sociology*, 65(3): 459–80.

Hay, C. and Wincott, D. (1998) 'Structure, agency and historical institutionalism', *Political Studies*, 46(5): 951–7.

Hay, C. and Lister, M. (2006) 'Theories of the state', in C. Hay, M. Lister and D. Marsh (eds) *The State: Theories and Issues*, Basingstoke: Palgrave Macmillan, pp 1–20.

Hay, C. and Farrall, S. (eds) (2014) *The Legacy of Thatcherism*, Oxford: Oxford University Press.

Haynes, P. (2018) 'Understanding the influence of values in complex systems-based approaches to public policy and management', *Public Management Review*, 20(7): 980–96.

Head, B.W. (2008) 'Three lenses of evidence-based policy', *Australian Journal of Public Administration*, 67(1): 1–11.

Head, B.W. (2015) 'Policy analysis and public sector capacity', in B.W. Head and K. Crowley (eds) *Policy Analysis in Australia*, Bristol: Policy Press, pp 53–67.

Head, B.W. (2016) 'Toward more "evidence-informed" policymaking?', *Public Administration Review*, 76(3): 472–84.

Head, B.W. (2019) 'Forty years of wicked problems literature: forging closer links to policy studies', *Policy and Society*, 38(2): 180–97.

Head, B.W. and Alford, J. (2015) 'Wicked problems: implications for public policy and management', *Administration and Society*, 46(6): 711–39.

Head, B.W. and Crowley, K. (eds) (2015) *Policy Analysis in Australia*, Bristol: Policy Press.

Head, B.W., Ferguson, M., Cherney, A. and Boreham, P. (2014) 'Are policy makers interested in social research? Exploring the sources and uses of valued information among public servants in Australia', *Policy and Society*, 33(2): 89–101.

Heclo, H. (2006) 'Thinking institutionally', in R.A.W. Rhodes, S.A. Biner, and B.A. Rockman (eds) *Oxford Handbook of Political Institutions*, Oxford: Oxford University Press, pp 731–42.

Heidbreder, E.G. (2017) 'Strategies in multilevel policy implementation: moving beyond the limited focus on compliance', *Journal of European Public Policy*, 24(9): 1367–84.

Heikkila, T. and Gerlak, A.K. (2013) 'Building a conceptual approach to collective learning: lessons for public policy scholars', *Policy Studies Journal*, 41(3): 485–513.

Heinelt, H., Sweeting, D. and Getimis, P. (2005) *Leadership and Participation in Cities: Searching for Innovation in Western Democracies*, London: Routledge.

Heinrichs, H. (2005) 'Advisory systems in pluralistic knowledge societies: a criteria based typology to assess and optimize environmental policy advice', in S. Massen and P. Weingart (eds) *Democratisation or Expertise? Exploring Novel Forms of Scientific Advice in Political Decision-making*, Dordrecht, NL: Springer Press, pp 41–61.

Heinz, J.P., Laumann, E.O., Nelson, R.L. and Salisbury, R.H. (1993) *The Hollow Core: Private Interests in National Policy*, Cambridge, MA: Harvard University Press.

Héritier, A. and Lehmkuhl, D. (2008) 'The shadow of hierarchy and new modes of governance', *Journal of Public Policy*, 28(1): 1–17.

Heyman, R. and Pierson, J. (2015) 'Social media, delinguistification and colonization of lifeworld: changing faces of Facebook', *Social Media and Society*, July–December: 1–11.

Higgott, R. (2007) 'International political economy', in R. Goodin, P. Pettit and T. Pogge (eds) *A Companion to Contemporary Political Philosophy* (2nd edn), Oxford: Blackwells, pp 143–82.

Hill, M.J. and Hupe, P.L. (2003) 'The multi-layer problem in implementation research', *Public Management Review*, 5(4): 471–90.

Hill, M.J. and Hupe, P.L. (2014) *Implementing Public Policy* (3rd edn), London: Sage.

Hoard, S. (2015) *Gender Expertise in Public Policy: Towards a Theory of Policy Success*, Basingstoke: Palgrave Macmillan.

Hodge, G., Greve, C. and Boardman, A. (eds) (2012) *International Handbook on Public-private Partnerships*, Cheltenham: Edward Elgar.

Hofferbert, R. (1974) *The Study of Public Policy*, Indianapolis and NY: Bobbs-Merrill.

Hogwood, B.W. and Peters, B.G. (1982) 'The dynamics of policy change: policy succession', *Policy Sciences*, 14(3): 225–45.

Hogwood, B.W. and Gunn, L.A. (1984) *Policy Analysis for the Real World*, Oxford: Oxford University Press.

Hood, C. (1983) *The Tools of Government*, Basingstoke, London: Macmillan.

Hood, C. (2010) *The Blame Game: Spin, Bureaucracy, and Self-preservation in Government*, Princeton: Princeton University Press.

Hoppe, R. and Wesselink, A. (2014) 'Comparing the role of boundary organisations in the governance of climate change in three EU member states', *Environmental Science and Policy*, 44(1): 73–85.

Houghton, D.P. (2008) 'Invading and occupying Iraq: some insights from political psychology', *Peace and Conflict*, 14(2): 169–92.

Howes, M., Wortley, L., Potts, R., Dedekorkut-Howes, A., Serrao-Neumann, S., Davidson, J., Smith, T. and Nunn, P. (2017) 'Environmental sustainability: a case of policy implementation failure?' *Sustainability*, 9(2): 165.

Howlett, M. (2008) 'Beyond good and evil in policy implementation: instrument mixes, implementation styles, and second-generation theories of policy instrument choice', *Policy and Society*, 23(2): 1–17.

Howlett, M. (2011) *Designing Public Policies: Principles and Instruments*, New York: Routledge.

Howlett, M. (2012) 'The lessons of failure: learning and blame avoidance in public policymaking', *International Political Science Review*, 33(5): 539–55.

Howlett, M. (2014) 'From the "old" to the "new" policy design', *Policy Sciences*, 47(2): 187–207.

Howlett, M. and Ramesh, M. (1995) *Studying Public Policy: Policy Cycles and Policy Sub-systems*, Oxford: Oxford University Press.

Howlett, M. and Lindquist, E. (2004) 'Policy analysis and governance: analytical and policy styles in Canada', *Journal of Comparative Policy Analysis*, 6(3): 225–49.

Howlett, M. and Ramesh, M. (2005) 'Policy subsystem configurations and policy change: operationalizing the postpositivist analysis of the politics of the policy process', *Policy Studies Journal*, 26(3): 466–81.

Howlett, M. and Migone, A. (2013) 'Policy advice through the market: the role of external consultants in contemporary policy advisory systems', *Policy and Society*, 32(3): 241–54.

Howlett, M. and Ramesh, M. (2016) 'Achilles' heels of governance: critical capacity deficits and their role in governance failures', *Regulation and Governance*, 10(4): 301–13.

Howlett, M., McConnell, A. and Perl, A. (2016) 'Weaving the fabric of public policies: comparing and integrating contemporary frameworks for the study of policy processes', *Journal of Comparative Policy Analysis*, 18(3): 273–89.

Huitema, D. and Meijerink, S. (2010) 'Realizing water transitions: the role of policy entrepreneurs in water policy change', *Ecology and Society*, 15(2): 26.

Hustedt, T. and Veit, S. (2017) 'Policy advisory systems: change dynamics and sources of variations', *Policy Sciences*, 50(1): 41–6.

ICA (Intelligence Community Assessment) (2017) *Assessing Russian activities and intentions in recent US elections*, ICA 2017-01D. Available at: www.dni.gov/files/documents/ICA_2017_01.pdf.

Immergut, E. (1990) 'Institutions, veto points, and policy results: a comparative analysis of health care', *Journal of Public Policy*, 10(4): 391–416.

Ingold, K. (2011) 'Network structures within policy processes: coalitions, power and brokerage in Swiss climate policy', *Policy Studies Journal*, 39(3): 435–59.

Jamieson, K.H. (2007) 'Justifying the war in Iraq: what the Bush Administration's uses of evidence reveal', *Rhetoric & Public Affairs*, 10(2): 249–73.

Jarvie, W. and Stewart, J. (2011) 'Working with complexity: community engagement and the Murdi Paaki COAG trial 2002–2007', *Australian Journal of Public Administration*, 70(3): 259–74.

Jasanoff, S. (2015) 'Serviceable truths: science for action in law and policy', *Texas Law Review*, 93(7): 1723–49.

Jessop, B. (1990) *State Theory*, Cambridge: Polity Press.

Jessop, B. (2006) 'The state and state-building', in R.A.W. Rhodes, S.A. Binder, and B.A. Rockman (eds) *The Oxford Handbook of Political Institutions*, Oxford: Oxford University Press, pp 407–30.

Jessop, B. (2008) *State Power: A Strategic-relational Approach*, Cambridge: Polity Press.

Jessop, B. (2016) *The State: Past, Present and Future*, Cambridge: Polity Press.

Jochim, A. and May, P. (2010) 'Beyond subsystems: policy regimes and governance', *Policy Studies Journal*, 38(2): 303–27.

John, P. (1999) 'Ideas and interests agendas and implementation: an evolutionary explanation of policy change in British local government finance', *British Journal of Politics and International Relations*, 1(1): 39–62.

John, P. (2016) 'The policy agendas project: a review', *Journal of European Public Policy*, 13(7): 975–86.

John, P. (2018) 'Theories of policy change and variation reconsidered: a prospectus for the political economy of public policy', *Policy Sciences*, 51(1): 1–16.

Johns, G. (2006) 'The essential impact of context on organizational behavior', *Academy of Management Review*, 31(2): 386–408.

Jones, B. (1982) *Sleepers Wake: Technology and the Future of Work*, Melbourne: Oxford University Press.

Jordan, A., Bauer, M. and Green-Pedersen, C. (2013) 'Policy dismantling', *Journal of European Public Policy*, 20(5): 795–805.

Jordan, G. (1990) 'Sub-governments, policy communities and networks: refilling the old bottles?', *Journal of Theoretical Politics*, 2(3): 319–38.

Katzenstein, P. (1984) *Corporatism and Change: Austria, Switzerland and the Politics of Industry*, Ithaca: Cornell University Press.

Kay, A. (2005) 'A critique of the use of path dependency in policy studies', *Public Administration*, 83(3): 553–71.

Kay, A. (2006) *The Dynamics of Public Policy: Theory and Evidence*, Cheltenham, UK: Edward Elgar Publishing Ltd.

Kay, A. (2009) 'Policy change as a hermeneutic problem', *Journal of Comparative Policy Analysis*, 11(1): 47–63.

Keast, R., Mandell, M., Brown, K. and Woolcock, G. (2004) 'Network structures: working differently and changing expectations', *Public Administration Review*, 64(3): 363–71.

Kellogg, W. and Mathur, A. (2003) 'Environmental justice and information technologies: overcoming the information-access paradox in urban communities', *Public Administration Review*, 63(5): 573–85.

Kellow, A. (2012) 'Multi-level and multi-arena governance: the limits of integration and the possibilities of forum shopping', *International Environmental Agreements: Politics, Law and Economics*, 12(4): 327–42.

Kennedy, G. and Crowley, K. (2018) 'Re-framing utilization focused evaluation: lessons for the *Australian Aid* programme?' *Journal of Asian Public Policy*. Available at: https://doi.org/10.1080/17516234.2018.1501172.

Kettl, D.F. (2014) *System Under Stress: The Challenge to 21st Century Governance*, Thousand Oaks, CA: CQ Press.

Kickert, W. (1993) 'Autopoesis and science of (public) administration: essence, sense and nonsense', *Organisation Studies*, 14(2): 261–78.

Kim, S., Ashley, S. and Lambright, H.W. (eds) (2014) *Public Administration in the Context of Global Governance*, Aldershot: Edward Elgar.

Kim, D.H. (1993) 'The link between individual and organizational learning', *Sloan Management Review*, 35(1): 37–50.

King, A. (1975) 'Overload: problems of governing in the 1970s', *Political Studies*, 23(2–3): 284–96.

King, A. and Crewe, I. (2013) *The Blunders of our Government*, London: Oneworld Publications.

Kingdon, J.W. (1995) *Agendas, Alternatives, and Public Policies* (2nd edn), New York: HarperCollins.

Kjaer, A.M. (2004) *Governance*, Cambridge: Policy Press.

Klijn, E.H. and Koppenjan, J. (2015) *Governance Networks in the Public Sector*, London: Routledge.

Kobrin, S. (2009) 'Private political authority and public responsibility: transnational politics, transnational firms, and human rights', *Business Ethics Quarterly*, 19(3): 349–74.

Koehn, P.H. and Rosenau, J.N. (2002) 'Transnational competence in an emergent epoch', *International Studies Perspectives*, 3(2): 105–27.

Krasner, S. (2016) 'The persistence of state sovereignty', in O. Fioretos, T. Falleti, and A. Sheingate (eds) *The Oxford Handbook of Historical Institutionalism*, Oxford: Oxford University Press, Chapter 31.

Lamberton, D.M. (1986) 'Review articles information, economic analysis and public policy', *Prometheus*, 4(1): 174–86.

Lamberton, D.M. (2001) 'An information infrastructure for development', *Prometheus*, 19(3): 223–30.

LaPorte, T. (ed) (1975) *Organized Social Complexity: Challenge to Politics and Policy*, Princeton: Princeton University Press.

Lasswell, H.D. (1956) *The Decision Process: Seven Categories of Functional Analysis*, Baltimore, MA: University of Maryland, Bureau of Governmental Research.

Laws, D. and Hajer, M. (2008) 'Policy in practice', in R. Goodin, M. Moran, and M. Rein (eds) *Oxford Handbook of Public Policy*, Oxford: Oxford University Press, pp 409–24.

Layzer, J.A. (2008) *Natural Experiments: Ecosystem-based Management and the Environment*, Cambridge: MIT Press.

Le Gales, P. and King, D. (2017) 'Introduction', in D. King, and P. Le Gales (eds) *Reconfiguring European States in Crisis*, Oxford: Oxford University Press, pp 1–44.

Levin, K., Cashore, B., Bernstein, S. and Auld, G. (2012) 'Overcoming the tragedy of super wicked problems: constraining our future selves to ameliorate global climate change', *Policy Sciences*, 45(2): 123–52.

Levitan, K. (1987) *Government Infostructures: A Guide to the Networks of Information Resources and Technologies at Federal, State and Local Levels*, New York: Greenwood Press.

Lieberman, R.C. (2002) 'Ideas, institutions and political order: explaining policy change', *American Political Science Review*, 96(4): 697–712.

Lindblom, C.E. (1959) 'The science of "muddling through"', *Public Administration Review*, 19(2): 79–88.

Lindblom, C.E. (1979) 'Still muddling, not yet through', *Public Administration Review*, 39(6): 517–26.

Lindquist, E. (2007) 'Organising for policy implementation', in J. Wanna (ed) *Improving implementation: organisational change and project management*, Canberra: ANU E-Press, pp 229–55.

Lipsky, M. (1980) *Street-level Bureaucracy: Dilemmas of the Individual in Public Services*, New York: Russell Sage Foundation.

Lowdnes, V. (1996) 'Varieties of new institutionalism: a critical appraisal', *Public Administration*, 74(2): 181–97.

Lowdnes, V. (2010) 'Institutionalism', in D. Marsh and G. Stoker (eds) *Theory and Methods in Political Science* (3rd edn), Basingstoke: Palgrave Macmillian, pp 60–79.

Lowdnes, V. (2018) 'The institutional approach', in V. Lowdnes, D. Marsh and G. Stoker (eds) *Theory and Methods in Political Science* (4th edn), Basingstoke: Palgrave Macmillian, pp 54–74.

Lowdnes, V. and Roberts, M. (2013) *Why Institutions Matter: The New Institutionalism in Political Science*, Basingstoke: Palgrave Macmillian.

Lowi, T. (1972) 'Four systems of policy, politics and choice', *Public Administration Review*, 32(4): 298–310.

Luhmann, N. (1993) 'Ecological communication: coping with the unknown', *Systems Practice*, 6(5): 527–39.

Luhmann, N. (2013) *Introduction to Systems Theory*, London: Policy Press.

Lukes, S. (2005) *Power: A Radical View* (2nd edn), Basingstoke UK: Palgrave Macmillan.

Lynn, L. (2001) 'The myth of the bureaucratic paradigm: what traditional public administration really stood for', *Public Administration Review*, 61(2): 144–60.

Maasen, S. and Weingart, P. (eds) (2005) *Democratisation or Expertise? Exploring Novel Forms of Scientific Advice in Political Decision-making*, Dordrecht, NL: Springer Press.

Maddison, S. (2016) *Conflict Transformation and Reconciliation*, London: Routledge.

Mahoney J. (2000) 'Path dependence in historical sociology', *Theory and Society*, 29(4): 507–48.

Majone, G. (1989) *Evidence, Argument, and Persuasion in the Policy Process*, New Haven CT: Yale University Press.

Maley, M. (2000) 'Conceptualising advisers policy work: the distinctive policy roles of ministerial advisers in the Keating government, 1991–96', *Australian Journal of Political Science*, 35(3): 449–70.

Maor, M. (2012) 'Policy overreaction', *Journal of Public Policy*, 32(3): 231–59.

March, J.G. and Olsen, J. (1983) 'The new institutionalism: organisational factors in political life', *The American Political Science Review*, 78(3): 734–49.

March, J.G. and Olsen, J. (1989) *Rediscovering Institutions*, New York: Free Press.

March, J.G. and Olsen, J. (2006) 'Elaborating the "new institutionalism"', in R.A.W. Rhodes, S.A. Biner, and B.A. Rockman (eds) *Oxford Handbook of Political Institutions*, Oxford: Oxford University Press, pp 3–20.

Marchak, P. (1985) 'Canadian political economy', *Review of Canadian Sociology and Anthropology*, 22(5): 673–709.

Marinetto, M. (2003) 'Governing beyond the centre: a critique of the Anglogovernance school', *Political Studies*, 51(3): 592–608.

References

Marks, G. and Hooghe, L. (2004) 'Contrasting visions of multi-level governance?' in I. Bache and M. Flinders, *Multi-level Governance*, Oxford: Oxford University

Marschak, J. (1996) 'Economics of inquiring, communicating, deciding', in D. Lamberton (ed) *The Economics of Communication and Information*, Cheltenham UK: Edward Elgar.

Marsh, D. and Rhodes, R. (1992) *Policy Networks in British Government*, Oxford: Oxford University Press.

Marsh, I., Crowley, K., Grube, D. and Eccleston, R. (2017) 'Delivering public services: locality, learning and reciprocity in place based practice', *Australian Journal of Public Administration*, 76(4): 443–56.

Matland, R. (1995) 'Synthesizing implementation literature: the ambiguity-conflict model of policy implementation', *Journal of Public Administration Research and Theory*, 5(2): 145–74.

May, P.J. (2012) 'Policy design and implementation', in B.G. Peters and J. Pierre (eds) *Sage Handbook of Public Administration* (2nd edn), London: Sage, pp 279–91.

May, P.J. (2015) 'Implementation failures revisited: policy regime perspectives', *Public Policy & Administration*, 30(3–4): 277–99.

May, P.J. and Jochim, A.E. (2013) 'Policy regime perspectives: policies, politics, and governing', *Policy Studies Journal*, 41(3): 426–52.

May, P.J., Sapotichne, J. and Workman, S. (2009) 'Widespread policy disruption: terrorism, public risks, and homeland security', *Policy Studies Journal*, 37(2): 171–94.

Maybin, J. (2015) 'Policy analysis and policy know-how: a case study of civil servants in England's Department of Health', *Journal of Comparative Policy Analysis*, 17(3): 286–304.

McConnell, A. (2010a) 'Policy success, policy failure and grey areas in-between', *Journal of Public Policy*, 30(3): 345–62.

McConnell, A. (2010b) *Understanding Policy Success: Rethinking Public Policy*, Basingstoke: Palgrave Macmillan.

McConnell, A. (2015) 'What is policy failure? A primer to help navigate the maze', *Public Policy & Administration*, 30(3–4): 221–42.

McCool, D. (1995) *Public Policy Theories, Models, and Concepts: An Anthology*, London: Pearson.

Mehta, J. (2011) 'The varied roles of ideas in politics', in D. Béland and R.H. Cox (eds) *Ideas and Politics in Social Science Research*, New York: Oxford University Press, pp 23–46.

Meijer, A. and Bannister, F. (2009) 'Using public administration theory to analyze public innovation', *Information Polity*, 14(4): 241–4.

Mercer, D. and Marden, P. (2006) 'Ecologically sustainable development in a quarry economy: one step forward, two steps back', *Geographical Research*, 44(2): 183–203.

Merklova, K. and Ptackova, K. (2016) 'Policy advisory councils (governmental and departmental advisory bodies) in the Czech Republic', in A. Vesely, M. Nekola and E.M. Hejzlarova (eds) *Policy Analysis in the Czech Republic*, Bristol: Policy Press, pp 157–76.

Metz, F. and Ingold, K. (2017) 'Politics of the precautionary principle: assessing actors' preferences in water protection policy', *Policy Sciences*, 50(4): 721–43.

Miller, C. (2001) 'Hybrid management: boundary organisations, science policy, and environmental governance in the climate regime', *Science, Technology and Human Values*, 26(4): 478–500.

Mintrom, M. and Norman, P. (2009) 'Policy entrepreneurship and policy change', *Policy Studies Journal*, 37(4): 649–67.

Mintrom, M. and Luetjens, J. (2017) 'Policy entrepreneurs and problem framing: the case of climate change', *Environment and Planning C: Politics and Space*, 38(6): 1362–77.

Moon, K., Dickinson, H. and Blackman, D. (2017) 'Not another review about implementation? Reframing the research agenda', Public Service Research Group, Issue Paper No 1, Canberra: University of New South Wales, pp 1–40.

Mosse, D. (2004) 'Is good policy unimplementable? Reflections on the ethnography of aid policy and practice', *Development and Change*, 35(4): 639–71.

National Audit Office (NAO) (2015) *Welfare Reform: Lessons Learned*, London: NAO.

Nelson, S.C. and Katzenstein, P. (2014) 'Uncertainty, risk and the financial crisis of 2008', *International Organization*, 68(2): 361–92.

Newig, J., Challies, E., Jager, N.W., Kochskaemper, E. and Adzersen, A. (2018) 'The environmental performance of participatory and collaborative governance: a framework of causal mechanisms', *Policy Studies Journal*, 46(2): 269–97.

Newman, J. (ed) (2005) *Remaking Governance: Peoples, Politics and the Public Sphere*, Bristol: Policy Press.

Newman, J. and Clarke, J. (2009) *Publics, Politics and Power: Remaking the Public in Public Services*, London: Sage.

Newman, J., Cherney, A. and Head, B. (2016) 'Do policy makers use academic research? Re-examining the "two communities" theory of research utilization', *Public Administration Review*, 76(1): 24–32.

Ney, S. (2009) *Resolving Messy Policy Problems: Handling Conflict in Environmental Transport, Health and Ageing Policy*, London: Earthscan/Edward Elgar.

O'Brien, M., Penna, S. and Hay, C. (1999) *Theorising Modernity: Reflexivity, Environment and Identity in Giddens' Social Theory*, London: Longman.

O'Connor, J. (1973) *The Fiscal Crisis of the State*, New York: St Martin's Press.

O'Flynn, J., Blackman, D. and Halligan, J. (eds) (2014) *Crossing Boundaries in Public Management and Policy*, New York: Routledge.

O'Leary, R. and Bingham, L. (2008) *The Collaborative Public Manager: New Ideas for the Twenty-first Century*, Washington DC: Georgetown University Press.

O'Toole, L.J. (1986) 'Policy recommendations for multi-actor implementation: an assessment of the field', *Journal of Public Policy*, 6(2): 181–210.

OECD (Organisation for Economic Cooperation and Development) (2008) *Concepts and dilemmas of state building in fragile situations: from fragility to resilience*, OECD/DAC (Development Assistance Committee) discussion paper, Paris: OECD.

OECD (Organisation for Economic Cooperation and Development) (2010) *Public Governance Review – Finland: working together to sustain success*, Paris: OECD.

OECD (Organisation for Economic Cooperation and Development) (2011) *Future global shocks: improving risk governance*, Paris: OECD.

OECD (Organisation for Economic Cooperation and Development) (2018) *Programme for international student assessment*, Paris: OECD.

Olsen, J. (2006) 'Maybe it is time to rediscover bureaucracy', *Journal of Public Administration Research and Theory*, 16(1): 1–24.

Osborne, D. and Gaebler, T. (1992) *Reinventing Government: How the Entrepreneurial Spirit is Transforming the Public Sector*, Reading, MA: Addison-Wesley.

Osborne, S.P. (ed) (2010) *The New Public Governance? Emerging Perspectives on the Theory and Practice of Public Governance*, London: Routledge.

Ostrom, E. (1990) *Governing the Commons: The Evolutions of Institutions of Collective Action*, Cambridge: Cambridge University Press.

Ostrom, E. (2011) 'Background on the institutional analysis and development framework', *Policy Studies Journal*, 39(1): 7–27.

Ostrom, E. and Cox, M. (2010) 'Moving beyond panaceas: a multi-tiered diagnostic approach for social–ecological analysis', *Environmental Conservation*, 37(4): 451–63.

Painter, M. and Pierre, J. (eds) (2005) *Challenges to State Policy Capacity: Global Trends and Comparative Perspectives*, Basingstoke: Palgrave Macmillan.

Parenting Research Centre (2014) *Implementation of recommendations arising from previous inquiries of relevance to the Royal Commission into institutional responses to child sexual abuse: final report*, Melbourne: Parenting Research Centre.

Parry, I. (2008) *Pricing Urban Congestion*, Washington: Resources for the future.

Parsons, W. (1982) 'Politics without promises: the crisis of "overload" and governability', *Parliamentary Affairs*, XXXV(4): 421–35.

Parsons, W. (1995) *Public Policy: An Introduction to the Theory and Practice of Policy Analysis*, Cheltenham, UK: Edward Elgar.

Patashnik, E.M. (2008) *Reforms at Risk: What Happens After Major Policy Changes Are Enacted*, Princeton: Princeton University Press.

Patton, M. (2011) *Developmental Evaluation: Applying Complexity Concepts to Enhance Innovation and Use*, New York: Guilford Press.

Peck, J. and Theodore, N. (2015) *Fast Policy: Experimental Statecraft at the Thresholds of Neoliberalism*, Minneapolis: University of Minnesota Press.

Perl, A., Howlett, M. and Ramesh, M. (2018) 'Policymaking and truthiness: can existing policy models cope with politicized evidence and willful ignorance in a "post-fact" world?', *Policy Sciences*, 51(4): 581–600.

Peters, B.G. (2001) *The Future of Governing* (2nd edn), Lawrence, KS: University of Kansas Press.

Peters, B.G. (2005) 'The problem of policy problems', *Journal of Comparative Policy Analysis*, 7(4): 349–70.

Peters, B.G. (2011) 'Institutional theory', in M. Bevir (ed) *The Sage Handbook of Governance*, London: Sage, pp 78–90.

Peters, B.G. (2012) *Institutional Theory in Political Science: The New Institutionalism* (3rd edn), New York: Continuum International Publishing Group.

Peters, B.G. (2014) 'Implementation structures as institutions', *Public Policy & Administration*, 29(2): 131–44.

Peters, B.G. (2015a) *Advanced Introduction to Public Policy*, Cheltenham: Edward Elgar Publishing.

Peters, B.G. (2015b) 'State failure, governance failure and policy failure: exploring the linkages', *Public Policy & Administration*, 30(3–4): 261–76.

Peters, B.G. (2016) 'Governance and the media: exploring the linkages', *Policy & Politics*, 44(1): 9–22.

Peters, B.G. and Pierre, J. (1998) 'Governance without government? Rethinking public administration', *Journal of Public Administration Research and Theory*, 8(2): 223–43.

Peterson Institute for International Economics. (2016) 'Why has trade stopped growing? Not much liberalization and lots of micro-protection', *Trade and Investment Policy Watch*. Available at: https://piie.com/blogs/trade-investment-policy-watch/why-has-trade-stopped-growing-not-much-liberalization-and-lots.

Pierre, J. and Peters, B.G. (2000) *Governance, Politics and the State*, Basingstoke, London: Palgrave Macmillan.

Pierson, P. (1993) 'When effect becomes cause: policy feedback and political change', *World Politics*, 45(4): 595–628.

Pierson, P. (1994) *Dismantling the Welfare State?* Cambridge: Cambridge University Press.

Plowden, W. (1987) 'Relationships between advisers and departmental civil servants', in W. Plowden (ed) *Advising the Rulers*, Oxford: Basil Blackwell, pp 170–4.

Pollitt, C. (2003) 'Joined-up government: a survey', *Political Studies Review*, 1(1): 34–49.

Pollitt, C. (ed) (2013) *Context in Public Policy and Management: The Missing Link?* Cheltenham: Edward Elgar.

Pollitt, C. and Bouckaert, G. (2004) *Public Management Reforms: A Comparative Analysis*, (2nd edn), Oxford: Oxford University Press.

Pollitt, C. and Bouckaert, G. (2017) *Public Management Reform: A Comparative Analysis into the Age of Austerity* (4th edn), Oxford: Oxford University Press.

Prasser, S. (2006) 'Providing advice to government', *Practice and Procedure Papers on Parliament*, Paper No. 46, Canberra: Australian Parliamentary Library.

Pressman, J.L. and Wildavsky, A. (1984) *Implementation: How Great Expectations in Washington are Dashed in Oakland* (3rd edn; 1st edn 1973; 2nd edn 1979), Berkeley: University of California Press.

Prince, M.J. (2007) 'Soft craft, hard choices, altered context: reflections on 25 years of policy advice in Canada', in L. Dobuzinskis, M. Howlett and D. Laycock (eds) *Policy Analysis in Canada: The State of the Art*, Toronto: University of Toronto Press, pp 95–106.

Pritchett, L. and de Weijer, F. (2010) 'Fragile states: stuck in a capability trap?', *Background Paper*, Washington DC: World Bank.

Productivity Commission (Australia) (2017) *Data availability and use: inquiry report*, Melbourne: Productivity Commission.

Rabe, B. (2016) 'The durability of carbon cap-and-trade policy', *Governance*, 29(1): 103–19.

Radaelli, C. (1995) *Journal of European Public Policy*, 2(2): 159–83.

Radaelli, C. (2008) 'Europeanization, policy learning, and new modes of governance', *Journal of Comparative Policy Analysis: Research and Practice*, 10(3): 239–54.

Radaelli, C.M., Dente, B. and Dossi, S. (2012) 'Recasting institutionalism: institutional analysis and public policy', *European Political Science*, 11(4): 537–50.

Radelet, S. (2017) 'Once more into the breach: does foreign aid work?', Washington, DC: Brookings Institute. Available at: www.brookings.edu/blog/future-development/2017/05/08/once-more-into-the-breach-does-foreign-aid-work/?

Ravetz, J. (2004) 'The post-normal science of precaution', *Futures*, 36(3): 347–57.

Rawls, J. (1993) *Political Liberalism*, New York: Columbia University Press.

Reed, M. (2005) 'Beyond the iron cage? Bureaucracy and democracy in the knowledge economy and society', in P. du Gay (ed) *The Values of Bureaucracy*, Oxford: Oxford University Press, pp 115–40.

Reid, R. and Botterill, L. (2013) 'The multiple meanings of "resilience": an overview of the literature', *Australian Journal of Public Administration*, 72(1): 31–40.

Reinecke, S., Hermann, A.T., Bauer, A., Pregernig, M., Karl Hogl, K. and Pistorius, T. (2013) *Innovative climate policy advice: Case studies from Germany, the Netherlands, Switzerland and the UK*, Research Report 1–2013, Vienna: Institute of Forest, Environmental, and Natural Resource Policy.

Reinicke, W. (1998) *Global Public Policy: Governing Without Government?*, Washington, DC: Brookings.

Rhodes, M. (2007) 'Strategic choice in the Irish housing system: taming complexity', *Housing, Theory and Society*, 24(1): 14–31.

Rhodes, R.A.W. (1995) 'The institutional approach', in D. Marsh and G. Stoker (eds) *Theory and Methods in Political Science*, London: Macmillan Press.

Rhodes, R.A.W. (1997) *Understanding Governance: Policy Networks, Governance, Reflexivity and Accountability*, London: Open University Press.

Rhodes, R.A.W. (2007) 'Understanding governance: 10 years on', *Organization Studies*, 28(8): 1243–64.

Rhodes, R.A.W. (2008a) 'Old institutionalisms', in R.A.W. Rhodes, S.A. Biner, and B.A. Rockman (eds) (2008) *Oxford Handbook of Political Institutions*, Oxford: Oxford University Press, pp 90–110.

Rhodes, R.A.W. (2008b) 'Policy network analysis', in R. Goodin, M. Moran and M. Rein (eds) *The Oxford Handbook of Public Policy*, Oxford: Oxford University Press, pp 425–47.

Rhodes, R.A.W. (2011) 'Thinking on: a career in public administration', *Public Administration*, 89(1): 196–212.

Rhodes, R.A.W., Biner, S.A. and Rockman, B.A. (eds) (2008) *Oxford Handbook of Political Institutions*, Oxford: Oxford University Press.

Riccucci, N.M. (2005) *How Management Matters: Street-level Bureaucrats and Welfare Reform*, Washington, DC: Georgetown University Press.

Rijke, J., Brown, R., Zevenbergen, C., Ashley, R., Farrelly, M., Morison, P. and van Herk, S. (2012) 'Fit-for-purpose governance: a framework to make adaptive governance operational', *Environmental Science & Policy*, 22: 73–84.

Rittel, H.W.J. and Webber, M.M. (1973) 'Dilemmas in a general theory of planning', *Policy Sciences*, 4(2): 155–69.

Roberts, J. (2014) *New Media and Public Activism: Neoliberalism, the State and Radical Protest in the Public Sphere*, Bristol: Policy Press.

Roe, E. (2013) *Making the Most of Mess: Reliability and Policy in Today's Management Challenges*, Durham NC: Duke University Press.

Rogge, K., Kern, F. and Howlett, M. (2017) 'Conceptual and empirical advances in analysing policy mixes for energy transitions', *Energy Research & Social Science*, 33: 1–10.

Room, G. (2016) *Actors in Complex Terrains: Transformative Realism and Public Policy*, Oxford: Routledge.

Rosenau, J.N. (2004) 'Emergent spaces, new places, and old faces: proliferating identities in a globalising world', in J. Friedman and S. Randeria (eds) *Worlds on the Move: Globalization, Migration, and Cultural Security*, London: I B Tauris & Co, pp 23–62.

Ruijer, E., Grimmelikhuijsen, S. and Meijer, A. (2017) 'Open data for democracy: developing a theoretical framework for open data use', *Government Information Quarterly*, 34(1): 45–52.

Sabatier, P.A. (1998) 'The advocacy coalition framework: revisions and relevance for Europe', *Journal of European Public Policy*, 5(1): 98–130.

Sabatier, P.A. (ed) (2007) *Theories of the Policy Process* (2nd edn), Boulder CO: Westview Press.

Sabel, C. and Simon, W. (2011) 'Minimalism and experimentalism in the administrative state', *Georgetown Law Review*, 100(1): 54–93.

Sandison, P. (2005) 'The utilisation of evaluations', *ALNAP Review of Humanitarian Action*. Available at: www.alnap.org/help-library/the-utilisation-of-evaluations-alnap-review-of-humanitarian-action-in-2005-evaluation.

Savoie, D.J. (2003) *Breaking the Bargain: Public Servants, Ministers and Parliament*, Toronto: University of Toronto Press.

Schandl, H. and Walker, I. (eds) (2017) *Social Science and Sustainability*, Melbourne: CSIRO.

Schmidt, V.A. (2008) 'Discursive institutionalism', *Annual Review of Political Science*, 11(1): 303–26.

Schmidt, V.A. (2009) 'Putting the political back into political economy by bringing the state back in yet again', *World Politics*, 61(3): 516–46.

Schmidt, V.A. (2010) 'Taking ideas and discourse seriously: explaining change through discursive institutionalism as the fourth "new institutionalism"', *European Political Science Review*, 2(1): 1–25.

Schneider, A. and Ingram, H. (1990) 'Behavioural assumptions of policy tools', *The Journal of Politics*, 52(2): 510–29.

Schneider, A. and Ingram, H. (1993) 'The social construction of target populations: implications for politics and policy', *American Political Science Review*, 87(2): 334–47.

Schneider, A. and Ingram, H. (1997) *Policy Design for Democracy*, Lawrence, Kansas: University of Kansas Press.

Schofield, J. (2004) 'A model of learned implementation', *Public Administration*, 82(2): 283–308.

Schön, D.A. and Rein, M. (1994) *Frame Reflection: Toward the Resolution of Intractable Policy Controversies*, New York: Basic Books.

Schultz, M., Bressers, D., van der Steen, M. and van Twist, M. (2015) 'Internal advisory systems in different political-administrative regimes', Presentation to International Conference on Public Policy, Milan, 1–4 July.

Schwartz, H. (1994) 'Small states in big trouble: state reorganization in Australia, Denmark, New Zealand, and Sweden in the 1980s', *World Politics*, 46(4): 527–55.

Scott, C. and Baehler, K. (2010) *Adding Value to Policy Analysis and Advice*, Sydney: University of New South Wales Press.

Self, P. (1993) *Government by the Market: The Politics of Public Choice*, Basingstoke: Macmillan.

Sellers, J.M. (2011) 'State-society relations', in M. Bevir (ed) *Sage Handbook of Governance*, London: Sage, pp 124–42.

Sellers, J.M. and Kwak, S. (2010) 'State and society in local governance: lessons from a multilevel comparison', *International Journal of Urban and Regional Research*, 35(2): 620–43.

Selznick, P. (1948) 'Foundations of a theory of organisation', *American Sociological Review*, 13(1): 23–35.

Selznick, P. (1957) *Leadership in Administration*, Evanston, IL: Row and Peters.

Seymour-Ure, C. (1987) 'Institutionalisation and informality in advisory systems', in W. Plowden (ed) *Advising the Rulers*, Oxford: Basil Blackwell, pp 174–85.

Shaw, R. and Eichbaum, C. (2011) *Public Policy in New Zealand: Institutions, Processes and Outcomes*, Auckland: Pearson.

Shergold, P. (2015) *Learning from Failure*, Canberra: Australian Public Service Commission. Available at: https://apo.org.au/sites/default/files/resource-files/2015/08/apo-nid62938-1162041.pdf.

Shipan, C.R. and Volden, C. (2012) 'Policy diffusion: seven lessons for scholars and practitioners', *Public Administration Review*, 72(6): 788–96.

Shrivastava, P. (1993) 'Crisis theory/practice: toward a sustainable future', *Industrial & Environmental Crisis Quarterly*, 7(1): 23–42.

Simeon, R. (1976) 'Studying public policy', *Canadian Journal of Political Science*, 9(4): 548–80.

Simons, A. and Voß, J-P. (2018) 'The concept of instrument constituencies: accounting for dynamics and practices of knowing governance', *Policy and Society*, 37(1): 14–35.

Skocpol, T. (1985) 'Bringing the state back in: strategies of analysis in current research', in P.B. Evans, D. Rueschemeyer and T. Skocpol (eds) *Bringing the State Back In*, Cambridge: Cambridge University Press, pp 3–37.

Skogstad, G. (ed) (2011) *Policy Paradigms, Transnationalism and Domestic Politics*, Toronto: University of Toronto Press.

Skogstad, G. and White, L.A. (2017) 'Revisiting Richard Simeon's "studying public policy"', *Canadian Journal of Political Science*, 49(4): 665–79.

Smith, H. (2018) 'Doing policy differently', Keynote address to Institute of Public Administration Australia, Canberra, 22 March.

Smith, K.E. (2013) *Beyond Evidence-based Policy in Public Health: The Interplay of Ideas*, Basingstoke: Palgrave Macmillan.

Smith, K.E. (2014) 'The politics of ideas: the complex interplay of health inequalities research and policy', *Science and Public Policy*, 41(5): 561–74.

Solon, A. (2018) 'How Europe's "breakthrough" privacy law takes on Facebook and Google'. Available at: www.theguardian.com/technology/2018/apr/19/gdpr-facebook-google-amazon-data-privacy-regulation.

Stark, A. (2014) 'Bureaucratic values and resilience: an exploration of crisis management adaptation', *Public Administration*, 92(3): 692–706.

Stark, A. (2018) *Public Inquiries, Policy Learning, and the Threat of Future Crises*, Cambridge: Cambridge University Press.

Stark, A. and Head, B.W. (2019) 'Institutional amnesia and public policy', *Journal of European Public Policy*, 26(10): 1521–39.

Starr, P. (2009) 'Goodbye to the age of newspapers (hello to a new era of corruption)', *New Republic*, 4 March. Available at: https://newrepublic.com/article/64252/goodbye-the-age-newspapers-hello-new-era-corruption.

Steenhuisen, B. and van Eeten, M. (2008) 'Invisible trade-offs of public values: inside Dutch railways', *Public Money and Management*, 28(3): 147–52.

Steinmo, S. (2008) 'Historical institutionalism', in D. Della Porta and M. Keating (eds) *Approaches and Methodologies in the Social Sciences: A Plurali*, Cambridge: Cambridge University Press, pp 118–38.

Stevens, A. (2011) 'Telling policy stories: an ethnographic study of the use of evidence in policymaking in the UK', *Journal of Social Policy*, 40(2): 237–55.

Stewart, J. (1994) *The Lie of the Level Playing Field: Industry Policy and Australia's Future*, Melbourne: Text Publishing.

Stewart, J. (2009) *Public Policy Values*, Basingstoke: Palgrave Macmillan.

Stewart, J. (2013) 'Public policy as information', *Prometheus*, 31(1): 3–19.

Stewart, J. and Ayres, R. (2001) 'Systems theory and policy practice: an exploration', *Policy Sciences*, 34(1): 79–94.

Stewart, J. and Jones, G. (2003) *Renegotiating the Environment: The Power of Politics*, Sydney: The Federation Press.

Stewart, J. and Jarvie, W. (2015) 'Haven't we been this way before? Evaluation and the impediments to policy learning', *Australian Journal of Public Administration*, 74(2): 114–27.

Stewart, J. and Prasser, S. (2015) 'Expert advisory bodies', in B. Head and K. Crowley (eds) *Policy Analysis in Australia*, Bristol: Policy Press, pp 151–67.

Stirling, A. (2008) 'Opening up and closing down: power, participation, and pluralism in the social appraisal of technology', *Science, Technology & Human Values*, 33(2): 262–94.

Stoker, G. (2019) 'Can the governance paradigm survive the rise of populism?', *Policy and Politics*, 47(1): 3–18.

Stone, D. (1997) *Policy Paradox: The Art of Political Decision-making*, New York: W W Norton.

Stone, D. (2008) 'Global public policy, transnational policy communities, and their networks', *Policy Studies Journal*, 36(1): 19–38.

Stone, D. and Ladi, S. (2015) 'Global public policy and transnational administration', *Public Administration*, 93(4): 839–55.

Sullivan, H. and Skelcher, C. (2002) *Working Across Boundaries: Collaboration in Public Services*, Basingstoke: Palgrave Macmillan.

Taylor, M.M. (2009) 'Institutional development through policymaking', *World Politics*, 61(3): 487–515.

Tenbensel, T. (2013) 'Complexity in health and health care systems', *Social Science and Medicine*, 93: 181–4.

Tenbensel, T. (2015) 'Complexity and health policy', in P. Cairney and R. Geyer (eds) *Handbook on Complexity and Public Policy*, Cheltenham: Edward Elgar, pp 369–83.

Tenbensel, T. (2018) 'Bridging complexity theory and hierarchies: markets, networks, communities: a "population genetics" framework for understanding institutional change from within', *Public Management Review*, 20(7): 1032–51.

Thacher, D. and Rein, M. (2004) 'Managing value conflict in public policy', *Governance*, 17(4): 457–86.

Thelen, K. (1999) 'Historical institutionalism in comparative politics', *Annual Review of Political Science*, 2(1): 369–404.

Thelen, K. (2004) *How Institutions Evolve: The Political Economy of Skills in Germany, Britain, the United States, and Japan*, Cambridge: Cambridge University Press.

Thelen, K. (2009) 'Institutional change in advanced political economies', *British Journal of Industrial Relations*, 47(3): 471–98.

Thomann, E. and Sager, F. (2017) 'Toward a better understanding of implementation performance in the EU multilevel system', *Journal of European Public Policy*, 24(9): 1385–407.

Thomas, O.D. (2017) 'Good faith and (dis)honest mistakes? Learning from Britain's Iraq War Inquiry', *Politics*, 37(4): 371–85.

Torfing, J. (2019) 'Collaborative innovation in the public sector: the argument', *Public Management Review*, 21(1): 1–11.

Torfing, J. and Ansell, C. (2017) 'Strengthening political leadership and policy innovation through the expansion of collaborative forms of governance', *Public Management Review*, 19(1): 37–54.

Trenholm, S. and Ferlie, E. (2013) 'Using complexity theory to analyse the organisational response to resurgent tuberculosis across London', *Social Science and Medicine*, 93: 229–37.

True, J. and Mintrom, M. (2001) 'Transnational networks and policy diffusion: the case of gender mainstreaming', *International Studies Quarterly*, 45(1): 27–57.

Van Asselt, M.B. and Vos, E. (2006) 'The precautionary principle and the uncertainty paradox', *Journal of Risk Research*, 9(4): 313–36.

Van Buuren, A. and Koppenjan, J. (2014) 'Policy analysis in networks: the battle of analysis and the potentials of joint fact-finding', in F. Van Nispen and P. Scholten (eds) *Policy Analysis in the Netherlands*, Bristol: Policy Press, pp 33–49.

Van Damme, J., Brans, M. and Fobé, E. (2011) 'Balancing expertise, societal input and political control in the production of policy advice: a comparative study of education councils in Europe', *Halduskultuur – Administrative Culture*, 12(2): 126–45.

Van den Hoven, J. (2005) 'E-democracy, e-contestation and the monitorial citizen', *Ethics and Information Technology*, 7(2): 51–9.

Van Hulst, M.J. and Yanow, D. (2016) 'From policy "frames" to "framing": theorizing a more dynamic, political approach', *American Review of Public Administration*, 46(1): 92–112.

Van Meter, D. and Van Horn, C. (1975) 'The policy implementation process: a conceptual framework', *Administration and Society*, 6(4): 445–88.

Veit, S., Hustedt, T. and Bach, T. (2017) 'Dynamics of change in internal policy advisory systems: the hybridization of advisory capacities in Germany', *Policy Sciences*, 50(1): 85–103.

Vickers, G. (1965) *The Art of Judgment*, London: Chapman and Hall.

Vickers, J. and Yarrow, G. (1991) 'Economic perspectives on privatization', *Journal of Economic Perspectives*, 5(2): 111–32.

Voß, J-P. and Simons, A. (2014) 'Instrument constituencies and the supply side of policy innovation: the social life of emissions trading', *Environmental Politics*, 23(5): 735–54.

Walgrave, S. and Dejaeghere, Y. (2016) 'Surviving information overload: how elite politicians select information', *Governance*, 30(2): 229–44.

Walker, B. and Salt, D. (2012) *Resilience Practice: Building Capacity to Absorb Disturbance and Maintain Function*, Washington, DC: Island Press.

Wang, W-J. and Chiuo, C-T. (2015) 'Exploring policy advisory committees in central government', in Y-Y. Kuo (ed), *Policy Analysis in Taiwan*, Bristol: Policy Press, pp 23–37.

Warren, M. (1993) 'Can participatory democracy produce better selves? Psychological dimensions of Habermas's discursive model of democracy', *Political Psychology*, 14(2): 209–34.

Weaver, R.K. and Rockman, B.A. (1993). 'Assessing the effects of institutions', in R.K. Weaver and B.A. Rockman (eds) *Do Institutions Matter? Government Capabilities in the United States and Abroad*, Washington, DC: The Brookings Institution, pp 1–41.

Weible, C. (2008) 'Expert-based information and policy subsystems: a review and synthesis', *Policy Studies Journal*, 36(4): 615–35.

Weible, C.M., Heikkila, T., deLeon, P. and Sabatier, P. (2012) 'Understanding and influencing the policy process', *Policy Sciences*, 45(1): 1–21.

Weick, K.E. (1995) *Sense-making in Organizations*, London: Sage Publications.

Weiss, C. (1978) 'Improving the linkage between social research and public policy', in L.E. Lynn (ed) *Knowledge and Policy: The Uncertain Connection*, Washington, DC: The National Academies Press, pp 23–81.

Weller, P. (1987) 'Types of advice', in W. Plowden (ed) *Advising the Rulers*, Oxford: Basil Blackwell, pp 149–57.

Weller, P. (2003) *Don't Tell the Prime Minister*, Melbourne: Scribe Publications.

Wellstead, A., Howlett, M. and Rayner, J. (2015) 'How useful is complexity theory to policy studies? Lessons from the climate change adaptation literature', in P. Cairney, and R. Geyer (eds) *Handbook on Complexity and Public Policy*, Cheltenham: Edward Elgar, pp 399–413.

Wendt, A. (1999) *Social Theory of International Politics*, Cambridge: Cambridge University Press.

White, H. (2016) 'Why implementation matters for impact and why impact matters for implementation', Paper at the Australian Implementation Conference, Melbourne, 6 October.

Wildavsky, A. (1979) *Speaking Truth to Power: The Art and Craft of Policy Analysis*, Boston: Little, Brown.

Wilkinson, K. (2011) 'Organised chaos: an interpretive approach to evidence-based policymaking in Defra', *Political Studies*, 59(4): 959–77.

Williams, P. (2002) 'The competent boundary spanner', *Public Administration*, 80(1): 103–24.

Williams, P. and Sullivan, H. (2011) 'Lessons in leadership for learning and knowledge management in multi-organisational settings', *International Journal of Leadership in Public Services*, 7(1): 6–20.

Wimmer, A. and Schiller, N.G. (2002) 'Methodological nationalism and beyond: nation-state building migration and the social sciences', *Global Networks*, 2(4): 301–34.

Winter, S. (2012) 'Implementation perspectives', in B.G. Peters and J. Pierre (eds) *Sage Handbook of Public Administration* (2nd edn), London: Sage, pp 265–78.

Workman, S., Jones, B. and Jochim, A. (2010) 'Policymaking, bureaucratic discretion and overhead democracy', in R. Durant (ed) *The Oxford Handbook of American Bureaucracy*, Oxford: Oxford University Press, pp 612–37.

World Bank (2017) *Governance and the Law*, Washington: World Development Report 2017.

World Bank Fragile and Conflict-Affected Countries Group (nd) *Fragility and Conflict: Supporting Peace and Development in Situations of Fragility and Conflict*, Washington, DC: World Bank.

Wu, X., Ramesh, M. and Howlett, M. (2015) 'Policy capacity: a conceptual framework for understanding policy competences and capabilities', *Policy and Society*, 34(3–4): 165–71.

Yamaya, K. (2015) 'Councils, policy analysis and policy evaluation', in Y. Adachi, S. Hosono and J. Lio (eds) *Policy Analysis in Japan*, Bristol: Policy Press, pp 139–48.

Yanow, D. (1996) *How Does a Policy Mean? Interpreting Policy and Organizational Actions*, Washington, DC: Georgetown University Press.

Zittoun, P. (2009) 'Understanding policy change as a discursive problem', *Journal of Comparative Policy Analysis*, 11(1): 65–82.

Index

Note: Page numbers for tables appear in italics.

A

abuse of older people 159
accountability 131, 136–7, 138, 145, 161
accumulation 13
Ackoff, R.L. 178
activists 171–2
adaptation 129, 188
adaptive governance 60, 105, 193, 194
adaptive management 156
adaptive system 17, 27
   see also Complex Adaptive Systems (CAS)
Adger et al 45
administrative capacity 130, 139
advertising revenue 137
advice 97–117, 165–6, 189–90, 191–2
advice brokerage 105
advisory bodies 112–13, *114*, 115
advisory subsystems 107, 108–9, 110, 111
advocacy 115, 166, 167, 171, 190, 192
advocacy coalitions 103, 172
advocacy groups 183
agency 34, 73, 82–3, 87, 167, 170
agenda content 123
agenda setting 122, 123–4, 169, 172, 175, 192
agents 17, 18, 20, 38, 42
aid 154, 182
Allison, H. 19
Althaus, C. 150
ambiguity 93, 153, 182–3
Anglo-governance school 61
armed conflict 152
ASEAN 90
Asia-Pacific 40
Asia-Pacific Economic Cooperation 86
Auditors-General 156
austerity 58, 167–8
Australia
   Aboriginal affairs 40
   international students 26–7
   international trade 86
   restructuring 51
Australian Productivity Commission 133
Australian Skills Quality Authority 26
Axelrod, R. 17, 32
Ayres, I. 68

B

Bacchi, C. 174–5
Baehler, K. 101
banking system 59
Barber, M. 150
Bardach, E. 147
Barrett, S. 145
Baumgartner, F. 122, 123–4, 126
Beeson, M. 172
behavioural-rationalism *41*
behaviourism 34–5
Behn, R.D. 157–8
Béland, D. 170
beliefs 42, 172
Bell, S. 42, 108–9
Benbow, S. 159
Benoit, E. 36
Bernanke, B. 90
Bernstein, S. 36–7
Bevir, M. 110–11
biofuels 82
blame 168
bonds 90, 91
borders 75–96
bottom-up approach 68, 148, 154
Bouckaert, G. 109
boundaries 24–6, 30, 115
boundary spanning 63, 80, 101, 106, 113
boundary spanning policy regimes 78, 93, 94–5, 191
Braithwaite, J. 8, 68
Brans, M. 14
Brinkerhoff, D.W. 154
broad values 172
brokerage 101, 105, 106
brokering 113, 115, 117, 171, 179

brokers 113, 115, 133, 166
Brown, A. 160
bureaucracy 124, 129, 138, 139, 156, 167
Burridge, A. 76

C

Cairney, P. 1, 20, 44, 88
Cairns Group 86
Cameron, David 58
Campbell Collaboration 158
capacity 149, 153, 155–7, 162, 169, 187, 192
   see also state capacity
cap-and-trade systems 67
capitalism 57
capitalist state 13
case studies 160
Castells, M. 130
change 48, 50, 66, 73, 159, 163–84, 185, 192–4
change interventions 25–6, 193
changing state 63–7
Checkland, P. 15, 22, 24
China 86
choices 153
citizens 116, 133, 139
city regions 71
civic engagement 137
climate change 18, 40, 52, 114–16, 146, 190
climate change policy analysis 9
climate policy 90, 176
closure 23
coalition-based states 136
coalition-building 71
coalitions 103, 166, 167, 169, 171, 172
coastal policy 52
Coen, D. 80
Cohen, M. 17, 32
'cold' advice 106
Coletti, P. 169–70
collaboration 101, 156, 179, 180, 184, 190, 192
collaborative capital 156
collaborative leadership 157
collective learning 158
colleges of technical and further education (TAFE) 26, 27
command and control 8, 17, 61, 62

communication technologies 129
comparative public policy 70
competence 150, 154, 155, 156, 158, 178
competitive advantage 69
competitiveness, institutional 69
Complex Adaptive Systems (CAS) 20, 27, 29–30
complexity 13, 17–22, 31, 32, 97, 148, 167
   and advisory mechanisms 109
   of the challenges 153
   and crises 49–50
   and Dryzek 177
   and implementation 161
   and information 126
   and institutions 52
   and policy change 163, 179, 183, 192
   and policy framing 176
   and policy learning 182
   and systems thinking 186–7, 188, 191
complex problems 109, 110, 112, 113, 117, 161
comprehensive rationality 88
conflict 148, 153, 155, 168, 169, 170, 174–7, 191
   and evidence 126
   and information 139
   between privacy and security 122
   and the state 63
conformance criteria 157
congestion pricing 25
constructivist-agency focused approaches 166
constructivist discursive institutionalism 42
constructivists 84, 85
contestation 5, 48, 50, 102, 107, 113, 116, 156
continuity 43, 134, 153, 163, 166, 168, 173
contracting, service delivery 146, 149, 155
control 26–7, 35, 51, 110
   and bureaucracy 129, 156
   and information 121, 137–8, 139
   and the state 61, 66, 134
coordination, policy 155

Index

Craft, J. 106, 107, 108, 112
crises 49–50, 51, 52, 58, 164, 167–70, 193
crisis management 160, 161
cross-border policy 78–9, 81–2, 85–8, 96, 189, 191
cross-sector collaboration 151
Crozier, M. 23
cyber-security 149
cybersurveillance 134
cyberwarfare 139

D

debureacratisation 105
decentralisation 67
decision-making 36, 87, 164, 167, 168, 171, 173, 175, 182
  and change 174
  and citizen engagement 116
  and implementation 143
  and information 129
  and policy advising 97, 98, 99, 100, 102, 107, 111
  and policy cycle 17
  political 124, 164
  and rational choice theory 84
  and the state 134
'deep state' 134
defence policy 176
de Greene, K. 15
Denmark 51
depression, 1930s 164
design, policy 153, 155, 177–80, 183, 188, 192
development aid 154, 182
devolution 156
de Weijer, F. 182
Dewulf, A. 176
diet, poor 24
diffusion, policy 182
digital communications 166
digitisation 149
direct democracy 131
disaster preparedness 45
discursive institutionalism 42
displaced people 176
Dispute Settlement Procedure, WTO 81
disruption 106, 168, 187
Doh, J. 92

Douglas, M. 89
drugs 36, 152
Dryzek, J.S. 177
Duit, A. 21–2
DuPre, E.P. 158
Durlak, J.A. 158

E

Easton, D. 12–13, 29, 41
economic theory 128
the economy, and the state 57
e-democracy 131
education, international 26–7
effectiveness 81, 89, 151, 154, 157, 158, 173, 178
efficiency 142, 148, 149, 150
e-government 139
electoral commitments 177
electoral systems 136
empirical policy writing 31
energy markets 18
engagement 25, 96, 136, 137, 143, 186, 189
  advisory 104
  citizen 16, 116, 132–3
  collaborative 101
  intergovernmental 81, 92
  and the state 45
entrepreneurs 166, 171–2
entrepreneurship 91, 171
environmental issues 8–9, 101, 146, 170, 175–6
epistemic communities 95
Eppel, E. 20
equifinality 27–8
Esmark, A. 121
EU (European Union)
  biofuels sustainability criteria 82
  climate policy 40, 90
  and competitive advantage 69
  Directives 143
  multilevel governance systems 152
  Renewable Energy Directive 93
European Commission 82, 83–4
evaluation 157–8, 182, 192
evidence 125–7, 138, 173, 181, 182
evidence-based advice 191
evidence-based policy 101, 173, 192, 194
evidence-informed debate 177

experience 68, 127, 152, 156, 174, 179, 180–1
   learnng from 157, 159
expert advice 112–16
expertise 116, 117
expert knowledge 190
experts 69, 83, 104, 133
external advice 104
externalisation 103, 106

F

Facebook 129
failure 11, 145, 146, 150, 158, 190, 192
   criteria for determining 156, 157, 177–8
Farrell, H. 89
far-right parties 168
'fast policy' 69
federalism 40
feedback 26, 27, 72, 188
feminism 170
finance, global 85
Financial Crisis, Global 6–7, 18, 34, 58, 79, 167–8
financial internationalisation 51
fine-tuning 157, 164
Finnemore, M. 89
first generation systems rationality 110
'first wave' analysis 106
Fischer, F. 172
flexibility 19, 37, 143, 148, 151, 190
focusing event 169
foreign interventions 152
foreign policy 176
formal institutions 38–9, 44
Forrester, J. 14
fragile states 29, 154
fragility 29
fragmentation 61, 67, 122, 131, 155, 162
framing policy problems 174–7
Frederickson, H.G. 183–4
freedom of information 133, 137
free trade 57
Friedman, T. 76, 86
front-line services 152
Fukuyama, F. 76

G

Galaz, V. 21–2
Galston, W.A. 168

global finance 85
Global Financial Crisis (GFC) 6–7, 18, 34, 58, 79, 167–8
global governance 79–80
globalisation 7, 78, 80–1
global public policy 77, 82–5
goal consensus 153
goals 141, 142, 183
Google 129
governance 2–4, 14, 154–5, 164
   adaptive 60, 105, 193, 194
   global 79
   and implementation 142
   and information 119–20, 127–31, 137–8
   and institutions 44–5
   multilevel 68–9, 152, 161
   networks 62, 162
   participatory 133
   plurilateral xi–xii
   and society 55–6
   and the state 61–3
   and systems theory 23
   urban 71
governance structures 129–30
governance theory 43, 52, 107, 108, 109–10, 187–8, 191
Governance turn xi–xii
Gray, J. 56
Great Depression 164
Gunn, L.A. 150

H

Haas, P. 95
Habermas, J. 13
Hajer, M.A. 162
Hall, P.A. 48
Halligan, J. 100, 102, 106, 108, 109
Hatton, T. 127
Hay, C. 59
Haynes, M. 22
Head, B.W. 126–7
health 24
health policy 79, 119, 145–6, 179
Heclo, H. 35
Heikkila, T. 1
Heinrichs, H. 103, 106, 191–2
Héritier, A. 66
high conflict-high ambiguity 153
high conflict-low ambiguity 153

Index

Hindmoor, A. 108–9
historical analysis 40–1
historical institutionalism 42, 72
Hoard, S. 28
Hobbesian state 56
Hobbs, R. 19
Hogwood, B.W. 150, 170
Hood, C. 63, 121, 160
Hooghe, L. 69
Hoppe, R. 115, 192
'hot' advice 106
Howlett, M. 70, 106, 112, 153, 177
human action systems 24
human rights 170
Hurricane Katrina 52
Hustedt, T. 116

I

ideas 113, 167, 171–4, 190, 192
ideational explanations 169, 170, 173
identity 62, 85
ideological approaches 170
ill health 24
Immergut, E. 49
immigration 168
implementation 20, 91–3, 141–62, 189, 190, 192
'Implementation Units' 151
incremental processes 170
indigenous peoples 40
informal institutions 38–9, 44
information 119–40, 189–90, 192
information flow 130, 131, 133, 137
information technology (IT) 130–1, 132, 138, 149, 192
information theory 120
infrastructure projects 144
Ingram, H. 182–3
innovation 50–2, 68, 69, 86, 106, 109, 122, 179–80, 190
  and crises 164
  and digitisation 149
  and disruption 106
  financial 59
  local 150
  and the state 60
instability 155
institutional analysis 31, 38–40
institutional change 170, 193
  see also institutions

institutional competitiveness 69
institutionalism 10, 41, 52, 186, 191
institutional reinvention 51–2
institutions 33–53, 189
intellectual property 128
interests, and policy 7–8
Intergovernmental Panel on Climate Change (IPCC) 114
intergovernmental policy solutions 81
internal advisors 105–6
international development aid 182
  see also aid
international institutions 36–7
international organisations (IOs) 81, 83, 84, 92
International Political Economy (IPE) 77, 84
International Standards Organisation 90
international students 26–7
Internet 137
Internet Corporation for Assigned Names and Numbers (ICANN) 91
interpretivist approach 172
investigative journalism 137
iron triangles 16
IT systems 152
  see also information technology (IT)

J

Jasanoff, S. 173–4
Jessop, B. 63, 64
job creation 147–8
Jochim, A. 94
John, P. 85
Jones, B. 122, 123–4, 126

K

Katrina, hurricane 52
Keynesianism 164, 170
Keynesian Welfare State 57, 58
key performance indicators (KPIs) 160
Kim, S. 84
King, A. 13
Kingdon, J.W. 123, 166
Kjaer, A.M. 46
Klijn, E.H. 37
knowledge, expert 190

knowledge brokering 113, 117
knowledge brokers 113, 115
knowledge types 126–7
Kobrin, S. 92
Koehn, P.H. 92
Koppenjan, J. 37
Krasner, S. 78
Kyoto Protocol on Climate Change 143

L

laissez-faire policy 57
LaPorte, T. 13
Lasswell, H.D. 13, 99, 110, 188
leaders 168, 170, 177
leadership 163–4, 169
learning 159, 160–1, 162, 168, 180–3, 188, 192
    collaborative 157, 158
the left 2
legitimacy 29, 30, 149, 154, 162
legitimation 13, 42
Lehmkuhl, D. 66
lesson drawing/learning 40, 160, 188
    see also learning
Lindblom, C.E. 68
Lindquist, E. 70
linear policy analysis 22–3
Lipsky, M. 148
local participation 67
low conflict-high ambiguity 153
low conflict-low ambiguity 153
Lowdnes, V. 45
Lowi, T. 8
Luhmann, N. 13–14, 23

M

March, J.G. 33–4, 35
the market 65
marketing, political 132
Marks, G. 69
Marsh et al 146
Matland, R. 153
May, P. 94, 154
media 128, 129, 131–2, 136, 137, 138, 166, 192
'mediatisation' 131–2
mental health problems 159
meta-analysis 135
metagovernance 62–3

migration 26, 27, 168, 174
Millennium Development Goals 143
mobilisation 167, 183, 190, 192
Mosse, D. 154
multilateral trade liberalisation 81
multilevel governance 68–9, 71, 152, 161
multinational corporations (MNCs) 80–1
multi-party governance 51

N

narratives 172
national identity 62
NATO 90
neo-liberalism 57, 105, 164, 170
network-based institutionalism 52
network coordination 151
network governance 43, 46, 61, 121, 162
network institutionalism 42–3, 45, 46, 53
networks 16, 37, 62, 189, 191
network theory 45
new constitutionalism 87
new institutionalism 38–9, 41–3, 47–8, 53, 89–91, 193
new network governance 46
New Public Governance (NPG) 63, 64, 72, 151
New Public Management (NPM) 3, 57, 69, 146, 149, 150, 165
New Zealand 51
'Next Steps' 142
Ney, S. 110
NGOs 80, 92, 171
NHS 159
nodality 92, 121
non-state actors 82, 83, 86, 87, 91–2, 108, 146
norms 143, 191
'nudge' factor 121
nutrition 24, 26

O

obesity 179
O'Connor, J. 6–7, 13
OECD countries, and implementation 155
Oliver, Jamie 24, 26

Index

Olsen, J. 33–4, 35
open advisory systems 103
open systems 28
organisational culture 159, 167
Osborne, S.P. 64
Ostrom, E. 160
outsourcing 145–6
overseas development assistance policy 89

P

Parsons, T. 13
Parsons, W. 33, 48
participatory democracy 132–3
participatory governance 133
Patashnik, E.M. 158
path dependency 37, 87, 166
Patton, M. 21
Pegram, T. 80
pensions policy 119
performance 158, 192
performance evaluation 157
performance-outcomes criteria 157
persuasion 130, 167, 172
Peters, B.G. 45, 49, 53, 61, 149, 170, 175
   on boundary spanning regimes 94
   on implementation 91
   on policy process 89
Peterson Institute for International Economics 79
Pierre, J. 61
Pierson, P. 58, 68
'place-based' collaborative models 146
place-based poverty 71
Plowden, W. 99
plurilateral governance xi–xii
policing 145
policy activists 171–2
policy advice 113, 189–90
   see also advice
policy advisory systems (PASs) 97, 98, 99, 100, 102–7, 109–10
   on climate change 114, 115–16
policy agenda 124, 169
Policy Agenda Project 70
policy brokerage 101, 106
policy brokers 166

policy capacity 155–7, 169
   see also capacity
policy change 159, 163–84, 185, 192, 193–4
policy coordination 155
policy cycle 16–17, 88
policy debate 167, 173, 174, 184
policy design 153, 155, 177–80, 183, 188, 192
policy diffusion 182
policy entrepreneurship 91
   see also entrepreneurship
policy evaluation 182
   see also evaluation
policy failure 11, 177–8, 190
   see also failure
policy feedback 72
   see also feedback
policy goals 141, 183
policy ideas 171–4
   see also ideas
policy innovation 51, 179–80
   see also innovation
policy learning 159, 162, 168, 180–3, 192
   see also learning
policy market 165
policy mixes 9, 171, 178
policy networks 16
   see also networks
policy paradigms 170
policy problems 174–7
policy process 88–9, 99, 188
policy reform 173, 180
policy regime 78, 80, 93, 94, 95, 154, 164, 191
policy reviews 160
policy shaping 48–52
policy style 70
policy subsystems 16, 81, 95
   see also subsystems
policy transfer 182
political activists 166
political advice 102, 106
political coalitions 169, 171
political economy 6–7, 69, 85–8
politically oriented knowledge 126
political marketing 132
political parties 132, 139, 168
politicisation 100, 103, 106, 117

politics 8, 138–9, 164, 166
The Politics of Information (Baumgartner and Jones) 124
poll tax 177–8
polycentricity 19, 20, 60, 67, 116
populism 187, 194
populist political parties 168
poverty 24, 71, 175
power 73, 94–5, 125, 137
    state 61, 72, 122, 188
Prasser, S. 100, 106
precautionary principle 176
preparedness 45, 155
the press 137
Pressman, J.L. 34, 147–8
Prince, M.J. 99
principal-agent model 91, 146, 157
Pritchett, L. 182
privacy 122, 128, 129, 133, 134, 149
private actors 82, 92, 108
privatisation 67, 146, 149, 164
problem 'framing' 174
problems, policy 174–7
problem-solving 48–52, 159, 185, 186, 187–8, 191, 193
    climate change 115
    and collaborative leadership 157
professional experience and expertise 126–7
protest movements 137
public choice theory 3, 66
public health 179
public inquiries 159, 160, 168, 181
public management 63, 68, 129, 130, 136, 142, 143, 164
    see also New Public Management (NPM)
public/private partnerships 67, 152
public spending 57, 58
punctuated equilibrium 124, 166

R

Radaelli, C.M. 49, 169–70
rational advice 106
rational choice theory 84
rationalists 84–5
rationality, comprehensive 88
Rawls, J. 77
realpolitik 139
real world orientation 48–9

reasoned argumentation 181
rebuilding 52
recessions 167–8
    see also Global Financial Crisis (GFC)
reflexivity 14, 50, 97, 103, 104
reform 61, 68, 154, 166, 168, 170–1, 180
    and case studies 160
    and coalitions 167
    financial 182
    ideas 173
    neo-liberal 105
    and Patashnik 158
    and policy advising 100
    and policy failure 150
    and policy learning 180, 181
    and public inquiries 159
refugees 168
regional participation 67
regulation 8–9, 26–7, 67, 128, 129
regulatory scholarship 65
Reinecke, S. 115
'Reinventing Government' movement 150
relational capital 156
reliability 143
renewal, institutions 51–2
research evidence 173
resilience 19–20, 45, 60
Rhodes, M. 20
Rhodes, R.A.W. 3, 33–4, 41–6, 53, 61, 151, 187
the right 2
risk 89–90, 169–70
risk aversion 159
Rittel, H.W.J. 47, 49, 110, 187
road congestion 25
road safety 181
Rockman, B.A. 36
Rosenau, J.N. 92
Rossbach, S. 14

S

Salt, D. 19
Schiller, N.G. 75
Schmidt, V.A. 42
Schneider, A. 182–3
Schofield, J. 159
Schwartz, S.H. 51
Science and Public Policy 135

Index

science and values, fusion 174
scientific evidence 173
scientific expertise 194
scientific information and analysis 126, 127
scientific research 184
Scott, C. 101
second generation systems theory 110
second wave analysis 106–8, 111
sectoral diversity 66
security 56, 122, 145, 154
self-steering 14, 23
Sellers, J.M. 55
sense-making 124–5
sequencing 70, 87, 150–1, 178
service delivery 152, 161, 165
service planning 149, 152, 161
sexual abuse 159
Seymour-Ure, C. 99
shocks 155, 170, 193
Simeon, R. 185, 186
situational policy change 169
Skocpol, T. 34
Smith, H. 106
Snowden, Edward 134
social-ecological system 45
social issues 101
social media 128, 129, 131–2, 137, 138, 192
social regulation 90, 91
social science information and analysis 127
social services 145–6
society-centric behaviourism 34
soft-systems methodology 15
sovereignty 76, 91
spending, public 57, 58
stability 90–1, 163, 164, 172, 192
stages models 88
stakeholder engagement 143, 189
stakeholder knowledge 179, 180
stakeholders, alliances of 166
Stark, A. 160
the state 3, 6, 13, 38, 45, 55–73, 189
  and affect of recessions 164
  and change 193
  and fiscal crises 6–7
  and governance 188
  and information 130, 136, 138, 139
  and secrecy 134
  and Skocpol 34
  and transnational public policy 92–3
state agencies 149, 168, 187
state capacity 3, 5, 6, 8, 29, 47, 48, 52, 64, 185, 187, 188, 193
  and expert advice 101, 112
  and implementation 143
  and quality of public policy 50
state change 63–7, 66
state legitimacy 29, 31
state power 61, 72, 122, 188
state regulation 67
  see also regulation
state-resilience 60
state-society relationships 66–8, 69, 71, 72
steering 14, 46, 62, 65, 121, 142, 164
  and advice 112
  and limitations 23
  and state agencies 149
Steinmo, S. 38, 40, 41, 48, 49
Stoker, G. 187
Stone, Deborah 125
Stone, Diane 77–81, 83, 85
Strategic Relational Approach (SRA) 63–4, 66, 72
strategy 25, 160, 170
Street-level Bureaucracy (Lipsky) 148
structural explanations 173
structural-institutionalist approaches 166
structure 52, 124, 167
sub-governments 16
subsystem networks 109–10
subsystems 14, 16, 17, 30, 43, 111, 187
  across borders 44, 81, 95
  and advisory systems 107, 108–9, 110–11
  and implementation 20
success 145, 146, 150, 156–7, 158, 178
surveillance 139
surveillance-related information 122
sustainable development 143
Sustainable Development Goals 143
Sweden 51
systemic institutionalism 10, 186, 191
A Systems Analysis of Political Life (Easton) 12

systems-based analysis 188, 189
systems models 14
systems theory 47–8, 108, 110–11, 190–1
systems thinking 11–20, 22–31, 56, 136, 167, 187
    and complexity 188
    and implementation 162, 190
    and information 126

T

tax policies 119
Taylor, M.M. 170
technology 128–9, 139
    see also information technology (IT)
Tenbensel, T. 21
termination 170–1
territorial diversity 66
Thatcher government 46, 149–50
Thatcherism 51, 57
Thelen, K. 170
tipping points 18
top-down approach 68, 147, 148, 151, 154, 157
trade liberalisation, multilateral 81
traffic congestion 179
transfer, policy 182
transnational private actor solutions 82
transnational solutions 80
transnational state-non-state policy solutions 82
transport 25
trigger event 169
Trump administration 166
trust 156

U

UK
    abuse in the NHS 159
    'Next Steps' 142
    place-based poverty 71
    poll tax 177–8
    and public sector reform 61
    Thatcher era 149–50
UN
    Framework Convention on Climate Change 114
    Millennium Development Goals 143
    Sustainable Development Goals 143

uncertainty 32, 155, 163, 167, 177, 183, 192
    and implementation 161
    and information 120–1
    and leadership 169
urban governance 71
US
    job creation 147–8
    and NPM 149–50

V

values 48, 50, 126, 172, 174, 191
Van Horn, C. 153
Van Meter, D. 153
varieties of capitalism 69
Veit, S. 116
Venezuela 29
vertical diversity 66
Vickers, G. 121
vocational education 26–7
voting 139

W

Walker, B. 19
'war on drugs' 152
water policy 171–2
Weaver, R.K. 36
Webber, M.M. 47, 49, 110, 187
Weberian state 58–9, 60
welfare state 58, 86
Weller, P. 99
Wellstead et al 21
Wesselink, A. 115, 192
wicked problems 31, 37, 40, 46, 47, 53, 97
    and evidence-based policies 101
    and implementation 155, 157
    and policy change 168, 177
Wildavsky, A. 34, 89, 147–8
Wilder, M. 106, 107, 108
Wimmer, A. 75
Workman et al 124
World Bank 29
WTO (World Trade Organisation) 81, 90, 91
Wu et al 169

Y

Young, W. 127

www.ingramcontent.com/pod-product-compliance
Lightning Source LLC
Chambersburg PA
CBHW070917030426
42336CB00014BA/2457